A SOCIOLOGY OF
CANADIAN
EDUCATION

Pat Duffy Hutcheon

Van Nostrand Reinhold Ltd. *Toronto, New York, Cincinnati, London, Melbourne*

To Sandy

ISBN paper 0 442 29917 6
         cloth 0 442 29916 8
Library of Congress Number 74-27503

Design by Brant Cowie/Artplus
Printed and bound in Canada by The Alger Press Limited

75   76   77   78   79   80   81   82   8   7   6   5   4   3   2   1

Preface

The relationship between sociology and education, from its beginnings in the work of Emile Durkheim, has been uncomfortable and ambiguous. University classes in "educational sociology", "social foundations of education" or "sociology of education" often have little in common other than a connotation of vague social concern. Available textbooks for such classes tend to be either collections of impressionistic readings about specific situations, or theoretical treatises devoted to abstract models and specialized terminology. These essays usually attempt to document presumed educational causes and consequences of social problems, or presumed social causes of educational problems. They are often written in a prescriptive or normative vein and in the American or British, rather than the Canadian context. The theoretical discussions are apt to be devoted to abstract sociological models and specialized terminology, with little attempt at application to educational settings.

The major disadvantage of the latter type of textbook is that the theoretical webs spun by the writer have a way of becoming disconnected from any empirical base in teacher-learner interaction. They tend to float far out of reach of the reluctant grasp of the reader who then feels justified in dismissing all theory as "idealistic" and impractical.

The weakness in the impressionistic approach is twofold. In the first place, the criteria for inclusion of educational events and social problems in the text (and subsequently, the class) become quite arbitrary. In the second place, such books are so time-and-space bound that any insights offered are non-transferable and obsolete almost at the date of publication.

It was in an attempt to compensate for just such inadequacies in available texts and references that I gradually acquired my own theoretical perspective and fund of instructional aids. This book is the result of almost a decade of experimenting with procedures for developing sociological understanding of educational events and processes in candidates for the teaching profession. It is the expression of a few basic assumptions about the nature of the disciplines of sociology and education, and of their relationship to one another. As a sociologist, I consider sociological concepts to be nothing more nor less than explanatory tools for the ordering of social phenomena—tools developed on the basis of a consensus in the relevant segment of the scientific community as to their meaning and use. As an educator I consider that training in the use of such tools requires both the laborious building, refining and sharing of abstract mental constructs, and much practice in their application to specific, concrete situations. And I am convinced that these situations must be as close as possible to the daily experience of the students.

Consequently, this book deals with eight key sociological concepts. They are the concepts which I judge to be most fruitful in terms of their potential for shedding light on current problems in education. They are analysed and interpreted as interrelated conponents of an "interactionist-evolutionary" theoretical framework: a model which draws on the work of Karl Marx, John Dewey, G. H. Mead, Julian Huxley, Jean Piaget and Thomas Kuhn, as well as the ideas of modern "general systems" theorists such as Walter Buckley, Von Bertalanffy, and Anatole Rapoport. The student is forced to apply theory to experience by working through specific case studies requiring the use of these key concepts as ordering tools. In a further attempt to encourage him to connect the concepts to his own experience and that of others, he is introduced to readings on educational issues, many of them comprising an overview of Canadian research over the past decade and serving as an intriguing source of data for sociological analysis.

The first sections of each of the two chapters in Part I present a model (or theory) of the learning process in human beings, along with some conclusions as to the nature of the teaching methodology implied by such a model. The entire book is carefully constructed in terms of this methodology, so that, throughout, the student is encouraged to *use* the sociological concepts dealt with in the process of acquiring them, and the instructor is discouraged from "giving" the student sophisticated definitions of terms and specific answers to educational problems.

The concluding chapter demands that the student detach himself temporarily from his own process of belief-construction about social phenomena in educational settings. (This is the process in which the book has involved him up to this point.) He is now required to examine the process itself: to distinguish between those beliefs (or explanations) in the human culture which can appropriately be termed components of reliable, tested knowledge, and those beliefs which are the largely unsubstantiated opinion of individuals or pressure groups. He is encouraged to probe into the differences between these types of beliefs and to picture them as ranged, in temporary positions, along a continuum from "subjective" to "objective"—rather than as categorized in two separate and immutable boxes. And finally, the student is faced with the dilemma that all educators must recognize sooner or later, and which educators and politicians in a pluralistic culture find particularly difficult to resolve. *What criteria are to be applied to the fund of experiences and beliefs available in the culture, when we set out to select from among them, the content of curricula for Canadian schools?*

I wish to thank all those students, colleagues, school teachers and trustees who have contributed, through the give and take of discussion, to the refining of the ideas expressed in the content and format of this book. Appreciation is due, as well, to all those scholars whose thoughts have shaped mine and upon whose work I have attempted to build; to my mother; to my son, Tom, from whom, in the course of his developing, I learned much; to Mr. Garry Lovatt of Van Nostrand Reinhold, Ltd., whose professional help and advice have been invaluable; to Mrs. Diane Mew for her excellence in editing; to Mrs. Beatrice Wrigley, whose generosity and diligence in typing have constantly amazed me; and to my husband, for his stimulation, support and criticism.

Contents

Introduction

This book is designed so that each chapter can be handled as a learning module in itself, for use in a variety of flexible scheduling and open-university approaches to the education of teachers. Each chapter is divided into five sections, in which the concept is (1) *explained* by reference to educational examples, (2) *demonstrated* by case studies in Canadian settings, (3) *applied* by the student to the analysis of Canadian research studies, (4) *amplified* through additional readings and (5) *reviewed* by the student through the use of ten items aimed at assessing the degree to which he has achieved understanding. Small-group discussion questions following each case study guide the student in the use of the concept as a tool for making sense out of educational events and information, as do the suggestions for independent study of the Canadian research. Lists of sources of data and a variety of current statistics on Canadian education are included in the appendix, for further use by teachers and students.

The book is divided into five parts—a structure based on the idea of a progression from the concrete and the immediate to the more abstract and all-encompassing. Throughout Part I, in our attempt to understand the processes of socialization and social organization, we look at the systemic aspects of the social relationships within the classroom. This is the familiar context in which every student and teacher can immediately locate himself. In order to begin to explain and understand what is happening in the classroom we must learn to recognize the crude and culture-bound categories with which we may have operated until now, and "try on" certain more refined and rigorously defined ones which are specific to the sociological perspective.

Part II of the book deals with the school as a formal organization. The teacher or student who has learned to see the interrelationships around him in terms of "socialization" and "social organization" soon realizes that the larger organization in which the person-to-person interaction occurs affects and is affected by that interaction in myriad ways. He is forced to penetrate a little deeper into the immediate occurrences and a little further beyond them, in order to get at the determining and determined characteristics of that encompassing structure—the formal organization. Two additional concepts, "role" and "authority" are introduced here, and we gradually begin to understand how schools or universities (as particular types of formal organizations) respond to challenges from within and without, and undergo or resist organizational change.

In the third section we move out beyond the school plant and into the society of which it is a functioning part. The urban society typical of industrialized countries throughout the world today is perceived as organized both into institutional complexes and into more or less hierarchically stratified layers. The school is therefore considered as a part of the educational complex and is analyzed in terms of its relationship with all the other organizations involved in the schooling enterprise. It is considered, also, in terms of how it is affected by, and in turn affects other institutional complexes such as the family and the economy, as well as the entire social structure in which it is embedded. The key concepts introduced in this section are "professionalization" and "social mobility", along with the related concepts of "urbanization" and "social stratification". With those expanded upon earlier, these concepts encourage the development of deeper insights into what is happening with schooling systems in modern urban societies.

Part IV allows us to stand back and view the educational process as a function of the evolution of human culture in its entirety. We look at the concept of "culture" and seek to understand how it is produced by a society, how it is instrumental to the survival of the group which carries it, and how it is transmitted and changed by its carriers. The significance of the concept for education becomes obvious when we consider cultural *change*. The role of education in the evolution of culture is examined against a background of the type of trial-and-error enculturation and innovation which has distinguished the cultural change process throughout the history of mankind. The concept of "values" is recognized as central to the problem of the determination of objectives for the guiding of education (objectives having the consequence of contributing, ultimately, to the direction in which the culture of the group will be shaped).

The final section is an attempt to assess the progress of sociology and education as disciplined approaches to knowledge-building. The question of whether or not a science of education is possible or desirable is discussed in depth, with the author's tentative conclusions being offered as a means of tying together the conceptual strands developed throughout the book.

Although the title is *A Sociology of* Canadian *Education*, this textbook is Canadian only in that all the examples and cases are drawn from the social and educational context of this particular country. The conceptual structure of the book and its mode of systematic analysis are of course generalizable to educational events and problems anywhere in the world. It is the author's hope that a student interested in the educational process in any country in this particular period of history will find offered here, both a fruitful way of making sense out of the teaching-learning relationship, and a workable set of conceptual tools for the improvement of that relationship.

Part One
The Classroom As A Social System

At first glance it may seem trite to maintain that a classroom could be regarded as a network of interrelationships in which group members participate more intensely than they participate in the interaction going on at the same time beyond their classroom boundaries. On second thought, however, one might begin to recognize that it is indeed a new and rather disconcerting way to look at a group of learners and teachers. We are in the habit of thinking of them as a number of individuals, gathered together momentarily within a particular room. A class is a group, we might want to insist, or a class is a room in a school plant. Both these definitions are obvious. Of what possible use is it to confuse the obvious by defining a class as a "system?"

But is the concept of "system" really that difficult? All of us have encountered it often in our daily experience. We say that a football team has developed a system for working together in particular ways to foil its opponents. We worry about our digestive system when we suffer stomach pains. We are all familiar with the solar system. We argue about the public transportation system of our city, or the telephone system which ties remote corners of the country together.

What is common to all these usages is the idea of a pattern of interdependent relationships. A telephone system is characterized not so much by those little boxes scattered across the nation as by the inter-connecting communication links or pathways which the telephone technology provides. A solar system is not merely a collection of heavenly bodies, but a collection of heavenly bodies interacting in regular ways, on the basis of certain principles of relationship.

Whenever the person studying the collection of entities in question discovers a pattern according to which each entity relates to the rest, he is beginning to see the group in terms of its "wholeness," or its systemic properties. Hall and Fagan define a system as "a set of objects together with relationships among the objects and among their attributes."[1] With this perspective comes the realization that fully as significant as the attributes of the parts is the nature of the relationships which bind the parts together into a functioning whole.

This interrelationship and interdependence among parts appears even more complex when we realize that all systems are sub-systems of larger encompassing systems which comprise their environment. Similarly, each is a supra-system for the smaller sub-systems for which it, in turn, provides the surrounding environment. The classroom is a sub-system of the school, whose supra-system is the schooling system of the province. The classroom at the same time is the supra-system for the small learning groups functioning within it.

[1] Hall, A. D. & R. E. Fagan, "General Systems", in L. Von Bertalanffy and A. Rapoport eds, *Yearbook of the Society for the Advancement of General Systems Theory* (Ann Arbor: Braun-Brumfield, 1956,) p. 18

One could even extend this understanding further and think of each member of the learning group as a personality or value system, just as we typically think of people as organic wholes.

The system perspective encourages us to conceive of reality as boxes within boxes, from the atom to the universe, with each box understandable in terms of the principles by which the boxes comprising it are related as well as by the nature of the member boxes themselves. The inorganic systems studied by physicists and chemists are simpler, less open and less dynamic than are the organic ones studied by biologists and physicians. Systems at the psycho-social level of organization are even more complex and open to change (and therefore more difficult to study) than are the still-largely-mysterious organic ones upon which they are based. This is why the study of the behaviour of human beings (covert as well as overt), as distinct from the study of their organic composition, is by far the most difficult that man could possibly tackle.

When we refer to individual human personalities or value systems, or the individual learning process, we are dealing with human behaviour at the *psychological* level of organization. When we refer to human groups and their processes of interactive behaviour we are forced to structure concepts involving the level of *social* organization. Because each personality or psychological system can only be fully understood as an interacting part of an encompassing social system (a family, a classroom, and so on) and each social system can only be fully understood in terms of the attributes and interrelationships of its psychological components, any comprehensive study of human behaviour would seem to require a *psycho-social* conceptual framework. In the same way, and for the same reasons, many psychologists use a *bio-psychological* systems framework in their attempt to understand individual personality development, while in medicine, a *bio-chemical* model provides the most fruitful theoretical perspective.

It is no accident that physics and philosophy are brought together by the best minds of every age in the development of an over-all conceptual framework or "world view" of the entire encompassing system of a universe of reality within which human social systems (from the new-born baby to the global community) are seen to interact. As physics progressed from the Newtonian universe to that of Einstein, philosophical models gradually began to move away from the idea of autonomous, free-wheeling individuals as the ultimate units of reality, to the idea that it is the nature of the *relations* within, among and around human beings that defines reality.

Philosophical models of the nature of knowledge have undergone a drastic alteration also. In the Newtonian universe knowledge was understood to be made up of building blocks comprising mirror-images of reality painstakingly discovered and accumulated, in an unchanged form, for posterity. We now realize that man can neither perceive nor formulate perfect pictures of an absolute reality. With considerably more humility, we are now satisfied with defining knowledge as structured sets of the most reliable hypotheses of relations yet constructed by man in the process of the public testing of human experience.

In viewing the classroom as a social system, then, we are employing a conceptual framework within which relations may be tested and knowledge about teaching-learning behaviours may be constructed. It is a model or framework which constantly reminds us of the network of interrelationships of which the individual classroom forms a small but vital connecting link. We are reminded that it is not sufficient to focus upon the *individual* pupil as the measure of all things; and to perceive the *group* as a "given" whose welfare supersedes that of the individual is no less distorting. We are forced to focus our attention upon teacher-pupil and pupil-pupil relationships and the nature of the learning process occurring for each member as a result of his participation in this particular pattern. And we are provided with a theoretical perspective that allows us to make sense out of what otherwise might appear as a jumble of meaningless behaviours ebbing and flowing around us as we strive to attain our goals of learning or of enabling others to learn.

1 Socialization

The Concept Explained

Human beings are changing continually from birth onwards as a result of environmental stimuli to which they are exposed willy-nilly. Some of these stimuli are aspects of the physical environment upon which the individual acts. Others are aspects of the social environment: the web of interacting human beings and their patterned ways of believing and behaving into which the child is propelled at birth and which we call society and culture, respectively. It is this process, by which stimuli from the social environment impinge upon the individual and act upon or are acted upon by him, that we call *socialization* or "socialization-enculturation."

When the socialization process is structured and controlled in conjunction with the physical environment in certain settings for certain periods of time, with the intent that individuals will develop the most effective beliefs and behaviours and thinking strategies possible, we say *education* is occurring. The person responsible for this structuring is the teacher. All human beings in the individual's milieu are socializing agents in relation to his development; we are all socializing agents for one another. A teacher is more than this for his students, however. In addition to the unintended socializing effect that his inadvertent emotional responses may have upon them, he influences them deliberately as an educational agent, as do, at times, their parents, priests, baby-sitters, and TV producers. These other educational agents can compensate for, corroborate, or contradict the educational efforts of the teacher. In addition, in any complex, pluralistic culture such as the Canadian one today, there are bound to be a myriad of unplanned and uncontrolled socializing agents producing barrages of stimuli which impinge upon the individual from all directions.

How can an understanding of the socialization process and its consequences for individual learning help the teacher? Perhaps the major benefit resides merely in the general awareness that the social as well as the physical environment is a source of the beliefs about "the real" and "the good" that the child begins to structure from birth onward, as he makes inferences on the basis of experienced regularities. In fact, for the learner, these twin aspects of the environment seldom occur separately. He learns about the physical environment in the context of the social. The concepts of physical relationships which allow him to "map" (and communicate to others about) the physical world are the same concepts which form the basis of the pool of scientific knowledge in the evolving culture of his species. To a large extent other human beings act as mediators in the individual's attempts to acquire these understandings. We learn about the world not only through acting upon it directly, but through the eyes and ears of our parents, teachers and friends. The highly verified and reliable knowledge about "the real" social as well as physical environment which has been produced by humanity over the course of centuries is acquired by the individual in social settings, and with the help (or hindrance) of other human beings.

It is by means of this socialization-enculturation process that the child becomes a member of the human group. By this means he is inducted into the conceptual structures developed over hundreds of thousands of years of human evolution: structures which enable him to order and perceive the world as a human being and to share what he sees and feels with others. When we say that the insane person has "lost touch with reality" we mean that, due to either genetic or environmental deficiencies, for him the socialization process has failed in that he has not acquired or sustained the social definition of reality shared by humanity. (The normal person experiences this "loss of touch" to some degree when he feels a condition of culture shock at encountering the way of life of a society very different from his own.)

As well as beliefs or explanations about "the real," beliefs about what is "good" for man in terms of social arrangements are transmitted by other human beings. However, this transmission occurs in conjunction with the individual's continuous process of testing these beliefs and "feeling" the consequences. This means that the individual is clearly not the passive recipient upon which some sort of static and omniscient society imposes a form from without. This earlier and now obsolete concept of socialization tended to give us a misleading picture of human growth as the shaping of helpless clay into a previously designed and unchanging mold. Such a concept is clearly deficient in explaining what even a cursory look at history indicates to us: the phenomenon of *change* in human societies.

Reliable explanations developed by social psychologists in recent years indicate that the potential exists for the child to be an active participant in the socialization process rather than a passive victim of it. We now believe that the child is born equipped with the embryonic means for constructing his basic concepts of the physical world by acting upon or bumping up against physical limits. (One falls when one crawls past the edge of the bed; if one touches fire one gets burned.) In the same way the social boundaries established by the dynamic but patterned behaviour of other people and which provide him with the bases of his concepts of the social environment are amenable to direct acquisition through active testing. (If one takes another child's candy one is likely to be hit by the victim or to have one's own candy taken away by a stronger child.)

Adults can interfere in these types of situations (and, indeed, must when the consequences brought about by the child's actions, if uncontrolled, would be harmful). However, adult interference that substitutes an entirely different consequence rather than merely controlling the natural result of a child's action can impede concept-building. For instance, the child may learn to avoid touching the fire or stealing another child's possessions because of the spanking or scolding which follows if he is observed by adults, rather than because of the consequences inherent in the situation. In this way he is socialized to believe that the source of rules for what constitutes "the real" and "the good" is certain human beings who possess the authority to determine consequences arbitrarily rather than that the source of these rules is the regularity which one discovers in the physical and social relationships being explored.

Probably the most serious dilemma for education has its source in this tendency of the adult, in his role of educational agent, to want to shortcut the socialization-enculturation process by giving the child the group's rules for what constitutes "the real" and "the good" and setting up a system of rewards and punishments based on the child's ready acceptance of these rules. It seems inordinately difficult for us to realize that the *process* by which the child acquires the human group's concepts is as important as the concepts themselves, and indeed determines the actual concepts acquired.

What does it matter that the father, acting as the child's first teacher, teaches the child that approaching the flaming fireplace is a "no-no", inevitably followed by a spanking? And that exactly similar "no-nos" and spankings follow the touching of countless perfectly harmless but costly knick-knacks in the same room? Before answering let us imagine an alternative approach to the same problem. The room is cleared of breakable heirlooms but is rich with objects of various size, shape and consistency which the child is allowed to manipulate. However, when the child approaches the fire for the first time, the father watches carefully, allowing him to touch it just enough to feel the heat and some pain. The father exclaims, "fire hot!" or something like that and might even go through a little act himself of touching the hearth and crying in pain. The child learns to discriminate between the fire and the other objects in the room. He has begun the process of acquiring the concepts in question by acting upon his physical environment and experiencing the consequences directly. Even more important, the source of authority as to the regularity that holds for him between his touching the fiery hearth and the painful consequence of that touch is the *testing* process rather than the adult.

This does not mean that the adult educational agent abandons the child to a random, hit-and-miss socialization (in this case to the disastrous consequence of burning to death in the fire). In fact, this approach makes greater demands upon the teacher than does the practice of "telling" and substituting external rewards and punishment. The teacher must be in control of the entire situation in order to structure the physical and social environment in advance and to have the objective of the experience to which the child is exposed clearly in mind.

In the case of our example the objective is for the child to begin to acquire the concept of "fire," one aspect of which is the association of pain and danger which will result in subsequent aversive behaviour on his part. We control the situation carefully so that he is encouraged to test his physical environment and to experience consequences that are real but not unduly harmful to his physical and emotional well-being. At the same time we repeat the words "hot" and "fire" so that he will begin to associate these symbols with the sensations felt. Depending on the rate at which the child learns, the experience may have to be repeated several times, until he can be depended upon to avoid the fire on his own. Eventually the words "hot" and "fire" will be sufficient to bring the whole set of experiences back to him, and he will infer that even an innocent-appearing white oven spells danger when he hears these particular words spoken urgently in connection with it.

Now what about the other educational approach, the more common one of the adult contriving rather than controlling the consequences which follow the child's behaviour? This time, as the child crawls toward the fire the father says "no! no!" in a firm voice and either restrains him bodily or slaps his hand. Because the fire arouses the child's curiosity he continues to try to approach it. Each time he hears the symbols "no! no!" and "bad!" and experiences the father as an obstacle to his progress or as a source of punishment. The concept which is constructed in him as the result of the generalization of these experiences is not one which helps him to make sense out of "fire" as a meaningful and potentially dangerous phenomenon in his environment. The concept is instead that of "badness" or "goodness" as related to him as a "self" and as defined by his father as the final source of authority on these matters.

He may even learn to associate the "no! no!" and "bad!" with the consequent punishment to such an extent that he looks enquiringly at his father for his reaction before he attempts to test anything new in his environment. At this stage the child has become highly socialized to accept the father as the ultimate source of authority as to the nature of "the good" and "the real." This may seem most desirable in the short run (and is indeed probably necessary to some extent during early socialization and enculturation, so that the child has a stable social world with certain definite limits to build his basic social concepts upon). But to the degree that it inhibits curiosity, and develops the habit of looking to individuals not merely as a valuable source of vicarious experience but as the source of ultimate authority instead of the habit of looking to the process of actively (or vicariously) experiencing and assessing the consequences of one's real or imagined actions, it is likely to have a debilitating effect upon the individual's intellectual and moral development in the long run. In this latter situation the testing that the child does is confined to a never-ending assessment of the boundaries of "bad behaviour" as defined in some arbitrary way by authority figures; the result is that, if there is any inconsistency at all in the responses of the adults to the child's forays toward the hearth, he may learn to indulge in a continuous teasing game which wears at the patience of the parents and teaches him that the regularities concerning reality which he has sensed hold only when those with the power to punish are present and in the mood to punish. This child soon begins to devote most of his curiosity and energy to the manipulation of other people in his environment rather than to the manipulation and control of his physical world.

We have been referring to the deliberate structuring of the socialization-enculturation process by the parents in the home—that aspect of the entire process which we term educational. There is, of course, a great deal going on that is not in any way so structured and intended. All the children in the home or the neighbourhood could be considered socializing agents for one another. All the adults in the vicinity contribute unintended inputs to the experience of the growing child as do the TV and movies to which he is exposed. The attitudes expressed by the parents and their ways of interacting with one another and with the rest of the children and the neighbours all contribute to the picture of the world that the child is structuring (largely unconsciously) or to that reflection of the culture of his family, nation and species which is now within him.

Once the child enters school he becomes exposed even more to the culture of the national society and the world community. It is here, in the school setting, that he encounters his society's systematic attempt to structure the socialization-enculturation process in directions deemed desirable by the group as a whole, if the polity is a relatively democratic one, or by the elite monopolizing the power, where the government is relatively totalitarian. Elites in various societies have used the educational system to perpetuate an aristocratic social structure by restricting opportunity for schooling to members of their own sub-society. Others have sought to maintain themselves in political power by using the schools to inculcate, in all young people, appropriately worshipful attitudes toward authority and toward conclusions about "the real" and "the good" proclaimed by those in authority.

John Dewey maintained that it is this attitude toward authority, rather than any particular set of values or facts to be inculcated, that is the key to the development of a democratic culture. However, he was not referring to authority in the usual sense of *respect for* the laws of the nation, the mores of the culture, or the rules of the organization. He was thinking more of the *source* and the *justification* of these rules, and whether or not they were seen as devised by men with certain objectives in mind, and therefore amenable to change by men on the basis of their consequences for human welfare. He did not question the necessity for civil, organizational, and family authority structures, and the agreed-upon rules on which they are based, if any of these social groups is to function as a system capable of guaranteeing a realm of freedom of action for all. At no time did he see authority and freedom as opposed to one another (as do the libertarians), any more than he saw the individual and the society in inevitable conflict. What he was mainly concerned with was the source of intellectual authority: the ultimate source of all continuity and change in the individual's (and therefore, the group's) beliefs about the nature of "the good" and "the real" which determine the knowledge and ideals defining reality for humanity as a whole.

Dewey concluded that, in order to ensure a democratic society and a free culture, we need more than democratic institutions of government. By these he meant those organized patterns of interaction which we have evolved over the past several centuries which guarantee that no government can decide to keep itself in power indefinitely, that an opposition group is always ready to assume the reins of government as soon as the majority of the people request it, and that all the people have the means of expressing their preference at fairly regular intervals, without fear of intimidation. He was not minimizing the importance of these institutions; he was saying that, although absolutely necessary for freedom and democracy, they were not, in themselves, sufficient. His point was that ways of behaving—even democratic procedures—tend to become habitual and mindless rather than reflective, unless the socialization process actively encourages reflection and inquiry. Therefore, even though our political institutions allow for optimal participation of all adults in the process by which the group's priorities are established and implemented, if that participation is on the basis of habit and blind emotion rather than wise and knowledgeable reflection, our political decisions will become so poor and the consequences for the group so grave that sooner or later the majority will opt for the destruction of its democratic political forms and a return to elite rule. There are many more signs today than in Dewey's time that we may be approaching such a crisis situation. This is evidenced by the number of our people now extolling the virtues of totalitarian forms of government in the belief that the weakness of western representative democracies resides in their institutional structures rather than in the quality of the decisions arrived at by means of a democratic process.

If we recognize that our problem is the quality of our political decisions and that this quality is a fairly accurate reflection of the quality of the private choices made by individuals in our society, then we are able to see the source of the problem as that *socialization process* which shapes the habits, behaviour and thought of individuals. Ironically, it is only in a relatively democratic polity that the wisdom and morality of all the people becomes a life and death matter to the society. Where totalitarian political forms prevail only the wisdom and morality of the governing elite matters; what is required of the masses is the habit of thought which encourages blind obedience to the authority vested in certain persons.

According to Dewey we will never achieve the free and democratic culture that our political institutions have made possible unless we structure the socialization process, at every level, with one major objective in mind. This objective is the development of reflective thinking in individuals: the habit of approaching any new problematic situation with the scientific temper; of observing and marshalling all the facts relevant to the task; of imagining alternative possibilities and of anticipating their probable consequences; of acting on these hypotheses (either overtly or mentally) in a controlled and orderly manner; and of observing, evaluating and communicating one's conclusions honestly. Dewey maintained that by the time the pupil is working at the high school level the problems structured for him should involve mainly intellectual rather than physical activity, but always he should be required, through reading and study, to find means to the achievement of designated ends or, given projected means, to infer the consequences which would follow from their use. Above all, our objective as educational agents must be to develop in the learner at every stage of his development respect for the scientific process rather than people or organizations as the ultimate source of authority.

This brings us back to the child and the fire. Which of the two approaches used is developing the habit of depending upon the process of testing one's environment as the source of authority; which, the habit of looking to high-status people as the source of answers?

Let us consider another example from a classroom situation. A child has learned that stealing is bad because his father says so. He knows that the consequence of stealing is a spanking from his father, if his father should find out about it. He sees a chocolate bar in the lunch box of one of the other children, and because no one is around he yields to temptation and steals the bar. The owner catches him eating it and attacks him. The teacher witnesses the event. What should he do?

Suppose he interferes by preventing the injured child from retaliating and telling him to turn the other cheek? Later he calls the father who administers the usual punishment; or else he punishes the little thief himself by denying him a treat that is passed out to all the other children at recess time. What has each child learned? A rule exists, out there, somehow apart from them, and imposed on them by people in authority. If the rule is broken, and known to be broken by these people, punishment follows. It is bad to break the rule because punishment will be meted out by someone external to the situation—maybe by God, if the act remains hidden from all human eyes. The thieving child has been labelled as "bad" and the injured party as "good" for not continuing the attack, in a public way that will affect the "self concepts" of both for some time to come.

What if the teacher had not interfered until after the first child had been allowed to experience the other's justifiable wrath (assuming of course, that no lasting damage had been done to him)? He would have learned in a very direct way that people do not like to have their property stolen; that stealing chocolate bars from one's friends does not work. Later, when he encountered the school rule and the societal law against stealing he would have possessed a store of experience to test the rule against. The idea of rules as having the function of making a society workable would then be a part of his concept of law. He would have begun to develop the thinking tools which might eventually enable him to assess all rules and laws in terms of their consequences for group life rather than in terms of some authoritative source which must never be questioned.

One unfortunate effect of teaching children by telling them the precepts rather than by structuring their immediate environment so that they will experience consequences directly and thus generalize the required set of understandings into a concept, is that the children will inevitably perceive the teacher as the final source of beliefs about "the real" and "the good." Rather, it is the environment and their means of testing it that the teacher must get them to see as this source, even though it is indeed he who is structuring that environment and arranging and capitalizing on their encounters with physical and social relationships in it. In other words, the teacher must always perceive himself as the responsible controller of the child's classroom experience and therefore as the indirect source of the learning that goes on, but he must operate so that the children do not perceive him as such. Most of the permissiveness and abdication of responsibility associated with yesterday's "progressive education" and today's "free school" and "informal education" movements stem from a serious misinterpretation of John Dewey on just this crucial point.

If children have been taught all through the elementary grades that verified knowledge and the scientific process by which it is tested and built is the source of authority, they will not feel dependent upon the teacher for the rewards of learning. Teacher approbation in the form of smiles, prizes and so on will be less significant as motivation than the delight of achieving new insights and increased power to act. The trouble with reliance upon teacher response as a source of motivation is that the learner may read it as the teacher's subjective evaluation of him as a person, rather than as the evaluation of the objective knowledge about the real world that he has managed to acquire in the form of a set of working concepts or motor skills. The pupil learns to ask "What does he want?" and to devote all his energies to random guessing, rather than to involve himself in a problem and see it through until it makes sense to him. In this latter case, a negative assessment of the work by the teacher is welcomed by him as it corroborates his own judgement as to his progress, aids him in his reality-testing, helps him diagnose his weaknesses and spurs him on to further effort.

Where the child has been socialized into an increasing dependence upon adults as ultimate sources of authority, both his natural curiosity and his confidence in his own powers of discrimination are progressively eroded. He may have acquired a large body of information because of his willingness to accept on faith the conclusions of authoritative "others" but it is likely that much of his repertoire will consist not of structured sets of concepts and related knowledge but of sets of symbols unrelated to everyday experience. He will have gradually learned to live in two different worlds: the world of formal education where he has become adept at manipulating symbols to the satisfaction of teachers and professors, and the world of direct experience where he continues to approach events in a random, habitual non-reasoning fashion. Most people who believe that "theory" is unrelated to "practice" are living in these two worlds. Jean Piaget's concepts of "figurative" as opposed to "operative" learning help to explain this phenomenon.[1] Dewey repeatedly emphasized the tragic consequences of this type of socialization for the culture of humanity.

The consequences for the individual are no less tragic. He will have learned to depend on others for his concept of "self," rather

[1] Jean Piaget, *Science of Education and the Psychology of the Child* (New York: Orion Press, 1970), pp. 33-36.

than upon his own developing powers of discrimination derived from an evergrowing complex of conceptual structures or instruments of knowledge with which he makes sense out of experience and which enable him to share his private experience with others and to test it in a social (or cbjective) context. If his work is negatively evaluated he will read this not as an objective assessment of his performance in relation to that of others where his ability to utilize knowledge is concerned, but as a rejection of his "self" or at least the labelling of it as inferior and inadequate. This is what we mean when we say that an individual "takes everything personally." He knows of no way to assess premises or conclusions except in terms of the authority of the person who holds them.

One could almost say that the child so socialized has been progressively enslaved and crippled to the extent that he has been conditioned to be more and more psychologically dependent upon the approval of others. According to Piaget it is only the child socialized, instead, to construct within himself the communicative and conceptual tools that would enable him to test and control his own surroundings who is likely to achieve the "formal" stage of cognitive development. This stage is necessary for the exercise of a responsible social morality, based on what Piaget terms "reciprocity." The person who has achieved this level of moral development will not behave according to the habit of following rules because they emanate from some ultimate source of authority, or simply because he has been taught to worship rules as rules. Rather, the intellectually developed person will have the capacity to observe and assess situations carefully, to imagine possible long-term consequences of alternative actions in terms of the anticipated feelings of himself and others, and to make moral choices on this basis. (He will have the capacity for such advanced moral behavior, according to Piaget, but other influences in his socialization process may prevent him from operating reflectively in the moral realm.)

B. F. Skinner claims that only to the degree that human beings become more sensitive to the long-term consequences of their behaviour for the human culture will we be likely to survive as a species. John Dewey, in his emphasis on the necessity for developing reflective thinking habits in young people, was talking about the same thing. He claimed over and over in his writing that the reflective, or broadly scientific, approach by the individual to his environment was both the prerequisite for a free and dynamic culture and the only basis for a process of cultural evolution directed by organized human intelligence rather than by random trial-and-error activities interspersed with violence.

The role of the educational agent in the socialization of each generation is therefore crucial. It is the responsibility of these agents (whether parents or teachers) to see that as much as possible of the process becomes *educational* — that it is not left to the accident of circumstance. Secondly, it is their responsibility to see that this educational process is carefully structured with the objective of rendering the child increasingly less dependent upon others as sources of authority and interpreters of reality. It must be deliberately structured so as to make him gradually more capable of operating on his environment reflectively and scientifically as a contributor to his culture's pool of organized intelligence rather than as a helpless victim of the products of the intelligence of others.

The Concept Demonstrated

CASE STUDY ONE

Anne Richmond had taken a number of sociology courses at university, and was enthusiastic about what she had learned. She was especially interested in group dynamics, and returned to her village school on the Alberta prairies determined to make use of her newly gained knowledge.

Certainly, there was need for sociological insight at Anne's school. A rather serious situation existed here. The problem was one of racial prejudice towards a handful of Cree children who accompanied their parents into the district every spring. The Indian group came from reservations in Saskatchewan to pick rocks from the rolling prairie "breaking" which was being prepared to produce the bumper wheat crops of the early postwar period. They were brought over by a white manager who hired them out to local farmers, and collected their wages. These people pitched their tents on the outskirts of the village every spring, and in due time a few grubby, sad-faced urchins arrived unceremoniously at the schoolhouse door.

These children were never accepted by the regular pupils. They suffered daily from the most extreme forms of discrimination. They were continually either being chased home ahead of a flurry of flying rocks or being ignored and avoided like the plague. The attitudes of the white children were, of course, reflections of those of their parents, who tried their best to pretend that the migrant workers on their doorstep did not exist. The unfriendliness and inhospitality of the village housewives by day was perhaps somewhat compensated for, however, by the frequency with which many of the town's respectable businessmen visited the camp by night. All in all, the situation was not conducive to the development of healthy inter-cultural relations.

Anne decided that she would try to use group dynamics in her classroom to combat the hate and anti-Indian prejudice which clouded the entire school. On the very day of the arrival of her three little migrants, she divided her grade six class into groups by means of sociometric techniques. She administered sociometric tests and constructed a sociogram from her data. These tests ask respondents to indicate with whom they would most prefer to work as well as with whom they would least like to work or spend time. If pupils answer the questions honestly the teacher is able to chart the responses on a sociogram so that "stars" (chosen by many) and "isolates" (whom nobody chose) can be identified. As she had expected, Anne discovered the existence of a number of cliques in her classroom. She was also able to single out two "stars" and, of course, her "isolates" — the three newcomers from the camp at the edge of town.

On the basis of her sociograms Anne formed her groups. She separated her stars and placed one isolate in each group. She then proceeded to organize all of her classwork on a group basis. Her hope was that as the Indian child in each group was drawn in and involved in the work, the other children would learn to accept him as a fellow human being. This failed to happen. Anne, not being one to give up easily, tried other ploys.

She managed to obtain some beginning story books in the Cree language and encouraged the newcomers to explain them to her and to the rest of the class. She started lessons for the whole class in the reading of the simple Cree words, and in the history and customs of the Cree in Western Canada: lessons in which the Indian children in each group shone suddenly and brilliantly. In conjunction with these lessons she organized academic contests among the learning groups, so that all of the members would be forced to cooperate in order to achieve group goals. She extended the competition to recess periods, and organized team games in which groups participated for prizes. Here again, the Indian children excelled, and in spite of themselves the other members of each group began to cheer their practised Indian athlete.

However, Anne noticed that the newcomers were still being ignored and sometimes scoffed at, when the learning groups were working at regular school subjects. She realized that they were far beyond their depth in subjects like arithmetic, reading and composition, and could not possibly show up well here. She reorganized the class once more, putting the Indian children together in their own group for these subjects, and using only problems and stories provided by them for her teaching materials. To her delight she was able to see immediate progress in their conceptual and skill development.

Weeks passed, however, with the Indian children still being totally left out of the friendship cliques which formed spontaneously whenever the children were left to their own devices. This indicated to Anne that she had not really succeeded. In spite of all the sociological theory to the contrary, she had failed to bring about the desired attitude change.

Then one day she looked out of the window, as the children were leaving school. The old, familiar, helpless anger engulfed her as she saw a number of grade seven pupils throwing rocks at one of her little Indian boys, and calling him names. She noticed four of her other boys approaching the scene. She watched with growing dismay as they, too, slowly picked up rocks. Suddenly they turned, and let fly with their missiles. And Anne gasped in surprise. For the rocks were winging, not at their fleeing classmate, but at the grade seven attackers!

QUESTIONS FOR GROUP DISCUSSION

1   What sorts of beliefs about "the real" and "the good," where Indians were concerned, had the majority of Anne's grade six class acquired as a result of their socialization-enculturation in home and community?

2   Teachers often try to combat prejudice by telling their pupils that it is bad and that they must love people who are culturally or racially different. Why do you suppose Anne chose not to use that approach?

3   What were the educational objectives that Anne had in mind? Discuss her attempted procedures for achieving these. In what way did she show herself to be flexible and capable of dropping or altering means that seemed not to be contributing to these objectives?

4   Why do you suppose Anne's original class structure (in which she placed one Indian child in each group) worked in some contexts and not in others?

5   Discuss Anne's decision to use only events from the lives of the Indian children as teaching materials for arithmetic, reading and language lessons. Give a justification for this in terms of the concept of socialization.

CASE STUDY TWO

Tom Bidwell was a grade twelve history teacher who had recently been assigned to a large collegiate institute in an Ontario city. His interest in political science and his desire to develop "good citizenship" prompted him to begin immediately to encourage extensive student participation in the forms and procedures of democratic government. Although his principal previously had not bothered much with student government, Tom was able to convince him that this was a necessary part of a student's educational experience.

Tom devoted much of his time during September to getting school elections under way. The rest of the staff agreed somewhat reluctantly to his idea. They watched the proceedings rather passively, but without interfering in a negative way.

It was Tom's intention that the students learn to be good citizens by *being* citizens; therefore he gave them as much freedom as possible, allowing voluntary student groups to organize the procedures for themselves. Candidates were nominated for all available positions, campaign managers were chosen, and the electioneering began in a blaze of enthusiasm. Various student groups, backing their candidates, began to devote most of their time and energy to campaigning. As the days passed, teachers began to complain of lack of interest in classwork, and wholesale neglect of assignments by the more popular of the students. A small "leading crowd" seemed to be participating most vigorously in the electioneering, both as candidates and as supporters of candidates. The majority of the student body seemed uninvolved in any active way, but unable to settle down to their regular work.

The election day had almost arrived when Tom realized with dismay that the candidates for all the top positions were not the most mature and responsible students, nor those with the best academic records. Instead, a small group who seemed to have a lot of money to spend, and a good deal of time for "goofing-off," had taken over the campaign. The entire procedure had come to be dominated by the circus atmosphere and even the corruption which Tom considered to be the most undesirable features of modern party politics.

Tom became particularly concerned when he was confronted with the platforms of the two candidates for president of the student council. Both were open attacks on the administration and most of the teachers of the school, full of threats, innuendoes, and half-truths. These were coupled with promises of more parties and an end to rules concerning the parking of cars and motorcycles in the schoolyard and drinking at school functions. No serious educational issue was touched upon. However, because he had insisted on complete student control of the entire elective process, Tom felt that he could not now interfere. Accordingly, the election took place as scheduled. The majority of the student body did not bother to vote, and a number of people whom Tom recognized as some of the most irresponsible "non-students" in the school were elected to the student council. The majority of the students seemed to consider the whole thing a big joke, while their new executive immediately began to battle with the principal for a suspension of all school rules.

During the unhappy strife-laden days that followed, Tom realized that whatever it was that the students were learning from their experience with student government, it was decidedly not what he would define as "good citizenship." But when the principal came to him, demanding that he salvage the situation which his decisions had helped to create, he was at a loss to know what action to take.

38651

QUESTIONS FOR GROUP DISCUSSION

1   In terms of socialization, did Tom's original concern for "good citizenship" involve the acquisition by his students of appropriate beliefs about the nature and prerequisites of democratic decision-making, or rather the development of habits such as campaigning and voting for candidates? Which of these do you consider to be a desirable educational objective?

2   In your opinion, what sorts of beliefs about group decision-making processes were actually being acquired, as a result of this experience, by (a) the student participants, and (b) the student observers? Are these the kinds of beliefs likely to contribute to the construction or destruction of democratic procedures in the larger society?

3   How could Tom control the consequences of the various student choices involved in this situation, so that desirable learning might now take place?

4   What would constitute *contriving* rather than *controlling* the consequences of what the students have done thus far? Think of a number of examples and discuss the possible result of each for the socialization of these students.

CASE STUDY THREE

In 1968 Mr. Warner became principal of a high school in Prince Edward Island. At the time of his appointment the superintendent had spoken glowingly of his new school, referring to it as one of the most successful in the province. Apparently this high·school had, over a period of many years, developed a reputation for producing a consistently high proportion of scholarship winners. This was a reputation, the superintendent implied, that a new principal would be expected to maintain at all costs.

During his first year Mr. Warner was quite happy about his school. Most of the staff members were old hands, and they worked well together. The pupils seemed to be studying hard inside school and playing hard outside. There were few discipline problems. The parents (mostly hard-working farmers who had chosen farming after high school) could be counted on to see that their children did their homework. Even the slowest learners usually managed to pass the final grade twelve exams, after much drilling by their teachers on the answers to the previous year's questions.

But as the second year of his appointment wore on, Mr. Warner began to feel a little uncomfortable about his role. He had embarked upon a follow-up study of the student population of the previous ten years and, as the results of his detective work began to come in, his dissatisfaction with the university-orientation of the school increased. He was gathering data on the school's few drop-outs as well as on those who had graduated and gone on to university, attempting to assess the contribution of their high-school experience to their effectiveness and fulfilment as human beings. And what he was finding was disconcerting, to say the least.

Mr. Warner discovered that a considerable proportion of the population that he was studying had indeed entered university, with very few enrolling in other forms of post-secondary education. However, their drop-out rate seemed excessively high. And of the university drop-outs, more were unemployed than were in the work force.

Upon interviewing randomly selected graduates of his school, Mr. Warner discovered a prevalence of attitudes which seemed to him to indicate cynicism and alienation. These attitudes occurred with great frequency among all products of the school, early high-school leavers, university drop-outs, and university graduates. Although most had been exposed to a number of classes of high-school math, science, English and social studies, they exhibited little curiosity about their physical environment, and no interest in regional, national or world affairs, beyond a willingness to make judgments. An inordinate concern with self was demonstrated by the majority of the interviewees. Most indicated that they read fewer than three books a year, other than those assigned for classes. Most of the drop-outs gave as their reason for leaving university their frustration at having to memorize uninteresting theories, techniques and information. The young people interviewed talked readily and rapidly, but Mr. Warner found himself struck continually by what he came to recognize as a common syndrome: a mumbling, expressionless style of speech, accompanied by a certain poverty of vocabulary, simplicity of sentence structure, and tendency to respond in cliches.

At the end of three years Mr. Warner emerged from his "evaluation" research with a strange Alice in Wonderland feeling. "How am I going to tell my dedicated and hard-working teachers," he agonized, "that the record of *schooling* success in which we have taken such pride appears, instead, to be a dismal record of *educational* failure?"

QUESTIONS FOR GROUP DISCUSSION

1   How might the procedures and priorities of this school have contributed to the intellectual, moral and emotional immaturity of its graduates?

2   How might the socialization-enculturation process to which these pupils had been exposed in the home and community have contributed to their lack of growth?

3   Might the complaint about having to memorize uninteresting theories, information, and so on in university indicate something about the teaching

methods employed by their instructors? Might it indicate something about the students themselves?

4 Is it possible to explain the cynicism and alienation of these young people in terms of a socialization-enculturation process that gradually forced them into the habit of operating in two separate worlds: one of routine, unanalysed, out-of-school existence, and one of symbols connected only with school? Discuss.

5 What sort of socialization-enculturation process is the first-year university student likely to be exposed to? Discuss the level of intellectual, moral and emotional maturity which might conceivably be required if one is to benefit from the typical university experience. Is the university a good place for an immature youngster to "find himself"? If not, what sort of an environment would you suggest for this purpose?

The Concept Applied
To Relevant Canadian Research

Cameron, A. and T. Storm. "Achievement Motivation in Canadian Indian, Middle, and Working Class Children." *Psychological Reports* 16 (1965): 459-463.
Sixty-six elementary school children from three subcultural groups (British Columbia Indian, white middle and white working class) were given fifty trials on a concept-learning task under conditions of material or non-material reward. There was a significant interaction between subculture and reward conditions, with middle class whites out-performing the other two on non-material and delayed-reward conditions.

Chabassol, David. "Prejudice and Personality in Adolescents," *Alberta Journal of Educational Research* 16, no. 1 (1970): 3-12.
Two hundred and seventy-seven junior and senior high-school students in a Maritime town were surveyed to discover whether Canadian adolescents, in the absence of French-Canadian, Negro and Jewish neighbours, would make prejudicial comments about these three minority groups. Fewest prejudicial statements were made by girls and "self-accepting" students, and about "Canadians," "Negroes," "French Canadians" and "Jews" in that order.

Clark, B. "The Brunswick-Cornwallis Pre-School: A Program for Disadvantaged White and Negro children." *Child Study* 29 (1967): 17-27.
This experimental program had two purposes: to provide planned experiences to prevent the academic retardation characteristic of culturally disadvantaged children, and to provide interracial experiences

that would prevent the effects of the prejudice so damaging to both white and Negro children. It was located in one of the most economically deprived areas in Canada. The findings indicate the existence of a major educational problem among lower-class children in Halifax. They also show that an enriched pre-school program can provide some of the learning necessary to elevate intelligence scores, even though not to the level attained by middle-class children of the same age.

Crysdale, Stewart. "Family and Kinship in Riverdale," in Mann, W. E., ed., *Canada: A sociological Profile* pp. 106-115. Toronto: Copp Clark, 1968.
A study of child-rearing patterns in a predominantly blue-collar Canadian community. A clear distinction between "working-class" and "middle-class" behaviours was not revealed by these findings.

Endler, Norman S. and Elizabeth Hoy. "Conformity as Related to Reinforcement and Social Pressure." *Journal of Personality and Social Psychology* 7 : 2 (1967): 197-202.
The effects of these variables on conformity among students at a Canadian university were studied by means of a sample of 60 male and 60 female students. Findings were (a) conformity was a function of the degree and type of reinforcement, (b) conformity in session 2 varied with the treatment received in session 1, (c) some students conformed more to perceptual than to verbal items, and (d) there were no sex differences in conformity.

Foster, Lois and Mary Nixon. "Language, Socio-economic Status and the School: An Exploratory Study." *Alberta Journal of Educational Research* 19, no. 3 (1973): 187-194.
This study was designed to test the following hypothesis in Alberta: the higher the socio-economic status (SES) the more complex the use of language. Contrary to the Bernstein theory of linguistic codes and the empirical work done by Lawton, there were few differences between high SES and low SES students.

Fowler, W. and Nasim Kahn, et al. "A Developmental Learning Approach in Infant Care in a Group Setting." *Merrill-Palmer Quarterly of Behavior and Development* 18, no. 2 (1972): 145-175.
Objectives of the investigation were to probe the significance of early experience as a foundation period for learning, through establishing a quality program of day care and education for infants to serve as a model for infant day care in Ontario and the rest of Canada. The most significant finding was that programs for infants can be developed to a level of quality that ensures adequate to high-level development in all types of children in all areas: cognitive, motor and socio-emotional.

George, P. M., and H. Y. Kim. "Social Factors and Educational Aspirations of Canadian High School Students," in Gallagher, J. E. and R. D. Lambert, eds., *Social Process and Institution: The Canadian Case*, pp. 352-363. Toronto: Holt, Rinehart and Winston, 1971.

This study analysed data collected from 1,069 high-school students of London and St. Thomas, Ontario, during 1968-69. Greater aspiration to pursue formal education was indicated by upper-class as compared to lower-class, male as compared to female, and urban as compared to rural students.

Greenglass, Esther R. "A Comparison of Maternal Communication Style Between Immigrant Italian and Second-Generation Italian Women Living in Canada," in Berry, J. W., and G. J. S. Wilde, eds., *Social Psychology: The Canadian Context*, pp. 335-344. Toronto: McClelland and Stewart, 1972.
In an experiment in which 89 mother-child pairs were employed as subjects, the relationship between maternal communication and ethnicity was examined. Italian immigrants tended to rely on direct imperatives. Canadian mothers relied on more indirect forms of control. Second-generation Italian mothers were even more likely than other Canadians to use indirect rather than authoritarian methods.

Hawthorn, H. B. "Socialization: Processes and Problems" in *A Survey of the Contemporary Indians of Canada*, Indian Affairs Branch, Ottawa, (1966) Vol. 2; 109-127.
A comparison was made of the typical child-rearing environments of the Indian and White children, along with a discussion of parental demands and routines.

Herman, A. B. "Effects of High School Program Choice on Self Concept." *Alberta Journal of Educational Research* 17, no. 1 (1971): 13-18.
This study sought to determine whether there is a difference between "self concept" and "ideal self concept" in matriculation and non-matriculation students in an Alberta high school. No significant differences were found, but there was some correlation with sex and intelligence groups. Chief concerns of these students were appearance and attitude of others.

Hostetler, J. A. "Socialization and Adaptations to Public Schooling: The Hutterian Brethren and the Old Order Amish." *Sociological Quarterly* 11, no. 2 (1970): 194-205.
The problem of this study was to establish that two small societies with similar Anabaptist cultures, but with different socialization structures, would adapt differently to educational demands in the surrounding

society. The Canadian Hutterites were compared with the American Amish. It was found that the Hutterites, with schools on the colonies and strong informal controls on the teacher and curriculum, and a stressing of dependency, suffered little loss of members, while the Amish, whose children were attending public schools, showed a gradual loss of members.

Ishwaran, K. "The Canadian Family: Variations and Uniformities," in Gallagher, J. E. and R. D. Lambert, eds., *Social Processes and Institutions: The Canadian Case*, Holt, Rinehart & Winston, 1971. This study used census data and the literature to support the thesis that Canadian families vary in organizational form from the "outpost" (aboriginal) families to the "rural" to the "urban," with complexity increasing as we move along the continuum. The author concluded that class and ethnic influences increase the complexity of Canadian kinship structures.

Kenneth, K. F. and A. J. Cropley, "Intelligence, Family Size and Socio-economic Status," *Journal of Biosocial Science* 11, no. 3 (1970): 227-236. The study involved the intelligence-testing of 170 Protestant children in grades six, seven and eight at two Board of Education elementary schools in middle- to upper-class areas of Regina, Saskatchewan. A relationship was found between intelligence and SES, but no significant differences were observed between mean I.Qs. for groups of children from different sizes of families. The findings support the hypothesis that the negative correlation between family size and intelligence (reported during the first half of the twentieth century) is primarily an artifact of an inverse relationship between family size and SES, which may no longer hold.

Kopf, K. E. "Family Variables and School Adjustment for Eighth-Grade Father-Absent Boys." *Family Coordinator* 19, no. 2 (1970): 145-150. The sample for this research was formed from the 26 highest and 26 lowest scoring children from an original sample of 145 boys in five moderate-size Canadian cities. The attitudes and behaviour of the mother were found to be significantly related to the child's adjustment in school.

Labercane, G. D., and R. D. Armstrong. "Socio-economic Status and the Meaning Vocabularies of Children." *Alberta Journal of Educational Research* 15, no. 4 (1969): 225-233. The purpose of this study was to analyse the relationship between SES and both recognition and recall vocabularies of upper elementary school children. (N=155 members of grades four, five and six from Edmonton public schools.) Significant differences were observed between upper and lower SES groups in vocabulary scores.

Lambert, W. E., et al. "Child Training Values of English Canadian and French Canadian Parents." *Canadian Journal of Behavioral Science* 3, no. 3 (1971): 217-236.
This article took the form of an analysis of parents' immediate reactions to a taped version of a child's demands for attention, etc.. The samples were of English-Canadian (EC) and French-Canadian (FC) working-class parents of six-year-olds. EC mothers and FC fathers were found to play the dominant socializing role. Both agreed in their treatment of boys versus girls. This contrasts sharply with the "cross-sex" permissiveness found in an American study.

Lewis, Claudia. "Doukhobor Childhood and Family Life," in Hawthorn, H. B., ed. *The Doukhobors of British Columbia*, pp. 97-121. Vancouver: U. of B.C. and J. M. Dent, 1955; 97-121.
This is an example of the "participant-observer" type of research, in which the author described how the Doukhobor child grows up within an authoritarian framework which communicates to him a value of controlled, submissive behaviour. Her thesis was that this makes him poorly suited to battle the stresses of Doukhobor life in Canada.

Linton, Thomas E. "Dogmatism, Authoritarianism, and Academic Achievement." *Alberta Journal of Educational Research* 14, no. 1, (1968): 49-53.
Rokeach's D scale, which is designed to measure rigidity of belief-structuring or "closed-mindness," was administered to 157 grade nine students who had been divided into three achievement categories ("failures," "mediocres" and "honours") on the basis of provincial departmental exams. An inverse correlation between achievement level and dogmatism was found.

MacArthur, Russell S. "Some Cognitive Abilities of Eskimo, White and Indian-Metis Pupils Aged 9 and 12 Years." *Canadian Journal of Behavioral Science*, 1, no. 1 (1969): 50-59.
When native pupils were scored on a standardized test, the least ethnic difference and least decline with age relative to whites occurred in ability to memorize and to reason from non-verbal stimuli. Almost no sex differences were discerned.

Mickelson, N. I., and C. G. Galloway. "Cumulative Language Deficit Among Indian Children." *Exceptional Children* 36 (1969): 187-190.
This is a description of an experimental summer educational program

sponsored during the summer of 1968 by the University of Victoria in cooperation with the Department of Indian Affairs, for three age groups of Indian children living on four reserves in the southern region of Vancouver Island. It was found that early language deficiencies tend to remain in the verbal repertoire of the child, but that this phenomenon can be corrected by means of specific and well-planned language experiences.

Pavalko, R. M. and D. R. Bishop. "Peer Influences on the College Plans of Canadian High School Students," *Canadian Review of Sociology and Anthropology* 3, no. 4 (1966): 191-200.
This study was based on the hypothesis that students whose best friends plan on college are most likely to plan to go themselves. A sample of 889 Ontario grade twelve students was used. The hypothesis was found to hold in general, except that peer plans had little influence on low SES girls—regardless of ability—while peer plans persisted as a factor in the plans of boys — partially independent of SES or ability.

Pedersen, Ergel. "Measured I.Q. Related to Teacher-Estimation of Intelligence: An Exploration in Bias." *McGill Journal of Education* 3, no. 1 (1968): 12-23.
By comparing the teacher-estimated intelligence to measure IQs of 657 students (from a larger sample of 6,465 grade eight and grade ten students in Quebec) this study found that teachers tended to overestimate the IQs of working-class boys and to underestimate the IQs of girls, regarless of their SES.

Rogers, R. S. and E. N. Wright. *The School Achievement of Kindergarten Pupils for Whom English Is a Second Language: A Longitudinal Study Using Data from the Study of Achievement.* Toronto: Board of Education, 1969.
Data were taken from the longitudinal study of 8,695 Toronto school children between 1960 and 1968. "English as a second language" (ESL) pupils were found to exhibit an average pattern of school performance distinctly different from that of the "monolingual" pupil, starting school with a considerable performance deficit which is more than overcome by grade three. It was concluded that the ESL pupils were not a homogenous group by any other criterion.

Schleifer, Michael and Virginia Douglas. "Moral Judgments, Behavior and Cognitive Style in Young Children." *Canadian Journal of Behavioral Science* 5, no. 2 (1973): 133-144.
This is a report of two studies of samples of six-year-old and pre-school children from middle-class and working-class districts of Montreal. In the six-year-old samples children characterized as immature in their

moral judgments were found to be more impulsive and more dependent. In the pre-school sample, children highest on moral maturity were seen as less aggressive by their teachers, as well as less impulsive and more independent.

Seeley, John R. et al. "The Family," in *Crestwood Heights: A Case Study of Culture in Canadian Suburban Life* pp. 160-223. Toronto: University of Toronto Press (2nd. ed.), 1963.
This chapter presents a description and analysis of primary socialization in an upper middle-class Toronto suburb during the early postwar years.

Singer, Benjamin D. "Violence, Protest and War in Television News: The U.S. and Canada Compared," in Gallagher, J. E. and R. D. Lambert, eds. *Social Process and Institution: The Canadian Case*, pp. 231-236. Toronto: Holt, Rinehart and Winston, 1971.
This is an example of content analysis employed as a research methodology, in which it was found that the American CBS network carried almost twice as many "aggression items" as did the Canadian CBC for the period under study.

Vaz, Edmund W. "Middle Class Adolescents: Self-reported Delinquents and Youth Culture Activities." *Canadian Review of Sociology and Anthropology* 2, no. 1 (1964), 52-70.
This study presents data on selected interests and activities and on peer orientations of middle-class Canadian adolescents which lend support to the notion of a middle-class youth culture. Their delinquency role was seen as a product of their role as "teenager."

Vernon, P. E. *Intelligence and Cultural Environment.* London: Methuen, 1969.
This book reports on a major survey of psychological theory and research relating to the differences between peoples in their levels of technological advance and "civilization" as they relate to variations in the pattern of abilities. In the last section (on cross-cultural studies) the author describes his comparative research on "deprived" groups, two of which were Canadian (Indian and Eskimo) and two of which were African. He concludes that the major differences between the thinking of "civilized" and "deprived" groups arises from the emphasis on conformity and social integration in the latter, plus their acceptance of magical beliefs which inhibit analytic perception and rational thinking.

Whitehead, Paul C. "Head or Brain? Drug Use and Academic Performance," in Gallagher, J. E. and R. D. Lambert, eds. *Social Process and Institution: The Canadian Case*, pp. 364-370. Toronto; Holt, Rinehart and Winston, 1971.

This study sought to explore the relation between drug use and academic performance in the Metropolitan Halifax school attendance area, using a 25 per cent random sample of classes from grades seven, nine, eleven and twelve. A linear and inverse relationship between the two was found.

Zentner, Henry. "Religious Socialization, Social Class and Academic Achievement: A Speculative Overview," in *Profiles of the Supernatural*, pp. 29-74. Calgary: Strayer Pub, 1972.
This chapter is an attempt to analyse findings concerning the impact of religious and social class factors upon the educational achievement of Canadian pupils.

INDEPENDENT STUDY

Select for careful reading, three studies, each of which deals with a different one of the following as an agent of socialization: (1) the family, (2) the peer group, and (3) the teacher, or (4) the media.

1   What sorts of beliefs about what is "real" and what is "good" are being constructed by the recipients of the socialization process in each case?

2   For each study, comment on whether the process being assessed could be termed education or unplanned socialization. Justify your answer in terms of the explanation of the concept in this chapter.

The Concept Amplified By Further Reading

Ashton-Warner, Sylvia. *Spearpoint*. New York: Alfred A. Knopf, 1972.
An eye-opening and often disturbing account of the results of the socialization process which today is shaping many middle-class children in America. Throughout the book are suggestions of *better* means of socializing children, (for example, the little sequence on "consequential discipline" on pages 174 and 175).

Hess, Robert D. and Virginia C. Shipman. "Early Experience and the Socialization of Cognitive Modes in Children," in Havighurst, Robert and Bernice Neugarten, *Society and Education*, pp. 125-136. Boston: Allyn and Bacon, (3rd. ed.), 1967.
Evidence is presented supporting the proposition that the structure of the social system and the structure of the family shape language which in turn shapes cognition.

Jensen, Arthur R. "How Much Can We Boost I.Q. and Scholastic Achievement?," *Harvard Educational Review* 39, No. 3 (1969), 1-123.
A carefully documented article attempting to explore the question of heritabil-

ity and variability of intelligence and its relationship to academic success. The author is careful to make the distinction between "individual" and "population" in addressing himself to the controversial issue of whether or not certain intellectual abilities are disproportionately distributed among groups in the U.S. today. His failure to distinguish equally carefully between biologically and socially related groups weakens his total argument considerably.

King, Edith W. and August Kerber. *The Sociology of Early Childhood Education*. New York: American Book Co., 1968.
This is an easy-to-read source, prepared in a textbook format with thought-provoking questions, a professional reading list, and reference to materials for use in teaching young children. It is written from an instrumentalist-evolutionary perspective.

Levine, Robert A. "Culture, Personality and Socialization: An Evolutionary View," in Goslin, David A., ed., *Handbook of Socialization Theory and Research*, pp. 503-541. Chicago: Rand McNally, 1969.
The author attempts a preliminary application of the Darwinian model to the interaction of culture and personality, with specific references to the process of socialization. He examines traditional anthropological, psychological and sociological approaches to socialization which view the process as one of enculturation, acquisition of impulse control, and training in social participation (in that order). He suggests that these are not incompatible with one another and that a more explicit application of the Darwinian model might lead to a comprehensive view of socialization.

Mead, George Herbert. *Mind, Self and Society*. Chicago: University of Chicago Press, 1934.
This book provides a large part of the theoretical basis for the "interactionist-evolutionary" model presented in the present text. It lays the groundwork for a view of man as a social self for whom every choice to act is a moral one with inevitable consequences for the fabric of interaction in which each self is embedded.

Petras, John. "George Herbert Mead's Theory of Self: A Study in the Origin and Convergence of Ideas." *Canadian Review of Sociology and Anthropology* 10, no. 2 (1973): 148-159.
An up-to-date interpretation of Mead's theory of self which views Mead's model of the socialization process as one of continuous interpretation, by the individual, of the data furnished him by the social situation of which his behaviour forms a part.

Piaget, Jean. *The Moral Judgement of the Child*. Glencoe, Ill.: The Free Press, 1932.
Here Piaget presents his theory of the development of morality in human beings. He explains and documents the existence of a genetic parallelism between the formation of the logical and moral consciousness. He shows how social life is necessary if the individual is to move away from egocentrism, with logical thought being both the means and consequence of this evolution; how

intellectual and moral constraints function in similar ways during certain stages of development; and how the cooperation which alone leads to moral autonomy and reciprocity is only possible given a correspondingly advanced stage of logical, or intellectual development.

Piaget, Jean, *The Psychology of Intelligence*. Paterson, N.J. Littlefield, Adams and Co., 1960.
The basis for the author's integrated model of cognitive and affective development is presented here.

Piaget, Jean and Barbel Inhelder. *The Psychology of the Child*. New York: Basic Books, 1969.
This is probably the best primary source for use as an introduction to the Piaget model of learning (or socialization).

Prince, J. R. "Science Concepts in New Guinea and European Children." *Australian Journal of Education* 12, no. 1 (1968): 81-89.
This is an example of research based on the Piaget model. Group questionnaires mainly concerned with the conservation of length, quantity, weight, area and volume were administered to 2,700 indigenous children spread over seven grades of primary and high school, as well as to a European sample. The Piagetian stages were readily observed, but the indigenous children were about four years behind the European children in the achievement of conservation.

Pulaski, M. A. S. *Understanding Piaget*. New York: Harper and Row, 1971.
This is an excellent secondary source to use as an introduction to the theory and research of Jean Piaget. It is written with clarity and ample reference to concrete examples.

Rossides, Daniel W. *Society as a Functional Process*. Toronto: McGraw Hill, 1968.
See pps. 109-121 for a discussion of the concept of socialization.

Schreiner, John. "What China Needs, China Teaches in the Schools." *Financial Post*, August 26, 1972.
Interesting data and impressions on contemporary Chinese education are presented here. (An example of the use of planned socialization as a vehicle of government policy.)

Schwebel, Milton, and Jane Raph, eds. *Piaget in the Classroom*. New York: Basic Books, 1973.
This is a timely attempt to unite one of the most fruitful social scientific models available today with actual classroom practice. A number of scholars and teachers whose interests bridge the behavioural sciences and education have contributed ideas and practical suggestions for the student who asks, "So how does all this theory help me to decide what to do Monday?."

Skinner, B. F. *Beyond Freedom and Dignity*. New York: Knopf, 1971.
This book identifies the philosophical assumptions underlying the modern

"operant conditioning" model of socialization. The author emphasizes the significance, for the understanding of human behaviour, of the Darwinian model of evolution, in which it is established that living organisms continually adapt on the basis of the experienced consequences of past behaviours or adaptations.

Swift, D. F. "Social Class and Achievement Motivation" in Swift, D. F., eds., *Basic Readings in the Sociology of Education*, pp. 182-198. London: Routledge and Kegan Paul, 1970.

The author stresses that how the individual behaves depends upon three aspects of the environment which he perceives: how he recognizes or understands the situation, how he values it, and the kind of pleasure or pain he expects from it. The author attempts to explain the relationship between success in school and social class by showing how the socialization process, which varies to some extent with social class, in turn influences the degree to which the individual values (and therefore strives for) academic achievement.

Utech, David A. and Kenneth L. Hoving. "Parents and Peers as Competing Influences in the Decisions of Children of Differing Ages." *Journal of Social Psychology* 78, no. 1 (1969): 267-274.

One hundred and eighty boys and the same number of girls from five grades in sixteen schools in a semi-rural, middle-class area were randomly selected. The hypothesis that conformity to the advice of parents is a decreasing function of age (when parents and peers offer conflicting advice) was supported. There was a significant decline in conformity to the advice of parents and a concomitant increase in conformity to advice of peers. Sex differences were not noted.

The Concept Reviewed

1   For the sociologist of education, the relationship between "socialization" and "education" can best be expressed as follows: (select one)
   a.   education is that part of the socialization process which is systematically structured and intentional
   b.   education and socialization are synonymous, both terms referring to the social process to which the child is exposed from birth onwards, which shapes his knowledge and values
   c.   the best education is an incidental process, while socialization is always the deliberate process by which the society forces the individual to conform to the status quo
   d.   with education there is always the intent to impose a certain set of values on the individual while socialization refers to friendly interaction in which the individual is free to choose his own values.

2   The teacher's role as an agent of socialization differs from that of all the other agents in a child's social environment in that:
   a.   the teacher's every interaction with the child is likely to affect the intellectual, emotional and moral development of the child in some way
   b.   the teacher is the one agent specifically designated by the social group to socialize the child in a systematic and purposeful way

c. the teacher intends that the child will acquire certain beliefs and habits (concerning both the physical and social environment) rather than others
d. the teacher is the only person in the child's environment who could be considered an educational agent.

3   In the complete absence of socialization the child would conceivably be:
a. non-conforming and creative
b. "de-humanized," if not insane
c. rational and international in outlook
d. aggressive and anti-social.

4   The model of socialization developed in this chapter views the human being as:
a. propelled at birth into his physical and social environment, and compelled to act upon (and be acted upon by) it
b. inevitably shaped into the mould fashioned for him by society
c. by nature seeking to rid himself of the societal constraints that operate to stultify his potentiality
d. requiring civilizing by his society so as to tame the brute that is within him at birth.

5   Which one of the following is *not* an example of the tendency of teachers and parents to shortcut the socialization process by "telling" or "giving" the child the physical or social rules?
a. the parent who permits the child to eat candy whenever he wishes during the day, then scolds him for not cleaning up his supper plate
b. the teacher who gives paper stars to all those pupils who come to school with their homework done
c. the parent who scolds a child for biting his twin brother, and prevents the brother from biting him back
d. the teacher who assigns, for homework, only those activities obviously required for the next day's projects, so that those pupils not prepared are readily recognized and necessarily excluded by the rest of the pupils
e. the kindergarten teacher who tells the pupil not to pile the blocks up too high, because they will fall down.

6   Which one of the following is an example of desirable procedures for socialization?
a. A youth wrecks the family car by drag-racing while drinking. His parents require him to contribute half of his pay check from a part-time job, for a year, toward the cost of a new one, while suspending his driving privileges for that period
b. A pupil achieves two years below his grade level in reading but has no trouble in handling arithmetic, science or social studies. He fails the grade and is required to repeat all the units of work involved.
c. A pupil in identical circumstances is passed to the next grade and required to read at the advanced level
d. A pupil in the opposite situation (one who reads with facility, but has failed to acquire the concepts being developed throughout the year) is

passed to the next grade and required to work at the advanced level

e. A youth wrecks the family car. The family purchases a new car immediately, and the youth is punished by being scolded angrily, and reminded frequently of his mistake. However, within a week he is driving the new car.

7 Which of the following is an example of unplanned, hit-and-miss socialization, rather than of the type that we could term education?

a. A teacher decides to go for "open education" and sets up a grade one classroom in which she carefully arranges materials, selected on the basis of their probable contribution to the construction of a number of skills and concepts which she has identified as desirable and necessary.

b. A teacher decides to go for "open education" and encourages her grade one pupils to bring anything they want from home to work and play with, making sure that she does not interfere in any way with their choices or activities.

c. The manager of the local TV station decides to run a series of programs dealing with the social causes and consequences of tobacco and alcohol addiction.

d. A church group plans its annual Sunday school program with the objective of reducing inter-ethnic hostilities in the community.

8 Which one of the following is the expression of a real issue in education today (and one to which Piaget speaks) rather than merely the expression of a popular educational fad or slogan?

a. "Classes must be child-centred rather than teacher-centred."
b. "Learning is an active rather than a passive process."
c. "Children must learn not knowledge but how to think."
d. "Our goal in education must be freedom rather than conformity."

9 For educators, the chief significance of Dewey's ideas is in his belief that:

a. the schools in a democracy must teach that each man's opinion is as good as the next, and that all opinions must be respected equally
b. if Western representative democracy is to survive, the schools must teach that all of our institutions are the best possible
c. the schools must see that what is taught and how it is taught is based on the objective of the formation of the scientific attitude in all children
d. equality of opportunity for schooling must be provided for everybody, in order to guarantee the survival of democracy
e. the schools should ensure that all members of society become specialized scientists.

10 If the child has been socialized into an increasing dependence upon adults as ultimate sources of authority, a number of consequences are likely to follow. Select the least likely consequence, according to the model of socialization developed in this chapter:

a. he will tend to live in two different worlds: that of school and of "real life"

b. he will tend to believe that theory has nothing to do with practice

c. he will tend to lose his natural curiosity and his faith in his own powers to test reality

d. he will tend to approach "real life" problems in a systematic, scientific manner

e. he will tend to seek certain and absolute answers to problems encountered throughout life.

Answers: 1 (a); 2 (b); 3 (b); 4 (b); 5 (d); 6 (d); 7 (a); 8 (b); 9 (c); 10 (d)

2 Social Organization

The Concept Explained

Most people, if they think of social organization at all, consider groups of human beings to be either organized or not organized. And, depending upon the direction of their ideological biases, they tend to see one of these categories as "bad" and the other as "good." That is, the tendency is to conceptualize the phenomenon at an extremely crude level and in value-laden terms. Two large "bins" are constructed, and all our experiences of social groupings are placed in either the "desirable" or the "undesirable" one. Educators who think in this way tend to refer quite uncritically to structured or organized classrooms as bad, and to non-structured or "informal" ones as inherently good, or vice versa. Much of the current wave of "reform-oriented" literature in education—as well as the bulk of the "tradition-oriented" response to it—is sadly illustrative of this low level of sociological awareness.

Some people, a little more sophisticated in behavioural studies, recognize that all human interaction is organized to some extent. This realization requires considerable refinement of the "organized" bin or category. It is perceived as being divided into a number of discrete sub-categories which have been labelled by terms such as "social system," "informal grouping," or "bureaucracy." All too often, however, these categories are still surrounded by an aura of magic. ("Bureaucracy" is bad because the sociology professor implied as much; "social system" is some sort of bourgeois apology for the status quo; "informal" is natural and therefore inherently good, while "formal organization" is somehow against nature and bad.) Sometimes these labels, acquired through reading or imitation of the speech of others, remain as mere symbols which we glibly define by the use of more symbols—especially as answers to exams in university classes, or in a variety of pseudo-intellectual games played by people who have been too long in the role of student.

However, in many cases, sufficient descriptions and simulated experiences are provided for the behavioural science student so that he actually succeeds in acquiring a set of concepts (meaning that the appropriate feelings, images and connections have become embedded in his thought processes) to the extent that he understands these various types of social arrangements intuitively. At this stage we could say that the learner has a good grasp of the concept of social organization as a set of discrete bins which enable him to order his experiences with social groupings so that he can at least categorize and map them.

A teacher at this stage of development of sociological understanding would be able to identify certain classrooms as informal settings, certain ones as functioning social systems, and certain ones as bureaucratic. He would be able to fit his memories of past school experiences into these categories as well, so as to make sense in a different way out of remembered events.

But there is an additional step which would render the concept much more powerful as an ordering tool: one that would make it potentially more useful for the process of knowledge-construction and for the practice of schooling. This is the step that begins to *relate* the discrete bins or types of social organization to one another, while continuing to refine them on the basis of finer and finer shades of difference. It allows us to ask questions such as "What are the features of a bureaucracy that make it different from an informal grouping?"

This step begins to build, within the thought processes of the student of human behaviour, a *conceptual structure* which allows for more than the increasingly refined categorizing of immediate experience relevant to social organization. It opens the way for the explanation, prediction and control by human beings of *changes* in the manner in which they arrange their interaction. And of course it is with the bringing about of controlled change in patterns of interaction in the classroom that teachers who talk of informal education are really concerned. For example, we begin to find a way to solve the problem of how a teacher can alter the organization of his classroom so as to change it from the random collection of non-communicating individuals thrown together on the first day of school to a social system functioning to enhance the intellectual, moral and emotional growth of each member.

The necessary first step at this stage is to explain the concept of social organization not as a set of discrete categories, but as a *continuum*. This means that we will not be satisfied merely with describing the various recognizable types of organization such as social system and bureaucracy, but that we will endeavour to explain the mechanisms by means of which a social system becomes a bureaucracy and vice versa. Only when social scientific concepts are perceived as dynamic continuums rather than as sets of discrete, static categories, will we possess the necessary tools for constructing testable explanations of changes in human interaction. And the central concern of education is the *process of change* in the individual, in the formal organization, and in the culture. A model of social organization which cannot explain how one type of structure changes to another is worse than useless for educators, as it is likely to result only in stereotyping and sloganizing. Terms representing ambiguous, crude concepts which do not allow us to discriminate among the phenomena that we encounter encourage sloppy over-generalizing, or prejudging on the basis of too few, or irrelevant criteria. Or we are encouraged to use the terms as symbols for the arousing of emotions. (What student does not feel a warm glow when he hears the term "humanistic education"? And what student has any profound understanding of how he as a teacher would proceed specifically in humanizing what goes on in the classroom, or even in comparing one classroom to another as to degree of humanization?)

How do sociologists explain social organization as a continuum? The first step is to go back to the beginning and posit the distinguishing feature of that type of social interaction we term "organized" as opposed to an imagined condition of "non-organization." We begin to see that it has something to do with predictability. Where the behaviour of the participant seems to be obviously patterned and according to rule we have no doubt about labelling it "organized." For instance, most people would recognize the behaviour of the Mounties in the Musical Ride as organized. But they might have a little more difficulty seeing that their own behaviour at work and even at play follows patterns that would be more or less easy for their closest friends to predict. However, a little more thought in this vein brings us to the realization that the behaviour of no human being is totally unpredictable. Nor is it ever totally predictable. This element of predictability arises from the need for collective action in the pursuit of group goals, a pursuit that requires prior group consensus. Group consensus is dependent upon durability of the interaction, which in turn only becomes possible with geographical (or artificially contrived) proximity of the participants. It is the proximity of human beings to one another which gives rise to the need for collective action in the first place, while at the same time allowing the development of those patterned responses which will achieve the group's goals over time. A group of teachers, all required to teach science in the same school, are highly likely to develop routines and approaches that, in a few years' time, will enable each teacher to make reasonably reliable predictions about what the others are doing. So predictability of interaction is a matter of degree, especially degree of proximity and durability of the relations concerned. It is clearly not an either/or proposition involving a state of organization versus one of non-organization.

Social organization, then, is part and parcel of all human interaction, and is characterized by more or less predictability, or formal patterning of behaviours. We could say that this formal patterning of behaviours is the theoretical dimension along which our various categories of social organization could be arranged.

Identifying the precise mechanisms by which one category changes to another is the next step. It is by far the more difficult one, and the step which will, in fact, comprise the actual construction of publicly verified knowledge in the field of social organization: knowledge which does not yet exist to any great extent. And it may well be teachers, working jointly with educational researchers in assessing the consequences of different structural arrangements in schooling situations, who will be making major contributions to the construction of such knowledge.

As a start toward an understanding of the continuum of social organization, we can identify the two extreme end-points first. We would expect to find neither extreme mirrored anywhere in the real world; they are "ideal types." This does not mean that they are preferred or desired types. It means, instead, that we try to imagine some extreme state of non-organization among human beings. We try to imagine this even though, in real life, the very moment that two people approach one another and begin to interact, a degree of formality of patterning, predictability, or mutual expectation of one another's reaction inevitably enters the picture. At the other end of the continuum we try to imagine a state of total formality or predictability where every individual is a cog in a social machine which operates precisely as programmed, and with no possibility of self-corrective feedback. These ideal types are useful, but not because they provide bins into which we can fit pieces of experience—this they definitely do not do. They are useful because they mark the extreme limits or boundaries of the yardstick (or conceptual framework) in terms of which we can locate our various bins and thereby relate our experiences of social interaction to one another.

We can now begin to picture our total concept, or conceptual structure, as follows:

Extreme of Non-organization ⟶ Aggregate ⟶ Informal Grouping ⟶

⟶ Social System ⟶ Formal Organization ⟶ Bureaucracy ⟶

⟶ Extreme of Formality of Organization

At the extreme of non-organization we can imagine a situation of social chaos in which undifferentiated, autistic organisms bounce off one another randomly. At the extreme of organization we can picture a tightly programmed, non-cybernetic social machine for which the only change possible would be its destruction and complete replacement with different members and a different blueprint. The "aggregate" represents a momentary gathering of individuals in geographical or technical proximity. Any section of a crowded street is a good example, or a bus-load of university students on the first day of classes. A class list of names of people who have not yet even met could be termed a statistical aggregate. This illustrates a form of technical, rather than geographical proximity.

The "informal grouping" is characterized by increased duration of gathering and a degree of interaction, as well as an awareness on the part of the members of belonging to a group for some reason. Here we can think of a class of pupils—all strangers—as they gather together daily during the first few weeks of school. Or the members of a political party, beginning to meet regularly for the first time, in order to name candidates and hammer out a program.

Where the "social system" level of organization pertains the interaction has endured long enough for a degree of interdependence to have been established. Roles (ways of behaving associated with each person) are emerging. Norms (group habits) are being established. Beliefs and sentiments (or a culture) are being shared. Group consensus on goals is continually evolving. The class (or the party) is beginning to work together, with leaders and laggards being recognized by all. Tasks have been assigned. Routines have developed, as have "in" jokes, memories of shared experiences, and commitment to certain group goals.

Where a "formal organization" exists, roles are pre-defined and the specific expectations and tasks assigned to them survive the tenure of individual members. (The principal's job is described on paper, with his responsibilities and spheres of jurisdiction clearly set out and shown to applicants.) Norms are pre-established in the form of rules for communication to incoming members. (A teacher goes first to his Department Head with a complaint, not to the principal; one does not criticize fellow teachers to pupils; and so on.) Common beliefs and sentiments are spelled out (as in the case of an educational philosophy) along with a plan for their transmission and continued construction (a curriculum). Specific objectives for group action have been agreed upon prior to the structuring of the organization. In fact, they are its reason for being. (The school is expected to provide all the children in the community with the skills and beliefs necessary for functioning in a complex urban environment.)

With the development of "bureaucracy" we find a rigidity of all these roles, rules, relationships and packages of beliefs. (Not only curriculum, but instructional procedures and resources are specifically defined for the teacher.) Major channels of communication have become technical rather than face-to-face. (The principal relies upon the intercom and the memo; the teachers submit forms on pupils consisting of test data, rather than engaging in conferences and interviews.) Goal substitution begins to occur, with the survival and intact maintenance of the organization replacing the original objectives for the achievement of which the organization was formed. (Smooth administrative functioning and economies of scale may be emphasized by the school's administrators at the cost of a healthy learning environment. The size of the school then increases, with the teachers becoming more specialized, each one teaching fewer and fewer concepts to more and more pupils. Increasing numbers of rules are listed, with ever more detailed behaviours being prescribed and proscribed.) All this tends to result in increased resistance to change, whether initiated within or outside of the organization.

It can be seen that *change* (if conceptualized as a process amenable to direction by human goal-seeking endeavours) would be inconceivable at either extreme of the continuum. This is an important idea for an educator, considering that education is defined as a planned process of individual growth or change. A type of organization conducive to the achievement of such systematic change in individuals would seem to be a prerequisite for education. Human beings are changing from birth onwards as a result of experience. However, education can never be merely the provision of an arena for more of the same trial-and-error experiencing to which the child is exposed through the accident of his birth. Neither can it ever be an excuse for stultifying individual development. What is attempted through education is the structuring and controlling of at least some of the environmental stimuli impinging on the individual for at least some periods of time so that his intellectual, moral and emotional growth process is not left entirely to chance.

In this effort to systematize and control change-producing environments so that individuals will develop in directions deemed desirable by the group, the teacher is not alone as an educational agent. This is a role that parents perform much of the time, some more consciously and rationally than others, and some with more power than others to control their children's environments. There are many other educational agents in the environment of every developing individual: the priest, the music teacher, the baby-sitter, and the communications media, for example. In addition, each individual is likely to be exposed to numerous uncontrolled socializing agents injecting barrages of stimuli into his environment. And his forays into his physical surroundings also provide him with either an enriched or impoverished milieu for development, depending on chance factors such as the location of his home, and opportunities for travel.

When we speak of the school we are considering a physical and social setting organized for the purpose of encouraging learning or growth in specified directions rather than in the random manner encouraged by the informal and uncontrolled shaping process to which the child is subjected in many other settings. When we speak of a teacher we are considering an educational agent: a mature and knowledgeable individual selected and certified by his community to bring about this individual change process in the direction of the goals of the group.

It is clear that, if schooling is to be provided for all youthful members of the group, the degree of social organization required will inevitably approach the "formal organization" level; for we are dealing here with collective action on behalf of very large numbers. This means that physical plants must be planned, financed and built, specialized roles such as that of teacher, principal and student must be defined, and perhaps an even more complex division of labour must be provided for, depending on the nature and extent of the goals assigned to the school and the size of the school plants and boards. If the provision of schooling were to be completely decentralized, and left to the desire and ability of the parents concerned, the function would be extremely costly (in terms of the resources devoted to it) and extremely exclusive, with the under-privileged being left out in the cold.

Obviously it can be argued that a degree of formal organization of schooling is required in order to provide equal opportunity of access to education for the children of the poor and the geographically isolated. In addition, formal organization of available resources clearly prevents costly duplications and omissions. Another advantage is that it ensures that all adult members of the group have been exposed to that common core of symbols and concepts necessary for the communication which serves as the glue which prevents a society's disintegration. However, the particular *form* that the schooling structure might take could conceivably be far removed from what we have at present. And the *degree* of formal organization necessary or desirable is a question requiring much further study. Ivan Illich's recommendation for "de-schooling" (or de-organization of education) seems instead to be an argument for radical change in the form and degree of formal organization. His "learning networks" are examples of a formal organization of social systems, according to our model, not examples of the absence of organization.

However, critics like Illich force us to ask whether we are blindly assuming that the more formal the organization, the better the schooling process. They also encourage us to question the assumption that every aspect of the educational setting should exhibit the same degree of formality of organization. Indeed, if the organizational context should be that which is most conducive to the nurturing of a continous process of systematic change in humanly fulfilling directions in both the individual and his community, perhaps we should be aiming at the minimum degree of formal organization required to guarantee opportunity of access and a core of common culture for all.

Perhaps we should be thinking in terms of levels of organization and the degree of formality most appropriate for the function being performed at each level. What about the classroom level of organization? Is there any reason for it to mirror the formality of the larger school structure—a structure made necessary by the size and complexity of the institutional complex of which it forms a part? The classroom is the milieu in which learners and teachers interact, in which the learning process which is the object of all this network of formal organization actually occurs. What pattern of social interaction is most desirable here?

First of all, we should understand that it is the teacher who is responsible for structuring the organizational context in which the planned and systematic part of pupil learning takes place. It is the teacher who must decide which degree of formality of structure is most desirable, given what we currently know about how learning occurs in the individual. Secondly, the teacher is responsible for determining the type of structure possible in his classroom at any particular time within any particular school, given what he knows about his own competence and the sociological imperatives of the situation. (These imperatives comprise such variables as the constraints imposed by the size, complexity and degree of formality of the encompassing organization—the school or school unit—within which one operates; the expectations of the pupils as to their own and the teacher's role; and the expectations and demands of the parents and other members of the immediate community.)

Thirdly, the teacher must know *how* to structure his classroom so that it operates at the most appropriate level of social organization. Even assuming that a teacher possesses an understanding of the concept of social organization, he might conceivably be totally lacking in knowledge of the more specific techniques by which one can alter social structures or patterns of interaction in order to make them more conducive to the achievement of specific learning outcomes.

At this point it is necessary for the teacher to know something about how informal small groupings form within a social system and of how this informal or "peer group" structure can either impede the realization of learning outcomes or be made to enhance it. He should know that a teacher can deliberately use small groups to achieve and maintain the social system level of formality of organization, if he decides that learning occurs best within that context.

How are teachers to make the decision that any particular level or style of organization—the social system, for example—is better than another that is either more or less formal? This is surely the same type of question that we might ask of other educational means such as types of physical resources and content, and as such it is equally open to systematic testing procedures. But it can be tested only if the teacher avoids the trap of viewing the social interaction or the group project as ends in themselves. It is necessary to sound this warning, for already there is evidence that educators who have finally learned that content is merely the vehicle by which learning outcomes are attained, rather than the goal, are now substituting yet another vehicle—social interaction—for learning goals.

Perhaps we would avoid these pitfalls if we always insisted that our learning objectives be expressed in individual terms. Learning is an individual growth process. Only if a change in the degree of formality of social organization enhances this individual growth is the teacher justified in adopting it. How, then, are we to compare the relative effectiveness of different organizational climates as means to individual learning? The first step is to define our desired outcomes precisely and to identify what types of written or orally expressed (or motor) behaviours on the part of the student we would be prepared to accept as indicative of the achievement of those outcomes. This list will include appropriate answers to carefully constructed test items designed to tap the attainment of concepts as well as a variety of possible activities: our instruments of measurement, in other words.

At this point some people will raise the objection that valuable emotional growth may be occurring in certain organizational contexts and impeded in others, but that this may not be amenable to assessment. Probably the most fruitful response here is that which is implied by Piaget's work. He sees emotional and intellectual growth not as separate, but as an intricately interrelated and interdependent process. To him, the feelings, or affective components, are the "energetics" of intellectual growth. The learner is motivated (by feelings of pleasure associated with past activity) to act upon his environment and to experience the consequences of his acting: to take in or "assimilate" data and to "accommodate" his thought structures to the new data. Feelings of anxiety at being confronted with new environmental demands, or a store of unpleasant sensations associated with reaching into his environment will serve to stultify resultant "accommodation" or intellectual growth.

To the teacher, then, the Piaget model implies that the objective of teaching can never be emotional development. Emotions or feelings are important in that they enhance or impede intellectual growth. But it is the intellectual and moral development that we are after as educators, and we should beware of confusing a highly desirable by-product and a contributing factor with the learning outcomes which are, in fact, amenable to some degree of reliable and valid assessment—as emotional development is not.

Piaget views intellectual development as being necessary but not sufficient for corresponding progress in the ability to make moral choices. Moral development is here understood as the increasing ability to operate as a *socially responsible* being: one whose choices are based on an awareness of the reciprocal nature of human relationships, along with the ability to hypothesize alternative consequences and to imagine the cumulative effect of these on all human beings in terms of one's own feelings. The identification of learning outcomes for moral development is a task scarcely considered by educators as yet, but one to which considerable time and resources could well be devoted at once. Small-group activity in a social system setting may prove to be a highly effective means of achieving desirable objectives in this area. However, until we identify such goals, along with their verbal and motor behavioural indicators, we are still groping in the dark.

Small-group work in most classrooms would require a decrease in the formality of the organizational climate. The teacher electing to move in this direction would be well advised to frame his objectives in terms of intellectual and moral development but not in terms of what he hopes may happen to the emotions of his students. And he should measure this growth in individual terms, not by means of collective tasks or projects.

All this has been intended to deal with the question of *why* one might wish to structure one's classes either more or less formally. It is in order to better enhance the intellectual and moral growth of one's students. It is not to provide for either an increase or a decrease in social interaction in the classroom as an end in itself nor to produce more grandiose projects than could be accomplished by students working alone. Only if we are clear about our objectives, and our means of evaluating them, will we be able to make the comparisons that will allow us to arrive at conclusions about the relative value of different levels of social organization in the classroom.

The second question concerns what is possible within the particular organizational context in which the teacher is working. Probably the best way to discover this is to record, over a period of time, the behavioural regularities pertaining within at least two classrooms in the school. A number of systems of interaction analysis are available for this purpose. Once this is done, one can identify those regularities that are the logically necessary consequences of (a) the rules and programs of the school, (b) the cherished norms of the community, and (c) the laws of the land. All other regularities may be dispensed with; usually these have their source in traditional expectations regarding teacher-student role relationships, and it is precisely these expectations governing classroom social interaction that the experimenter is setting out to change.

This brings us to the third question: how does a teacher go about altering the social structure of his classroom? Let us assume that the teacher considers it desirable and possible to decrease the level of formality of organization. On the basis of his survey and analysis of the interaction in his classroom he has concluded that the present teacher-dominated structure could be loosened up considerably. However, he does not intend to abandon his responsibility to control the organizational climate by allowing the situation to become so fluid and informal that the prevailing peer-group structure will determine how people will relate to one another in his classroom. In other words, he intends to build and maintain a relatively open social system rather than an informal grouping or a formal organization.

To make a class a functioning social system a teacher must establish interdependence and boundaries as quickly as possible. Probably the best way to accomplish the first is through the formation of small groups operating as necessary parts of the whole. Three criteria for the structuring of these groups should be kept in mind.

1   Within each group there should be as much variation as possible in terms of student developmental level and experiential background.

2   As much as possible, students should be allowed to select their group in terms of the topics or themes in which they are most interested.

3   As much as possible, close friendship pairings or cliques should be broken up.

Why is it desirable that groups be organized on the basis of heterogeneity of abilities and homogeneity of interests, that the element of student choice be provided for, and that the informal peer group structure not be confirmed and perpetuated by the teacher? There are many arguments in favour of homogeneity of abilities. In fact, many see grouping in the classroom merely as an administrative device for making a formally organized classroom more effective; the teacher can better move a number of students along over the same content at the same pace if their abilities are similar. Others argue that students who read at about the same level, who have similar ability to generalize and hypothesize, and to anticipate and to accept responsibility for the consequences of their actions will be able to operate on content in similar ways and therefore learn more from one another in a social system setting. Arguments in favour of heterogeneity, however, are based on the following assumptions:

1   These three significant types of abilities are not always uniformly developed: that is, the same student might have poor communicative and reasoning skills but a high degree of social responsibility and self-discipline. In order to achieve homogeneity on all three, one's groups might have to be much smaller than the optimal size of seven to ten.

2   Students learn a great deal from one another if the class structure allows it. The best teacher for someone having difficulties might well be the student who has only recently worked his way through the steps involved himself.

3   Because teaching something is often the best way to learn it, the more able student in a group may benefit a great deal from helping others.

4   The type of small group most conducive to learning is that which provides a challenge to all of its members: a challenge in this case resulting from the diversity of learning needs to be satisfied, the requirements of leadership on the part of the most able, and the impetus for the weaker students to approach the level of achievement of the leaders.

The major reason why the groups should be formed on the basis of student interest is that commitment to the objectives of the class is a prerequisite for the interdependence and boundary maintenance so necessary for a functioning social system. Cutting across the peer group structure also contributes to this; otherwise small-group work could result in the segmentation of the class into warring factions, committed to the destruction of class objectives rather than to their achievement. For the same reason it is usually desirable to change the membership of groups at least once every ten weeks.

It is not enough simply to form small groups; one must see that they are actually functioning as mutually interdependent parts of the whole. Each individual must be helped to forge out a role which contributes to the achievement of the learning tasks of the group, while each group is encouraged to see that it has a role in the achievement of the objectives of the entire class. Group presentations to the larger class must occur regularly, but should be seen as valued inputs to the learning culture of the whole rather than as end-products to be evaluated in themselves. In order for this to work there must be a degree of awareness of class objectives and of shared commitment to these on the part of the students. It is the teacher's responsibility to make these objectives explicit at the beginning of each unit of work, and to justify them in terms of the students' past, present and future experience.

It helps to establish the boundaries necessary for a social system to function if the learning tasks and content vehicles (but of course not the learning outcomes) of one's classes differ. A mildly competitive situation among classes will contribute to the internal integration of each, while cooperation among the groups within each class is desirable. Norms unique to each class and generated by the members also help to establish boundaries and interdependence. A shared culture evolves fairly rapidly as learning occurs in the social system setting, both at the small group and larger class level. A teacher can encourage this by providing full-class experiences in the form of field trips and good large-group lectures, and by promoting the keeping of a class history, small-group logbooks, and a file of programmed materials constructed by learning teams (consisting of a "tutor" and two "pupils") within the small groups.

To sum up, for the teacher experimenting with various levels of social organization in the classroom setting, evaluation is all-important. It must be evaluation of the curriculum-based learning objectives, expressed in terms of intellectual and moral growth and assessed by means of precise indicators previously identified by the teacher. It must be on the basis of individual rather than collective performance. And it must allow us to make comparisons among classes with different organizational climates. If this is done conscientiously we should eventually have available the data necessary for making rational decisions about the type of social organization in which learning best occurs.

The Concept Demonstrated

CASE STUDY ONE

Alice Graham was new at teaching, but she had begun her first year as a junior high school literature teacher with much commitment and high hopes. She was resolved not to teach as she had herself been taught. The idea of teacher exposition of *anything* filled her with horror, as did the demand that students acquire knowledge of factual material and be required to indicate the degree to which they had done so in examinations. Her favourite classes at Sir George Williams University had been those in which small-group discussion had predominated. Consequently, she set about on the first day of school to organize her five grade eight literature classes into discussion groups.

She allowed her pupils to select the groups of their choice, in order to ensure greater work satisfaction and group loyalty. The groups were then asked to meet during the regular class sessions (usually one in each corner of the room and one in the centre) and to decide what they wanted to do for the next month. Alice considered it imperative to keep the situation as unstructured and democratic as possible, so she steadfastly refused to offer the groups guidance or direction.

As the weeks wore on Alice found herself growing concerned about what was happening, and especially what was failing to happen in her groups. They discussed and argued loudly but seemed unable to arrive at any consensus as to what they should do. Some individuals were beginning to come to her expressing boredom and frustration and demanding that she discipline the lazy and noisy.

Finally, after some pressure from neighbouring colleagues and administrators, Alice decided to assign discussion topics to her groups. These were grasped eagerly and tossed about by the students, with all group members seemingly becoming authorities overnight. Sometimes Alice experienced vague stirrings of misgivings as she listened to the dogmatic restatement of unsubstantiated opinion being shouted into the hubbub around her. But after all, she told herself, what is really important is that I've made them aware of these important issues and encouraged them to be unafraid of expressing opinions about them. "And," she would add, "it's obvious that their discussion is relevant to them and that they are actively participating rather than assimilating facts passively and regurgitating them on exams."

Toward the end of the term Alice became disturbed about the administration's insistence upon the need to evaluate her students' progress. A sensation of being trapped in the all-powerful system engulfed her. She opposed all evaluation on principle, but finally was persuaded by her colleagues to conform at least to some extent. She felt intuitively that the enthusiasm of her students as they engaged in heated discussion was sufficient evidence that they were learning. But how to decide just who was learning what in order to measure individual progress?

She decided on oral examinations but found them too time-consuming to administer individually. For Alice the after-school hours had become a valued respite from the exhausting class discussion periods, and she was reluctant to use them for teaching duties. So she settled on questioning students in their groups, but soon found, to her dismay, that her questions and interference were highly resented. When she asked a student to rephrase a statement, try to develop an argument more logically, define his terms, or do some reading on a subject with which he was revealing a very superficial acquaintance but an overwhelming authoritativeness, she found her authority to make such suggestions being rudely questioned.

And when a student declared, "What right have you to criticize me; I have just as much right to my opinion as you have!" she was at a loss to answer. Where, she agonized, had she missed the boat?

QUESTIONS FOR GROUP DISCUSSION

1   Was Alice correct in assuming that the successful discussion groups in which she had participated in university had just happened naturally? Was she correct in assuming that a level of social organization that had worked for university students would necessarily be appropriate for grade eight pupils?

2   Did Alice's decision to allow her pupils to select themselves into groups on the basis of friendship have the result of imposing any sort of structure on her classes? If so, how might this structure have contributed to the problems that developed?

3   What were the learning objectives that Alice had defined for her pupils? How had she planned to structure her classes so as to achieve them? By what means did she intend to determine her degree of success in achieving these objectives?

4   How did Alice plan to cope with the sociological imperatives of her teaching situation? What were some of these?

CASE STUDY TWO

Jim Taylor found himself facing an extremely hostile grade eleven math class at the beginning of his third year at Calvin High. Partly in response to the Hall-Dennis Report, the southern Ontario school had broken away from homogeneous grouping the year before and was now endeavouring to avoid the streaming or tracking of students which had been its practice for many years. Many of the superior students and their parents were resentful and confused about the recent changes. A few of the most vocal of these former academic stream students were in Jim's home room class. In addition, he had drawn a disproportionate number of those individuals from the general and vocational stream who had been labelled as troublemakers the previous year. All in all, it seemed to him on the first day of classes in September, that he could literally feel the hostility coming at him in waves from the silent bodies slouched in five rows of six before him.

By the end of the first week it was clear to Jim that a radical change in approach was necessary if any advantages associated with heterogeneous grouping were to be realized by the class that year. He hit on a plan that seemed a natural. Why not utilize the great disparities in ability and knowledge among his students to the benefit of all? Why not divide the class into "helpers" and "helpees," assigning to each of the latter group a tutor from among the more gifted students?

As Jim acted at once to implement his plan more ideas came to him, all equally exciting. He decided to develop a program which would consist entirely of independent learning, with the tutors "contracting" with him and researching the topics and concepts to be dealt with, while at the same time involving the "pupil" member of the team in the researching activities and teaching him the materials. These "learning pairs" could meet with him regularly for help with their planning and teaching-learning techniques. He would assign marks on the basis of the progress of both tutor and pupil, as indicated by regular bi-monthly tests.

Jim evaluated his experiment carefully, noting with satisfaction that the generalized hostility of the first few weeks was gradually giving way to a reluctant interest and involvement in learning on the part of tutor and pupil alike. However, a number of signals puzzled and distressed him. A group of parents of the more gifted students wrote a joint letter of complaint to the Director of the Board of Education expressing concern that the progress of their offspring was being sacrificed for the sake of problem students. Administrators in the school expressed criticism of the fact that each learning team was dealing with different material and that Jim seemed to have failed to impose any structure on the class as a whole. Within the class Jim noticed a growing competitiveness as the tutors pitted their students against one another in a race for the marks which were assigned periodically on the basis of individual tests.

Jim realized that continued inability on his part to analyse the situation and to identify the sources of his problem would soon condemn his experiment to failure. What was he doing wrong, he wondered — or was the entire idea simply inherently unworkable?

QUESTIONS FOR GROUP DISCUSSION

1   To what extent were Jim's problems due to a faulty implementation of organizational change in the school as a whole?

2   Was it likely that a social system would gradually evolve in Jim's classroom, given the structure that he had established? How would you classify his structure on the continuum of social organization? Was the extreme competitiveness among the learning pairs related to this structure in any way?

3   In your opinion, were the parents of the gifted children justified in worrying about the progress of their offspring? Why or why not?

4   How could Jim have avoided the negative reactions of the administrators and parents?

5 Discuss the possible advantages and disadvantages of Jim's approach in terms of learning objectives.

CASE STUDY THREE

Bill Mumford had studied group dynamics in university and had come to his first high-school teaching post in a little town in Manitoba resolved to put his knowledge to practical use. It was not surprising, therefore, that his first move the day after meeting his social studies classes for the first time was to administer sociometric tests, in the hope that these would reveal the friendship patterns of his students.

Bill couldn't help but be aware that in some of his classes the sociometric technique was taken as something of a joke. The smirks and snide asides pervading the room made him wonder about the validity and reliability of his results. However, he decided to plunge ahead. He drew up sociograms for all of his classes and proceeded in each case to pick out his stars. He named these people to a special four-man steering committee and gave them the responsibility for planning large-group or class-discussion topics for the entire year. In addition, he divided each class into four small groups on the basis of the preferences expressed by the sociogram and to each of these he allocated one member of the steering committee.

Once the group structure was established for each class Bill hastened to involve his steering committee in planning a program of small-group experiences which could be articulated with the class activities which the steering committees had listed previously. In most cases it was decided that each small group would be responsible for one class presentation per month, on a topic checked out with the steering committee. Bill was to mark these and to allow the group members to allot individual marks, the only requirement being that the latter would have to average out to the teacher-assigned group mark.

Bill's system worked fairly well in two of his classes, with the steering committee assuming a large share of the leadership function which he would otherwise have had to bear alone. In the remaining three classes, however, his steering committees were a disappointment. As he became better acquainted with his students he realized that these so-called stars were not the real class "influentials" at all; that in at least one case they were instead the most unpopular members of the entire class.

These steering committees were of little help to him in planning and when he found himself forced to pass off his own ideas to a particular class in the name of its steering committee, little enthusiasm or cooperation resulted. Even in those classes where the steering committees were providing leadership, he was not without problems.

In those cases, his steering committee members seemed to be dominating the small groups to which they had been assigned, to a rather alarming extent.

As time passed another problem became increasingly apparent. Competition among the groups for marks was becoming more and more severe. By spring the competition was erupting into pronounced inter-group hostility, expressing itself ever more frequently in ugly verbal combats. The large-group sessions were becoming painful encounters in which Bill found himself involved, in spite of himself, in inter-group antagonisms.

By May Bill saw no way out of the dilemma, as he observed the competition within his classes reaching fever pitch. His plan should have worked. What was there about these particular students, he asked himself, that had caused them to react in this unexpected fashion?

QUESTIONS FOR GROUP DISCUSSION

1   To what extent does the successful use of sociometric devices depend upon the level of sophistication of the participants? Discuss in terms of Bill's experience.

2   Comment on some of the problems involved in structuring a class for the development of responsible pupil-leadership. Is it sufficient merely to confirm and legitimize the informal peer group structure? How could Bill have improved his attempt at developing leadership?

3   In what ways could systematic evaluation and increased flexibility on Bill's part have prevented serious problems from arising?

4   How could Bill have struck a better balance between cooperation and competition, so that both processes could have contributed to the evolution of social systems in his classrooms?

The Concept Applied
To Relevant Canadian Research

Anderson, G. J. and H. J. Walberg. "Class Size and the Social Environment of Learning." *Alberta Journal of Educational Research* 18, no. 4 (1972): 277-286.

Fourteen dimensions of social climate of learning in high school classes were examined in their relation to the size of the classes concerned. Two data samples included in the study were 149 classes participating in the 1967 evaluation of the Harvard Project Physics Course and 61 classes in the Montreal Metropolitan Area in a variety of subjects. Eight of the hypotheses supported by the Harvard data were again supported in the Montreal sample, though only two reached statistical significance. Small classes were perceived both as more difficult and more cohesive.

Armstrong, R. D. and N. M. Purvis, "Trends in the Patterns of Staff Utilization in the Elementary Schools of Alberta: Implications for Teacher Education." *Alberta Journal of Educational Research* 19, no. 1 (1973): 12-21.
Results from a 1968 and a 1971 study were compared. In 1968 team teaching received less support, and the self-contained classroom more support from teachers than from either principals or superintendents. In 1971, findings indicated that both subject specialization and team teaching had increased: a major and rapid change in the direction of a form of organization deemed desirable by administrators in 1968.

Black, D. E. and W. E. Goding, "An Experiment in Classroom Management." *Alberta Journal of Educational Research* 18, no. 1 (1972): 15-29.
Fourteen graduate student instructors were responsible for conducting class discussions after TV lectures in an introductory psychology course. One group of students participated in a series of group process workshops; the other attended no extra meetings (experimental and control group). No significant difference was found in academic achievement. In the affective domain, the experimental group was found to be no different on anxiety level, less reticent, but more dogmatic.

Diemert, N. E. and E. A. Holdaway. "Teacher Satisfaction in Team and Conventional Teaching Situations." *Alberta Journal of Educational Research* 16, no. 2 (1970): 111-122.
Data were collected from sixty-nine teachers working in team teaching schools and seventy-nine teachers working in more conventional Alberta schools, to compare job satisfaction. The team teachers expressed significantly less satisfaction with "teacher salary" than did the conventional teachers, but were significantly more satisfied with "current issues," "community support of education," and "school facilities and services."

Friesen, D. "Variations in Perception of Organizational Climate," *Alberta Journal of Educational Research* 18, no. 2 (1972): 91-99.
This study made an assessment of "openness" as viewed by administrators, teachers and students. The perceptions of climate by the three groups were compared in two schools: one, an open campus school, and one, a traditionally organized school. The school that was

considered to have a more open climate by experts was also perceived by the teachers to be more open. However, pupils in the "open" school did not perceive their organizational climate to be any more open than did those in the school classified as "closed."

Hersom, Naomi. "Organizational Dimensions of Schools." *Alberta Journal of Educational Research* 16, no. 2 (1970): 63-77.
This study was concerned with determining the basic dimensions underlying the organization of public elementary and secondary schools in Canada. Dimensions which theory and research had suggested as relevant were: production, maintenance, adaptation boundary spanning and administrative activities. Differences in emphasis were found between elementary and secondary schools.

Holdaway, E. A. and John Seger. "The Development of Indices of Innovativeness." *Canadian Education and Research Digest* 8, no. 14 (1968): 366-379.
In a sample of forty urban elementary schools in Western Canada, the researchers assessed three indices of innovation ("number of innovations adopted," "extent of adoption" and "relative earliness of adoption") in relation to five particular innovations: (1) departmentalization of staff in grades four to six, (2) parent-teacher interviews during school hours, (3) regular and systematic use of central office consultants, (4) teaching French in grades five and six, (5) regular use of TV as a teaching aid. They concluded that the three indices were related to different aspects of innovativeness as a general characteristic.

King, A. J. C. and R. A. Ripton. "Teachers and Students: A Preliminary Analysis of Collective Reciprocity." *Canadian Review of Sociology and Anthropology* 7 (1970): 35-48.
A model proposing the existence of reciprocal relationships was derived to explain interaction between students and teachers in secondary schools. It was hypothesized that the priority influences of career on teachers and the concept of education as instrumental on students produce a reciprocity characterized by routinized curriculum and evaluation procedures. Students and teachers from three secondary schools in Ontario were surveyed by questionnaire, attitude inventory and interview. The factors of career, ideology and instrumentality of education were supported as operational constructs, and the elements of reciprocity were found to be present.

Miklos, E. and E. A. Breitkreuz. "Analysis of Influence and Social Structures in Schools." *Alberta Journal of Educational Research* 14, no. 4 (1968): 239-251.

Influence and social structures in schools were investigated through an analysis of communication and interaction patterns among staff members in a small Canadian school. It was concluded that this method of analysis could be a useful supplement to other methods.

Miller, John P. "The Effects of Human Relations Training on Teacher Interpersonal Skills." *Alberta Journal of Educational Research* 19, no. 1 (1973): 37-47.
This study attempted to assess the effects of in-service human relations training on teacher interpersonal competence. The results indicated that, although the teachers gained significantly in interpersonal skills in a counselling relationship, the acquired skills did not transfer to interaction in the classroom.

Punch, Keith, "Bureaucratic Structure in Schools: Towards Redefinition and Measurement." *Educational Administration Quarterly* 5, no. 2 (1969): 43-57.
This was an empirical study carried out in forty-eight schools in five Ontario centres, which aimed to refine the concept of "bureaucracy." It was found that bureaucratic structure in schools is realistically conceptualized as a unitary, homogeneous variable only if restricted to the dimensions of hierarchy, rules of incumbents, procedural specifications and impersonaltiy. If specialization and technical competence are included it becomes a two-factor concept.

Richer, S. and R. Breton. "School Organization and Student Differences: Some views of Canadian Educators." *Canadian Education and Research Digest* 8, no. 1 (1968): 20-37.
This is a partial report of a national survey of public secondary schools in Canada during the 1965-66 year, using a stratified probability sample designed to include composite, technical-vocational and academic-commercial schools. Responses were elicited from teachers, principals and counsellors. Most of the schools administered mental ability tests, although only a minority had ability grouping. The majority favoured co-education. The most significant finding was the pronounced interprovincial difference of opinion, reflecting Canada's decentralized system of education.

INDEPENDENT STUDY

Select the research study which most interests you and locate it in the appropriate journal. After reading it carefully respond to the following:

1   What sort of a model of social organization does the researcher seem to have in mind?

2   Analyse and interpret the data differently than the researcher did, by applying to them the concept of social organization as it has been developed in this chapter. Does this shed any additional light on the reported findings?

The Concept Amplified
By Further Reading

Amidon, Edmond J. and J. B. Hough, eds. *Interaction Analysis.* Reading, Mass.: Addison-Wesley Pub. Co., 1967.
A collection of studies of patterns of interaction in school and classroom settings. The studies are analysed and discussed in terms of their contribution to the development of the new research tool of interaction analysis.

Bales, Robert F. "A Set of Categories for the Analysis of Small Group Interaction." *American Sociological Review* 15, no. 2 (1950): 257-263.
A simplified, introductory description of the small-group theory and methodology underlying interaction analysis.

Barth, Roland. *Open Education and the American School.* New York: Agathon Press, 1972.
A valuable book about the currently popular movement toward less formal organization in school classrooms. The author tries to analyse the movement in terms of its premises about the nature of the learning process and of knowledge as well as its implications for social organization in the schools of America.

Bierstedt, Robert. *The Social Order.* New York: McGraw-Hill, 1963.
This introductory sociology textbook is a classic, and is highly recommended for students who wish to acquire a solid foundation in the subject. The continuum idea of social organization is introduced here, with the author's model of "statistical," "societal," "social" and "associational" groupings.

Brunetti, Frank A., et al. "Studies of Team Teaching in the Open Space School." *Interchange* 3, nos. 2-3 (1972): 85-101.
The author concludes that the entire social climate of classes is so changed in the open space situation that substantial changes in the organization of activities and influence are forced on the participants.

Eisenstadt, S. N. "Bureaucracy, Bureaucratization, and De-bureaucratization," in Mizruchi, Ephraim, *The Substance of Sociology,* pp. 395-407. New York; Appleton-Century-Crofts, 1967.
The author points to possible improved ways of investigating various structural aspects of bureaucratic organizations, as well as the nature of the process of bureaucratization. (An example of a dynamic systems approach.)

Goodlet, G. R. "Nongrading and Achievement: A Review." *Alberta Journal of Educational Research* 18, no. 4 (1972): 237-242.

A review of research on non-grading and achievement suggests that the case for non-grading is not yet established, and because of methodological problems in many studies, may not yet even have been adequately tested.

Gorman, Alfred H. *Teachers and Learners: The Interactive process in Education*. Boston: Allyn and Bacon, 1970.
A practical book for teachers, based on an interactive model. Presents many pointers on how to organize one's pupil groups effectively.

Herman, Wayne, et al. "The Relationship of Teacher-Centred Activities and Pupil-Centred Activities to Pupil Achievement and Interest in 18 Fifth Grade Social Studies Classes." *American Educational Research Journal* 6, no. 2 (1969): 227-239.
Teachers, matched according to their verbal behaviour, were randomly assigned to teacher-centred and pupil-centred activity treatments for average, above-average and below-average classes. After six weeks the treatments were reversed. No significant differences in interest or achievement were revealed. These findings suggest that the considerable volume of material implying that pupil-centred instruction is better than teacher-dominated modes requires careful appraisal.

Homans, G. C. *Social Behavior: Its Elementary Forms*. New York: Harcourt, Brace and World, 1961.
A good discussion of the nature of sociological explanation, as well as a presentation of a set of general propositions about social behaviour as an exchange of activity (tangible or intangible) and more or less rewarding or costly, between at least two persons.

Little, A., J. Russell, and C. Mabey "Do Small Classes Help a Pupil?" *New Society* 18, no. 473 (1971): 767-771.
The authors consider several studies of class size in relation to pupil attainment, as well as the results of their own investigations in this field. Findings indicate that pupils appear to do better in larger classes.

Lutz, Frank W., and L. Iannaccone, *Understanding Educational Organizations: A Field Study Approach*. Columbus, Ohio: Charles E. Merrill, 1969.
This book is an example of an attempt to apply general systems theory to the field study of power in educational organizations.

MacDonald, W. Scott. *Battle in the Classroom: Innovations in Classroom Techniques*. Toronto: Intext Educational Publishers, 1971.
A report of a program of anthropological-psychological research into the community and schooling system of a group of Hawaiian residents. It includes a number of analyses of what actually went on in classrooms. A simple but useful instrument of interaction analysis for classroom settings is presented.

Musgrove, Frank. "Historical Materials for the Study of the Bureaucratization of Education," in History of Education Society, *History, Sociology and Education*, pp. 33-47. London: Methuen, 1971.

An attempt to make a systematic study of the process of bureaucratization in schooling as a historical development.

Northway, Mary L. *A Primer of Sociometry.* Toronto: University of Toronto Press, 1967.
A thorough explanation of the use of sociometric techniques.

Oakley, K. A. "The Stability of Teacher Behaviour in Conditions of Varying Class Size." *British Journal of Educational Psychology* 40, no. 3 (1970): 253. (abstract of an M. Ed. thesis).
This study concluded that changes in class size do not appear to affect (1) the teacher's basic verbal behaviour pattern, (2) the amount of effort needed to control and discipline the class, (3) the amount and variety of activities, and (4) the amount and type of pupil-pupil interaction.

Sarason, Seymour B. *The Culture of the School and the Problem of Change.* Boston: Allyn and Bacon, 1971.
An enlightening book which looks at organizational sources of obstacles to change (in fruitful directions) in school settings. The author examines the role of the "outsider," the principal and teacher in the change process, from an evolutionary-ecological perspective.

Schmuck, R. A. and P. A. Schmuck. *Group Processes in the Classroom.* Dubuque, Iowa: Wm. C. Brown, 1971.
A good discussion of interaction within groups in the classroom situation, with social organization being viewed as a dynamic process involving an experimental history, current climate, leadership, attraction, norms, communication, cohesiveness and developmental stages.

Taylor, M. T. and R. M. Sharp. "Classroom Analysis for Pre-service Teachers," *Education for Teaching* 86 (1971): 16-23.
The authors claim that to provide student teachers with an understanding of teaching, both a cognitive framework to improve perception of pupil behaviour and an understanding of the impact of teacher behaviour on the learning process are required. A course designed to accomplish this, developed by the authors and using the work of Flanders and Amidon, is described in detail.

Thelen, Herbert A. *Classroom Grouping for Teachability.* New York: John Wiley and Sons, 1967.
A procedure (compatibility grouping) which "fits" pupils and teachers is evaluated by an experiment involving thirteen teachers and their classes. The investigations concluded that using compatibility grouping, classes showed greater application to work, more enthusiasm, fewer discipline problems, higher solidarity, greater cohesiveness and better morale. Practical procedures for this type of grouping are described.

Vogel, F. X. and N. D. Bowers. "Pupil Behavior in a Multi-age, Non-Graded School." *Journal of Experimental Education* 41, no. 2 (1972): 78-86.

This study examined the form of elementary school organization in relation to pupil behaviour. Measures of attitude and performance were collected from 473 pupils in ten non-graded and ten traditional classrooms. The experimental pupils scored significantly higher on conceptual maturity, but lower on attitudes and academic achievement.

Walberg, H. J. "Predicting Class Learning: An Approach to the Class as a Social System." *American Educational Research Journal* 6, no. 4 (1967): 529-542.

This study is a replication and extension of prior empirical work using the Getzels-Thelen model of the class as a social system. From a national sample, data were collected on the characteristics of 144 classes. Both the organizational climate and the biographical variables were found to be highly significant and equally efficient in predicting learning.

The Concept Reviewed

1   Sociological concepts should be expressed as continuums because:
a.   human social behaviour is dynamic rather than static
b.   discrete, isolated categories are not very useful in helping us to understand how behaviour changes from one category to another
c.   we need to develop such yardsticks if we are ever to be able to relate and compare concrete social situations, groups or events to one another
d.   the identification of "ideal types" (imaginary polar extremes or limiting cases) helps us to see any concrete example in perspective
e.   all of the above
f.   all but (d) and (e)
g.   none of the above.

2   The most important defining characteristic of a social system is:
a.   geographical or technical proximity of members
b.   interdependence of members and roles
c.   interaction
d.   consciousness of belonging.

3   If a teacher wishes to experiment with altering the social organization (or the organizational climate) of his classroom, he must be prepared to evaluate carefully in terms of:
a.   the emotional development of individual pupils
b.   the group projects produced
c.   the intellectual and moral development of individual pupils
d.   the quality and degree of social interaction pertaining.

4   Competition and cooperation both have a place in the development of a classroom social system. Which of the following is likely to be the *least* constructive use of these processes?
a.   encouraging your various classes to compete with one another in terms of class averages

b. encouraging your various small groups within a particular class to compete with one another in terms of marks

c. encouraging mild competition among your classes, but cooperation among the small groups within each class by changing the membership of the groups periodically

d. encouraging small group contributions to the learning of the class as a whole, while allowing some friendly competition among tutoring pairs or three-man learning teams within each small group.

A social system is considered desirable as a classroom learning environment for the following reasons: (select the *least* valid reason)

a. pupils are involved in an active way in the culture-building enterprise in which hopefully they will engage all their lives as adults

b. pupils are involved in the building of norms and the construction and implementation of explicit rules which reflect these, just as, as voting adults, they will be expected to participate in the creation, changing and upholding of their society's laws

c. pupils work on tasks which require the cooperation of others and which require them to resolve differences by compromise rather than by conflict

d. pupils have the freedom to follow their own interests of the moment

e. pupils see the need for people to assume different roles in a dependable way, and learn that, as social beings, we cannot avoid responsibility for the effects of our actions upon others.

Arguments in favour of grouping on the basis of heterogeneity of ability include all but one of the following. Which *does not* support that position?

a. pupils learn well from one another by having to teach one another, if the class structure allows for a tutoring relationship

b. the teacher can administer the classroom more efficiently if the pupils who can cover the same content at the same rate are working together

c. pupils in a small group learn best where they are continually challenged both to excel and to lead others toward excellence

d. individuals are not always uniformly strong or deficient in all the types of abilities significant for learning; therefore, because some variability will always be present among small groups, it might better be planned for and capitalized upon

e. moral development might well be encouraged, if pupils work in a situation which demands tolerance of and a sense of responsibility for the less able, and respect for exceptional expertise and performance.

For the classroom as well as for the school as a whole, when the "informal" level of social organization pertains, one of the following is not likely to occur. Which is *least likely*?

a. the person or clique with the most power (due to physical strength, charisma or control of physical resources) will tend to assume control

b. the peer group structure resulting from out-of-school influences will tend to be confirmed and perpetuated

c. the teacher or principal will tend to lose the function of leadership

d. conflict will tend to erupt among factions

e. the goals of the system tend to be displaced by the interests of competing groups

f. the system will tend to become more and more impersonal.

8 According to our model of social organization, all the Canadian males between the ages of twenty-one and twenty-five would be termed:

a. a statistical aggregate

b. an informal grouping

c. a formal organization

d. a geographical aggregate.

9 On our continuum of social organization, what distinguishes a bureaucracy from merely the formal level of organization is:

a. the formalizing of group norms as rules

b. pre-defined roles

c. detailed prescriptions for interaction that are relatively resistant to change

d. an official philosophy or ideology.

10 When a social system begins to operate as a formal organization, an observer would likely notice:

a. the emergence of interdependence

b. the formal acknowledgment and spelling out of goals, roles and rules

c. the development of an awareness of belonging on the part of the group members

d. a tendency toward group disintegration.

Answers: 1 (e); 2 (b); 3 (c); 4 (b); 5 (d); 6 (b); 7 (f); 8 (a); 9 (c); 10 (b).

Part Two
The School As
A Formal
Organization

As we move from the classroom level of conceptualization to the perspective of its encompassing social system, the scene before us changes. (Just as it does for the nature lover who moves from an examination of a particular wildflower in a crevice to a vantage point from which his eye takes in the entire valley stretched below him.) In our case the supra-system is the school in which a number of class-room social systems are functioning in the pursuit of common goals.

If the school is a social system in its own right, then obviously it must comprise parts, with interrelationships holding among these parts and their attributes. These parts are the various classes, each of which is dependent on all the others for the care and sharing of the physical environment (for example, library holdings and playground equipment) and for the cooperative structuring of daily and yearly activities so that the efforts of each class are enhanced rather than impeded or cancelled out by those of the others. This sort of coordination does not just happen, even where only two sub-systems are involved. It requires a conscious effort on the part of the two teachers to articulate the functions over which they have control, and on the part of the pupils to do the same.

Even in a two-room school the classes are in a particular relation-ship to one another; this places certain constraints upon each, so that the benefits to be derived from their joining together can be max-imized. The graduates of the primary room move on to the secondary one eventually, and their level of concept-and-skill acquisition at that point will determine what the secondary teacher can do. The entrance requirements of the secondary teacher will in turn contribute to the shaping of the instructional objectives of the primary teacher. The daily coming and going of each class must not prevent the achieve-ment of the learning goals of the other.

The task of coordination becomes more difficult and involved when the number of pupils in the school increases, necessitating more classes. Or when the enterprise of educating each pupil is broken down into a number of separate stages, so that each year a different teacher is responsible for him. Or when the total enterprise of educating each pupil is separated into a number of discrete tasks, to be performed by different teachers during the same stage (as when we have a departmental set-up with subject area specialists, each of whom sees each pupil only briefly each day.) Or when we opt for team teaching within the same subject area, and have each specialist perform only one of the instructional tasks involved in teaching the subject at that grade level.

As the need for coordination increases (due to the increase in numbers of members, or to complexity of division of labour, or both) we find the emergence of two additional groups of specialists. The first are specialists in this very process of keeping the system functioning with as little waste of time and materials as possible, and with as few detours and roadblocks as possible in the pursuit of its goals. The second group are specialists in giving the pupils the sustained, personal attention which the specialist teachers no longer are able to provide, or in patching up the emotional problems caused by teaching failures. We call these people administrators and counsellors, respectively.

At this point in its development, the supra-system becomes what we call a formal organization. Because each individual decision to act has immediate and long-term consequences for other individuals and sub-systems, limits must be set on each member's freedom to make arbitrary moves. The defining, communicating and maintaining of these limits requires time, effort and expertise on the part of those members designated as administrators. To avoid confusion and conflict, the responsibilities for the various tasks within the organization are spelled out carefully, usually before candidates for membership are recruited. For the same reasons, routines which have been found to work well and to reduce friction, omissions and redundancy, are communicated to incoming members. This way, the entire process of working out compromises and group strategies need not begin all over again with each newcomer.

In ongoing societies, few associations actually go through this gradual changeover from a non-formal social system to formal organization. More often the larger society, through its political arm, has identified priorities for group action and designated specific goals, for the attainment of which specific associations are brought into being, formally organized from the start. Schools (except for experimental "free" schools) seldom grow from one classroom to a dozen, with members gradually recognizing the need for formal organization and increasingly implementing it along the way. Seldom, too, does an association of members who are formally organized from the start deliberately move in the direction of a lower level of organization, although this is possible. And in many situations, where size of membership has decreased, or a change in the goals of the association seems to require a generalist rather than specialist approach, less formality of organization may well be desirable.

Where considerable specialization of function within the association has been deemed necessary and desirable, members will tend to relate to one another in terms of their own special contribution to the job being carried out by the association as a whole, rather than in terms of their sub-system membership. Within the classroom the members act as "instructor" (or group leader) and "learners." But in order for the business of the school as a whole to be carried on, they are grouped with others with common tasks and interests transcending each particular classroom, as "pupils," "teachers," "administrators" and "counsellors." As such, they relate to one another, and to parents and higher-level administrators. When this change in relationships occurs, we say that a different and more specifically defined set of ways of responding to the school situation has come into being: ways determined by the particular responsibility that each has, for the achievement of the school's goals. We call these group-recognized ways of responding, "roles." They are the basis for the interaction that holds the formal organization together and allows it to function as a supra-system. Without these formal role relationships, a school would be no more than an aggregate of isolated classroom social systems which merely happened to be located in the same general geographical space.

3 Role

The Concept Explained

Perhaps the best way to begin to acquire the sociological concept of role is to picture a man from Mars in a spacecraft poised above a typical Canadian high school. He knows nothing of what is going on inside the human organisms in the "beehive" in question, but the strange sounds of their efforts at communication are interpreted immediately by his computer. This advanced computer also notes every movement in the vicinity of the school (indoors and out) and is capable of identifying any and all regularities in the motor and verbal behaviours of the strange little figures below him. Gradually patterns begin to emerge from the seeming chaos of interaction.[1]

Certain people arrive a little earlier than the majority, gather momentarily in one particular region, and then fan out into other box-like areas. When the crowds arrive they distribute themselves among these areas, often settling into neat rows, facing the one early arrival who seems to have been waiting, and who immediately begins to talk. At the same time the members of the crowd become relatively silent. At certain times during the day, however, they burst into chatter irrelevant to the communication just ended, as they swarm into narrow runways and then redistribute themselves into different areas. One of the early arrivals goes immediately to a smaller enclosure near the main entrance and seems to spend most of his time there (either alone or closeted with individuals) or in the narrow runways. And so on and on....

What the man from Mars is observing are behavioural regularities. Individuals seem to be behaving in this particular social setting in more or less regular ways, depending upon the position that each one holds. Each position has a certain status in the social system in question. By status is meant the current consensus among the various role performers as to the relative worth or prestige of that position. These observable behavioural regularities (both motor and verbal) are what we term the *objective* aspects of the individual's role. On the basis of past performance (charted by the all-knowing computer)

---

[1] Seymour B. Sarason, in *The Culture of The School and The Problem of Change,* uses this "man from space" analogy.

the man from Mars would soon begin to predict that certain individuals whom he had previously classified as belonging to the same position or category (because of similarities in behaviour) would do and say certain types of things in certain ways at certain times. That is, certain *expectations* regarding their probable future behaviours would have been formed by him.

Our observer, from his position external to the beehive, would probably have difficulty in comprehending that each of these little figures, on the basis of his own extremely complex inner computer, also had recorded certain generalized perceptions of the regularities in the behaviours around him, and had developed a whole nest of expectations of how others in his environment would likely behave in response to him and to one another. Much less would the man from Mars be able to realize that each little figure had also constructed, by means of his incredibly intricate inner mechanism, a second set of expectations: expectations of the expectations that "significant others" held concerning his behavior. These complex, double sets of expectations, derived from past behavioural regularities, we term the *subjective* aspects of role. This means that we have to think of our concept as comprising both *role performance* (which can be observed objectively by an outsider) and *role expectations*, the so-called subjective influences on behaviour which can only be inferred by the observer as he listens to and watches the individual in question in his relationships with others.

These regularities in human behaviour and the expectations to which they give rise simplify social life, at least to the extent that it is sufficiently predictable for human survival. For if every individual social interaction were indeed as random and meaningless as the beehive appeared from the perspective of the man from Mars at his initial viewing of it, human social life would be impossible. But it is obvious to the sociologist that social interaction is somewhat ordered both from the subjective and objective point of view. And it is the sense of this ordering that we try to express by the concept of role.

The man from Mars examined a social setting which is more or less formally organized: a school plant. In such a setting one would expect to find a network of clearly delineated roles, operating in a coordinated manner for the efficient achievement of specified goals, even though within this organization there may be much less formally structured classroom systems. The formal organization is the most effective social instrument yet devised by humans for the implementation of policy on a group basis. It corresponds to technology as a tool in the physical realm. In fact, there is a continuous interaction between the two, as advances in technology demand corresponding changes in the formal organizations which utilize it, and vice versa.

Like any other formal organization, the school is assumed to have a set of goals known to all its members and to which they are committed. Indeed, that is its reason for being as well as the source of the positions established within it and the reciprocal roles that have become attached to these positions. Sometimes, however, role expectations become ambiguous and the relation of role performance to the school's stated objectives questionable, due to incompatibility or substitution of goals. When role performers in the school (teachers and pupils, for instance) hold incompatible educational goals, confusion reigns. There is bound to be trouble in a classroom where the teacher's goal is merely to cover the content in the text by the end of the term, while the goal of the pupils is to understand what the text is about. Or vice versa. Or where the pupils see the school's goal to be the provision of a permissive and non-demanding social milieu, while the teachers consider it to be the development of knowledgeable and logical critical thinkers.

During recent years in Canada, we have been witnessing a clash between the expectations of affluent middle-class and working-class parents. The latter tend to want the school to equip their children with the qualifications for becoming affluent, while the former want the school to provide their (already safely affluent) children with the means of enjoying the fruits of affluence, such as leisure time and travel. Usually this conflict of goals is reflected among teachers, pupils and administrators as well.

An example of goal substitution is the tendency for the original educational goals of the school to be replaced by the desire to perpetuate the organization itself, or the administrative positions within it, or even the particular people currently holding those positions. In the same way it is easy for a teacher, when teaching jobs are scarce, to convince himself that the security of his tenure has first priority as a goal of the school.

Problems also arise when goals are expressed as untestable abstractions, so that no one has any means of evaluating the degree to which his own role performance is contributing to their achievement. Schools and educators are especially prone to this weakness. How, one wonders, can a group of teachers reliably assess their progress toward development of "creativity," "individuality," "humanism" and "good citizenship" among their pupils?

It could be argued that Canadian schools today suffer, to some degree, from all of these problems. The original objective in establishing a complex of formal organizations for schooling was twofold: the provision of equality of educational opportunity for all children in a country plagued by a sparsely settled population and serious regional disparities; and the transmission of that minimum core of common ideals, norms and symbols which would comprise the glue to hold the emerging pioneer society together. It is no longer as clear as it once seemed that equality of tenure in school is equivalent to equality of opportunity to be educated, nor is there agreement on the necessity for and the components of a common core of culture. All this is bound to result in great role confusion among the members of the school organization.

There seems to be little disagreement, however, about the need for some degree of formal organization of the schooling enterprise. One could easily imagine what would happen in a school of three hundred students and limited resources in terms of teacher time, materials and space, if each individual "did his own thing." It simply would not work as a means of achieving collective action in the pursuit of the group's goals. Obviously, the larger the numbers involved, the more formality of organization will be necessary. But at some point the law of diminishing returns sets in, and beyond that point increasing formality becomes dysfunctional for effectiveness. The possibility that this point may be reached more quickly in schools than in other social settings, because of the necessarily open-ended nature of the teaching-learning role relationship, has perhaps too often been overlooked by decision-makers in education. This may be due to the business administration model upon which much of their training has been based.

An added difficulty stems from the fact that the Canadian school today is embedded in an increasingly complex and interrelated web of role relationships in the larger society. The more complex social life becomes the more the same individual comes to hold positions in a variety of social organizations, rather than in merely one. It is this multiple group membership, resulting in a multiplicity and diversity of roles, that is the distinguishing feature of life in industrialized urban settings as opposed to rural or tribal ones. And it is this factor of multiple group membership that greatly increases the difficulty and complexity involved both in the daily operation of the school and its relations with other parts of the society.

We implied earlier that, to the man from Mars, a human social setting would look like a beehive. But roles in an actual beehive are single, simple and inflexible. Bee societies do not change, do not evolve from simplicity to complexity of organization as have human societies. It is likely that both the patterned role performance and the expectations are programmed into the individual bee at birth. In the case of human societies roles are programmed (or acquired through experience) after birth. And because even in the most totalitarian societies the socialization process never produces perfect "copies" (due to the extreme complexity of the interaction among genetic predispositions, perceptual processes and environmental demands) changes in roles are virtually guaranteed.

If the learning process of humans is too complex and interactive to enable them to be socialized like peas into pods, we could expect that, even if the positions available from generation to generation remained the same, the role performance and the role expectations would still vary tremendously. This would be due to differences in the value systems (and consequently the predispositions to behave in certain ways) of the incumbents. In other words, there will likely always be a certain amount of tension between what the individual perceives his role expectations to be and his actual performance. For the latter will be determined by the value system, or "self" that he brings to the position as well as by the expectations aroused in himself and others by the performance of past incumbents. This means that even in the most bureaucratic of organizations, some alteration of role during the tenure of each individual is inevitable. And as we move back along the continuum of social organization toward ever greater informality, role change becomes increasingly likely, until the rate of change becomes so great that there is insufficient stability for group life. Anomie (a state in which there are no clear cultural standards or guides for behaviour acknowledged by the social group) becomes commonplace, as does the "future shock" discussed by Alvin Toffler in his book by that name.

A second source of role change is the continual increase in complexity of organization mentioned earlier. As human beings develop more and more ways of adapting to and reconstructing their environment they are required to create many new types of positions, with roles attached to them. In addition, each individual during his lifetime is required to assume positions (and thereby to perform roles) in more and more social systems. In the urban society the teacher is no longer the tribal priest who devotes his entire life to controlling the group's socialization process. The teacher is often also a parent, an alderman, a part-time university student, a member of the Teachers' Federation, a church elder, a member of a glee club, a boy's club leader, a member of a political party, and so on.

This complexity of social organization is a further cause of tension for the role performer. These various roles compete for the individual's most precious resource — his time — and there must be some sort of trade-off between different role expectations. In addition, these competing expectations may come into conflict. Some may demand behaviours which are incompatible with those demanded by another role or with the individual's value system. The more complex the social organization, then, the greater is the possibility of such *role conflict*.

There is an important difference between *tension* (the source of all role change) and *conflict* (which may well be, instead, an impediment to change.) Tension inevitably exists between value system and role expectation. Tension is also aroused as the result of the competing claims of the individual's multiple roles. Conflict enters the picture, however, when competing demands are so incompatible that no compromise seems possible. Again, the idea of a continuum best helps us to understand this relationship between tension and conflict. At some point, what has been a healthy, change-producing tension becomes an unhealthy, change-preventing conflict. The two phenomena are not discrete and different in kind; they differ merely in degree of incompatibility between value system and role expectation.

Role conflict can take the form of extreme incompatibility among the various expectations one perceives to be held by "significant others," or between one's own expectations and those of significant others regarding the performance of one particular role. In the first instance, the principal, other teachers, students and parents all make contradictory demands upon you as a teacher. You are expected to be a pal, a therapist, a judge, an instructor, a priest and a custodian all at once. In the second case, the expectations of all these others are in general agreement, but they are incompatible with your own image of your role as a teacher. Here we could think of the teacher or principal who insists on introducing informal education over-night in a traditional school, or the teacher committed to the values of the counter-culture who goes to teach in a conservative farm community.

The above type of role conflict (sometimes referred to as "intra-role" conflict) results from role confusion which in turn is associated with the following:

1   informality of social organization with its consequent lack of precise definition and delineation of roles;

2   cultural pluralism, which makes possible widely varying value systems within the same society;

3   *widely* divergent and unplanned socialization processes occurring within the same society due to the weakness of the education system; and

4   resultant breakdowns in communication.

A second type of role conflict (discussed previously, and sometimes termed "inter-role" conflict) is associated with increased complexity of social organization. It is said to occur if the multiple positions assumed by the individual are so diverse that the role expectations attached to them become incompatible with one another. An example might be the female teacher who insists upon being the perfect housekeeper, which means meeting standards that few full-time homemakers attain, while at the same time trying to live up to her husband's expectations of her as a worshipful mate who meets him at the door with slippers and pipe in hand while attired in sexy lounging pyjamas. Or the male teacher who "farms on the side" insisting on seeding his one and a half section farm single-handed at the time of year when his grade twelve students most need extra help. Or the social studies teacher who is running as a political candidate, or is selling social science teaching materials for an American, British, or French firm.

Role tension, of course, has the same causes as role conflict. We have referred to role tension as inevitable and desirable in that it is implicit in the human social condition and is, in all probability, an important source of individual, organizational and cultural change. The more extreme situation which we refer to as role conflict, however, would seem to be both unnecessary and undesirable, in that it is probably a serious obstacle to rational social change. For the individual, it creates anxieties that feed on the energy required for reflective problem-solving activities, and arouses emotions which blind one to possible alternatives. All this renders one less effective as a human being. For the organization, conflict is invariably disintegrative as gross incompatibility of expectations makes the compromise required for rational decision-making difficult, if not impossible. Where conflict prevails, confusion is the order of the day, and one demand can only win out if the opposite is demolished. This tends to create an irrational, zig-zagging pattern of change as the organization moves from one extreme position back to another.

Rational change within an organization would seem to require effectiveness in terms of goals which are continually being evaluated against changing environmental demands. If the organization is to achieve its goals efficiently the roles within it must be coordinated with one another and must be operating in the service of these goals. Roles are reciprocal phenomena, created not only by one individual or by the generations of incumbents of one position, but by interaction among people holding related positions. It is possible to imagine them operating somewhat as gears, requiring a certain amount of meshing if the machine is not to grind to a stop or explode.

However, because a formal organization like a school is not a simple machine, nor the people in it merely mindless cogs, each role has a considerable range of possibilities within it. It is this range that provides the individual with his room to manoeuvre and that makes organizational change possible. Even in bureaucratic settings where role specifications are clearly spelled out, these establish minimal rather than maximal limits on performance. The area beyond these formal requirements is bound only by the "limits of tolerance" of the other interacting parties. Wise people, striving for change in a school setting, test these limits gingerly, expanding them slowly and being prepared to pull back if the reaction of significant others seems to indicate prudence.

Teachers or administrators seeking an excuse for not improving existing conditions tend to perceive their roles narrowly, in terms of minimal limits only. Accordingly, their tenure results in these very specifications being more strongly confirmed and confining, rather than changing shape or expanding so as to better adapt to changing circumstances. Such teachers are prone to make statements like: "The principal would never allow that." "I wouldn't dare not cover the textbook in case the superintendent found out." "Students demand authoritarianism (or permissiveness) and I wouldn't last two weeks if I tried to structure the class differently."

But roles do change, and as they change so, too, do the goals of the formal organization alter in response to new environmental demands; for this is how organizations remain effective. The alternative is to rigidify and become obsolete. There is always a tension between the need for *efficiency* within the organization and the need for *effectiveness*, with its requirement of continuous role change and adaptation. In striving for efficient use of the resources at hand, there is a temptation to standardize procedures and to treat all pupils alike. Effectiveness demands the maximum of accommodation to individual and local differences and adaptation to changes over time in the objectives of the system and the society. This is a second inevitable and desirable source of organizational change of which educators should be aware.

In order for formal organizations to remain both efficient and effective in their operation, *evaluation* and *integration* must be adequate. The first provides continuous feedback on the degree to which prevailing role definitions are contributing to the achievement of the organization's goals as well as the degree to which present goals are appropriate for environmental demands. In the school this means that student performance (as indicative of intellectual and moral growth) must be continually assessed and related to teaching style and organizational climate. It means, too, that the school's graduates should be assessed in the light of their effectiveness as adults.

Efforts at integration are necessary to combat the natural disintegrative processes at work within any formal organization. These are due to the phenomenon of informal organization: the tendency for people who interact in terms of formal roles to form into friendship groupings in which relationships shed their secondary or formal role-determined nature and become primary. (Here roles emerge in the course of face-to-face interaction and are determined, not by the rules of the organization, but by the personalities of the participants.)

Informal organization within the formal setting, although necessary, can be disintegrative if it gives rise to factions that repudiate the organization's goals, and replace them with conflicting ones based on a particular faction's perceived self-interest. In the school we can think of teacher cliques, student peer groupings, or a teenage subculture with its own definition of the teacher role as that of enemy, and with its rejection of the "student-as-learner" role. This informal organization inevitably poses a threat to the formal organization—a threat that can only be controlled if commitment to the organization's goals can be aroused in and shared by all the members, and role performance, effective in terms of these goals, is instituted. Techniques such as interschool scholastic and athletic contests, school parties, school songs and colours and graduation ceremonies are often deliberately designed with the goal of internal integration in mind.

The most lasting basis for integration, however, is effective *communication* within the organization. Communication problems tend to be related to the size of the membership. Perhaps schools, more than other formal organizations, should resist the pressures toward increased size which necessitates the bureaucratization of communication channels. In a bureaucracy there is a tendency for information to flow only in one direction, from the administration to the members, while feedback comes only irregularly and in response to specific demands. Only by means of continuous two-way communication can messages be conveyed and corrected simultaneously so that the sender and receiver are brought closer together. And only by means of the deliberate structuring of opportunities for effective communication among all the members can role conflict (as well as conflict between the requirement of the organization for both efficiency and effectiveness) be kept at the level of a healthy tension. Examples of such opportunities might be lunchtime staff seminars, regular meetings of small groups of teachers who work with the same age groups, frequent staff meetings at which more than administrative trivia are discussed, teacher-pupil-parent seminars on goals, and out-of-class activities in which teachers and pupils work together.

Just as communication is the key to the evolution of culture in the social system of the classroom, and to the individual learning that results, so too is it the key to the maintenance of the school as a network of dynamic roles, coordinated in the service of those educational goals deemed most desirable by the entire social group.

The Concept Demonstrated

CASE STUDY ONE

Mr. Renfrew is a Department of Education superintendent. He has been intimately associated with the progress of education in his province of Saskatchewan for thirty-five years. He is a competent scholar in his own right and has always endeavoured to keep abreast of current developments and fads in education, approaching them critically rather than with unquestioning acceptance. He takes his job seriously and feels a sense of personal responsibility for what happens in the schools under his jurisdiction.

Mr. Renfrew is beginning to feel himself to be a member of a disappearing species, as the trend in Saskatchewan (as in a number of other provinces) is to replace retiring departmental superintendents with locally appointed superintendents or directors of education. In spite of the change in status, however, these new people are experiencing the same conflicts and confusions that are now making Mr. Renfrew's position almost untenable.

Recently a number of problems have arisen in Mr. Renfrew's school unit—problems which he knows are shared by his fellow superintendents and directors. These problems seemingly involve conflicts among personalities, although Mr. Renfrew is aware that other factors are involved. He suspects that the local of the professional teachers' federation and some of the Faculty of Education people may be contributing indirectly to some of the problems.

One problem is in the area of the curriculum. A number of principals have been insisting on introducing new and different courses of study into their schools. These courses involve radical departures from the provincial curricula, and because of this, Mr. Renfrew feels that he must object. He considers that if this sort of procedure is allowed to gain headway, the maintenance of standards, which has always been his chief concern, would be an impossibility. The provincial Department of Education would no longer have the means of ensuring that children in small, isolated school districts were receiving equal educational opportunities.

If curricula varied from school to school, evaluation tools and procedures would have to vary likewise, and there would be no province-wide examinations. To Mr. Renfrew, the greatest advantage of these exams (aside from their elevating effect on standards) is the possibility that they provide for a province-wide, objective comparison of achievement from school to school.

Another closely allied problem encountered by Mr. Renfrew is a growing, thinly veiled resentment on the part of the younger and better qualified teachers of his supervisory function. These people seem to feel that because they have relatively adequate academic and professional preparation, they have nothing further to learn, even from someone with thirty-five years of experience in the field. They even question Mr. Renfrew's right and competence to evaluate their teaching abilities.

This issue came to a head recently when the unit board of trustees met with Mr. Renfrew to discuss the need to cut three teachers from the unit staff of one hundred and fity, due to the sudden drop in enrolment with which most of the schools were being faced. The board saw this as an opportunity to rid themselves of the least competent teachers, but in order to identify these they needed the cooperation of the superintendent and school principals. Mr. Renfrew agreed that the three teachers to be let go should be the least competent rather than merely the most recently hired, but he maintained that a rigorous and reliable evaluation of all the teachers was necessary if this was to be done. However, when he asked the principals to cooperate with him in this, he was faced with a wholesale refusal to "prejudice their colleague relationship with their teachers by sitting in judgement on them."

This confrontation is merely the most recent of a number of events that have made Mr. Renfrew feel increasingly frustrated in the performance of his appointed task. On the one hand, he is held accountable by both the local community and the Department of Education for what goes on in the school under his jurisdiction. On the other hand, he is finding it more and more impossible to ensure that principals will cooperate with him by performing their job responsibly, and to ensure that teachers will carry out his directives, or even that they will communicate the results of their classroom endeavours to him.

QUESTIONS FOR GROUP DISCUSSION

1   Is it true, as Mr. Renfrew assumes, that the criteria for evaluation would have to vary from school to school because of variations in the content, procedures and materials under study? In other words, does diversity in curriculum *content* necessarily mean that we are left with a "rubber yardstick" — with no reliable means to assess and compare pupil progress from school to school? What if the *objectives* in terms of skills and concepts to be acquired were uniform across the province? Discuss.

2   What implications does your answer to the above question have for the role of the teacher from school to school? For the role of principal and superintendent?

3   From which type of role conflict do Mr. Renfrew and the principals seem to be suffering? Give reasons for your answer.

4   Discuss the prospects and possible pressures for role change where principals and superintendents in Canada are concerned. Is the current emphasis on accountability likely to affect this?

CASE STUDY TWO

Judith Hemmingway had taken a teaching position in a little community in the British Columbia interior after having taught in Vancouver for two years. The prospect of greater freedom to be enjoyed by the country school teacher appealed to her.

Judith had been a rebel and an activist as a university student and had become a teacher because of an Existentialist commitment to freedom of choice for human beings. She was convinced that her chief responsibility to her pupils was to free them from the chains imposed upon them since birth by their culture. In the Vancouver school she had found herself in constant conflict with the principal and many of the other teachers on the subjects of school rules and curriculum. The prospect of her own school with no rules or set curriculum imposed from above upon herself and her pupils was an intriguing one for Judith, and she approached her new job with great expectations.

True to her philosophy, Judith immediately began to encourage her pupils to question any and all of the traditions, or norms, rules and laws which they had been previously conditioned to accept. No matter what the subject under study, Judith managed to work in her point of view. In the quest of freedom for her pupils she encouraged them to value nonconformity rather than conformity to the norms and laws of their culture. Because Christianity was the norm she encouraged agnosticism. Because representative parliamentary democracy was the Canadian governmental system she emphasized the advantages of one-party rule. Because the Canadian economic system was assumed to be more capitalist than socialist, she taught the merits of socialism. During the FLQ crisis she applauded the actions of the kidnappers and explained the imposition of the War Measures Act as an example of fascism. Because monogamy and heterosexuality represented ideals of the Canadian culture she brought articles to school that pictured group marriage and homosexuality as natural and desirable. When parents questioned her actions she argued that if their children were to learn to make free choices concerning their own behaviour they must be presented with the other side of every issue.

Although Judith did not realize it, as the fall months passed a storm was brewing around her in the small community. The incident that precipitated a general reaction by the parents was an assignment of Judith's. She had required her grade eight pupils to read Bertrand Russell's essay entitled "Why I am not a Christian," and to summarize his argument in their own words. One pupil took the essay home to show his father, who happened to be a Pentecostal minister. Phones buzzed for a couple of days; parents met with parents, then parents met with school board members. The result of all these deliberations was a petition signed by 90 per cent of the parents, requesting that

Judith be removed from her post immediately. The school board acted at once, with the chairman delivering the notice of dismissal in person.

Judith was surprised at first, then appalled and angry. These people seemed to have no conception of academic freedom, or the right of the teacher to professional autonomy. This, she felt, was liberal democracy at its worst, with the wishes of the unenlightened majority prevailing over the right of the individual to choose freely what he would be and do. For the first time Judith began to wonder whether it was possible in such a system to improve people and institutions by means of education.

QUESTIONS FOR GROUP DISCUSSION

1   What type of role conflict seems to be exemplified here? In what ways is it similar to, or different from, Mr. Renfrew's situation? According to the explanation of the concept of role in this chapter, what are the probable social sources of this type of conflict? How does this fit Judith's situation?

2   Why do you suppose Judith's perception of her role as a teacher failed to undergo any change during her two-year teaching stint in Vancouver? If roles are reciprocal rather than unilaterally determined, her perceived role as a teacher should have been undergoing a gradual evolution during that period. Can you explain how this may have failed to happen in this case?

3   Did Judith's perception of her role as a teacher change at all during her months at the country school? Discuss.

4   Does the idea of minimal and maximal role boundaries apply here? Try to explain what happened in terms of maximal boundaries of the teacher role, or limits of tolerance on the part of the community.

CASE STUDY THREE

Central Valley Collegiate in Toronto had for some time been considered a model of progressive education. It served an upper middle-class district and its teachers were better qualified than the average. Central Valley had pioneered in the matter of meaningful pupil participation in school government and in innovations such as individualized instruction and independent study. In fact, educators from various parts of Ontario had visited the school in recent years, looking for fresh ideas in high school education.

The news that Central Valley had been hit by pupil strikes and a sit-in therefore came as a distinct shock to parents and professional educators alike. It was difficult to determine the source of the trouble. Mr. Allen, the principal, had given his pupils a great deal of freedom.

He was considered by all who knew him to be a progressive educator, deeply committed to changing the school system and society. He had a strong student council which dealt not only with routine pupil affairs, but with actual matters of school policy. Their representatives attended staff meetings with voting strength equal to that of teachers. They had a say in the recruitment, hiring and firing of school personnel, and in curriculum issues.

Now Mr. Allen was being attacked by a group that referred to themselves as neo-Marxists. This group comprised a number of the brightest pupils in the school. They were claiming that Mr. Allen's reforms had been mere window-dressing; that they had not gone nearly far enough. They stated categorically that as long as teachers were allowed to evaluate pupils and to require that certain core classes be taken, the much-vaunted freedom of pupils to follow their own interests was illusory. Central Valley Collegiate, they said, was still operating as a servant of a sick society. In addition, they claimed that the student council had been co-opted by the principal and was not, in fact, acting in the real interests of the pupils.

Mr. Allen was severely disillusioned. He saw his teachers, now thoroughly intimidated, cowering in their classrooms after several days of abuse from the strikers. He saw the majority of the pupils hanging on the sidelines, ready to support the strikers as long as they appeared to be winning. Why had his progressive stance not prevented this confrontation, he wondered. Why had it happened in his school, of all the secondary schools in the city?

QUESTIONS FOR GROUP DISCUSSION

1   Discuss this problem in terms of the concept of informal organization within the formal. Is there any way that the disintegration that seems to be in the offing here could be avoided at this point?

2   Explain this situation by means of the concept of role conflict. How do you account for the fact that role conflict seemed to be more severe here than in the more traditional schools?

3   Is the organizational change process likely to occur in a steady, rational way here, or is it more likely to fluctuate from one extreme of role relationships to another? Why?

4   How might the idea of organizational goals shed light upon this situation? Is there any agreement on what these goals should be among the various teacher and pupil members?

The Concept Applied
To Relevant Canadian Research

Bergen, J. J. and D. Deiseach. "Dimensions of the High School Student's Role." *Alberta Journal of Educational Research* 18, no. 1 (1972): 8-15.
Six dimensions of role were identified in a study of the high school student's role as perceived by first-year Education students. Differences in attitude toward the role were found to be related to the type of school attended but not to personal variables such as sex, socio-economic background, or to teacher-education route. The importance of defining the role of the high school student is stressed as an initial step in attempting to find a more meaningful part in the school organization for the student.

Breton, Raymond, "Academic Stratification in Secondary Schools and the Educational Plans of Students." *Canadian Review of Sociology and Anthropology* 7, no. 1 (1970): 17-34.
This analysis of data collected from a Canada-wide sample of students in 360 secondary schools reveals that the program of study in which the student is placed has the strongest impact on his educational intentions. The data also show that the student's position in the school stratification system is more strongly related to his educational intentions than to the position of his father in the occupational structure.

Eddy, W. P. "The Relationship of Role Orientation of Teachers to Organization of Schools." *Alberta Journal of Educational Research* 16, no. 1 (1970): 13-21.
This study sought to determine whether teachers with differing local-cosmopolitan role orientation had differing perceptions of and satisfaction with the level of bureaucratization of the schools in which they worked. A number of hypotheses were tested using a sample of 339 teachers in twenty Alberta schools. Findings: teachers were more satisfied in high than in low bureaucratic schools; "locals" were generally more satisfied with and loyal to the organization than were "cosmopolitans"; little difference was apparent between the reaction of administrators to the two types of teachers.

Edman, Marion. *A Self Image of Primary School Teachers: A Cross-Cultural Study of Their Role and Status in 12 Cities.* Detroit: Wayne State University Press, 1969.
This book comprises a report on teachers in twelve major world cities, including Windsor, Ontario. Comparisons were made by eliciting information in connection with sex and family status of teachers,

formal qualifications, choice of profession, adequacy of income, occupational prestige, participation in culture, professionalism, political activities, time spent in teaching duties, decision-making in school matters, and regulations governing employment and retirement.

Egnatoff, John G. "The Changing Status of Saskatchewan's School Principals." *Canadian Educational and Research Digest* 8, no. 4 (1968): 354-365.
Communities under 25,000 population and containing schools employing four or more teachers in Saskatchewan were surveyed in 1954 and 1965 to ascertain changes in perception of the principal's role, with principals, teachers and school board members as respondents. The general finding was a heightened perception of the principal's role as an administrator, with less emphasis in 1965 than in 1954 on community leadership, organization of extracurricular activities, and teaching.

Finlay, J. H. and A. W. Reeves. "Expectations of School Boards for the Role of the Provincially Appointed Superintendent of Schools in Alberta." *Alberta Journal of Educational Research* 7, no. 1 (1961): 74-80.
A sample of 324 school board members returned the questionnaires used to collect the data for this study. It was found that boards expected superintendents to exercise independent action in instructional leadership and selection and management of staff personnel, with the area of finance ranked as their least important administrative function.

Gathercole, F. J. "The Role of the Locally Employed Superintendent of Schools in Alberta, Saskatchewan and Manitoba." *Ontario Journal of Educational Research* 6, no. 2 (1964): 93-98.
Data for a comparison of role behaviour and role expectations of the incumbents of forty-three superintendencies in the three prairie provinces were collected by means of a questionnaire. Findings: a high degree of consensus that their responsibilities include (1) maintenance of a high quality of instruction, and (2) provision of general leadership in education. Most see themselves as chief executive officers of boards.

Holdaway, E. A. "What Topics are Discussed at School Board Meetings?" in Stevenson, et. al., *The Best of Times/The Worst of Times: Contemporary Issues in Canadian Education*, pps. 415-418 Toronto: Holt Rinehart and Winston, 1972.
This report presents an analysis of the topic areas discussed, based upon 21,220 statements made in seventy-four hours of transcribed tape-recorded proceedings of meetings of thirteen Alberta rural and urban school boards.

Holdaway, E. A. "Characteristics of School Trustees in Alberta." *The Alberta School Trustee* (March 1973): 26-27.

Four hundred and twenty-three trustees responded to questionnaires eliciting background information. Only 16 per cent were female but, as a group, they had received a significantly higher education than had the male members. More of the females had been teachers. Thirty-two per cent of the respondents were farmers, 12 per cent housewives, 10 per cent merchant-businessmen, 5 per cent managers, 4 per cent civil servants.

Horowitz, Myer, et. al. "Divergent Views of the Principal's Role: Expectations Held by Principals, Teachers and Superintendents." *Alberta Journal of Educational Research* 15, no. 4 (1969): 195-205.

Significant differences were found to be present among teachers, principals, and superintendent groups in the sample made up of personnel from the Protestant School Board of Greater Montreal. Expectations of the role of the principal in secondary schools also differed from expectations of the role of the elementary school principal.

Lehtinieme, L. "A Tested Theory of Student Unrest." *Alberta Journal of Educational Research* 18, no. 1 (1972): 51-58.

This study tested the theory that protest activity is related to the stress caused by inconsistent role prescriptions. The data yielded by 225 questionnaires obtained from undergraduates at two Ontario universities during the 1969-70 year were used. Results of the analysis indicated that students who saw themselves as having adult rather than pre-adult status were more likely to have been actively involved in protest.

Mackie, M. "School Teachers: The Popular Image." *Alberta Journal of Educational Research* 18, no. 4 (1972): 267-276.

This paper describes the stereotypes of school teachers and explores the relationship between the occupation's prestige and its public image. Stereotypes were collected from 590 students located in twenty-five organizations.

Punch, Keith. "Interschool Variation in Bureaucratization." *Journal of Educational Administration* 8, no. 2 (1970): 124-134.

This study of forty-eight elementary schools in Ontario attempted to account for interschool variation in bureaucratization, particularly as it was associated with leader behaviour. It was found that leader behaviour was the biggest single determinant: size was inversely related.

Ricks, Francis A. and Sandra W. Pyke. "Teacher Perceptions and Attitudes That Foster or Maintain Sex Role Differences." *Interchange* 4, no. 1 (1973): 26-33.
This is a study of sixty Ontario secondary school teachers. Results revealed teacher perceptions of traditional male-female pupil behaviour in the classroom, teacher preference for male teachers and male pupils, and the reluctance of most teachers to facilitate sex role behavioural changes.

Sherk, H., and W. D. Knill. "The Role of the Alberta Superintendent." *Alberta Journal of Educational Research* 11, no. 2 (1965): 65-101.
A sample of 180 divisional and county school principals indicated their expectations for and perceptions of the role behaviour of the superintendent for each of fifty-three critical tasks. Many different and incompatible expectations were found.

Wiens, John. "Differences Between Influential and Non Influential Administrators." *Alberta Journal of Educational Research* 16, no. 2 (1970): 103-110.
Survey data from a study in British Columbia suggest that principals who are influential either in promoting or preventing change are different in several ways from principals who are not influential. In general, it was found that influential principals tend to be older and have more education than their peers, to have had more than one principalship, and to be aware of the existence of informal organization in their schools.

INDEPENDENT STUDY
Select the research study which most interests you and locate it in the appropriate journal. After reading it carefully, respond to the following:

1   How applicable to other Canadian situations do you consider these findings to be? Justify your opinion by referring to the methodology employed.

2   Describe the theoretical framework of the study, as implied by the implicit or explicit assumptions of the researcher. Compare and contrast it with the role theory explained in this chapter.

The Concept Amplified
By Further Reading

Chinoy, Ely. *Society: An Introduction to Sociology.* 2nd. ed. New York: Random House, 1967.
Pages 35-40 contain a good discussion of the concept of role.

Cohen, Louis. "School Size and Head Teachers' Bureaucratic Role Conceptions." *Educational Review* 23, no. 1 (1970): 50-58.
A sample of 196 heads of small schools and 147 heads of large schools was selected at random in England and Wales. Data supported the hypothesis that size of school is related to bureaucratized role perceptions of the head.

Coleman, James S. *The Adolescent Society.* Glencoe, Ill.: The Free Press, 1961.
A classic study of high school pupil role relationships that has been repeated in many different times and places since. The author's conclusions and suggestions concerning competition are especially interesting, as well as his general recommendations for taking the adolescent society as a given and using it to further the ends of adolescent education.

Coleman, Peter S. "Organizational Effectiveness in Education: Its Measurement and Enhancement." *Interchange* 3, no. 1 (1972): 42-52.
A good survey of the literature and a summary of findings on this topic. The author's final conclusions are (1) that teachers should be confronted frequently with the goals of the system, (2) that they should regularly be put in the position of discussing their policies and practices with their clients (pupils and parents), (3) that the policies carried on should be discussed frequently with teachers, (4) that at any given time the administrators should be able to express the organization's goals without hesitation, and (5) that all the above concerns should be considered appropriate professional concerns by the teachers so that control will be exercised by colleagues as well as the administrative hierarchy.

Fraser, G. S. "Organizational Properties and Teacher Reactions." *Comparative Educational Review* 14, no. 1 (1970): 20-29.
A study of the relationship between certain structural properties (size and organizational complexity) and certain compositional properties (age, sex of staff, and reactions of teachers in terms of job satisfaction and career commitment). Teachers in the United States, Australia and New Zealand were studied. Findings: organizational complexity was the strongest predictor of job satisfaction and career commitment, with schools at the middle level of organizational complexity producing the highest degree of teacher satisfaction and commitment.

Gordon, C. Wayne. *The Social System of the High School.* Glencoe, Ill.: The Free Press, 1965.
A participant-observer type of study of 576 students in an American suburban high school. The findings have implications for our understanding of pupil role perceptions and expectations.

Guskin, Alan E. and Samuel L. Guskin. *A Social Psychology of Education.* Don Mills, Ont.: Addison-Wesley Publishing Company, 1970.
Chapters 1 and 2 present good discussions of the concept of role; chapters 3, 4 and 5, the concept of social organization in the classroom setting, and chapters 6 and 7 the concept of socialization.

Rossides, Daniel W. *Society as a Functional Process.* Toronto: McGraw-Hill of Canada, 1968.
Pages 63-67 include an enlightening discussion of the concept of role.

Ryan, Kevin, ed. *Don't Smile Until Christmas*. Chicago: University of Chicago Press, 1970.
This book consists of the diaries of six first-year teachers. They demonstrate in a striking way the extent of the role confusion and conflict too often present in this situation. An important book for every beginning teacher.

Sarason, Seymour B. *The Culture of the School and the Problem of Change*. Boston: Allyn and Bacon, 1971.
Chapters 8, 9, 10, 11 and 12 are especially informative on the roles of the principal and teacher, and on the significance of these roles for the process of organizational change.

Smelser, Neil J., ed. *Sociology: An Introduction*. New York: John Wiley and Sons, 1967.
Pages 570-600 contain a good discussion of role as a dynamic concept.

Waller, Willard. *The Sociology of Teaching*. 2nd. ed. New York: John Wiley and Sons, 1965.
This book, first published in 1932, is still one of the most comprehensive treatments available of the complex teacher-pupil role relationship in the school setting.

The Concept Reviewed

1   Which one of the following is least likely to be an example of role conflict?
a.   the teacher who doesn't dare deviate from the details of the teaching materials and procedures suggested in the curriculum
b.   the teacher who feels that he is expected to be a pal, therapist, instructor and custodian all at once
c.   the teacher who is torn between staying home to nurse her sick child and conducting her classes
d.   the teacher on an Indian reserve today who sees himself as a Christian missionary.

2   The prevalence of multiple group membership in modern Canadian society contributes most directly to:
a.   role confusion
b.   role change
c.   inter-role conflict
d.   intra-role conflict.

3   Which of the following is a good example of the expression of goals as untestable abstractions (one of the major causes of role confusion in a formal organization)?
a.   A team teaching program requires that teachers spend so much time having meetings and arguing over goals and strategies that they are too exhausted to concentrate on their teaching during the day.
b.   A team teaching program has as its major objective the development of cooperative attitudes among pupils and teachers. However, the parents

of the district want the school to equip their children with the means of climbing to the top of the Canadian economic and social structure.

c. The school's team teaching program brings it to the attention of educators throughout the country. The project becomes a showpiece, with most of the teachers' and pupils' time being devoted to the preparation of productions designed to win audience approval.

d. A team teaching program has as its major objective individualized learning. However, each team member defines the concept differently.

4   Without the existence of roles, human social life would be:

a. impossible, because no one could predict how anyone else would respond to anything; no one could count on anyone

b. difficult, but workable and exciting, as everything would be unpredictable and the consequences of one's choices could never be anticipated

c. creative, because we would be freed from the chains forged by patterns of behaviour established in the past

d. more honest, because everyone would be authentic; there would be no more hypocritical acting of parts.

5   Which one of the following is not a necessary and desirable source of change within the Canadian school today?

a. the tension between the individual teacher's value system and the expectations associated with his role

b. the tension between the need for efficiency and the need for effectiveness of the school operation

c. the tension experienced by the teacher, principal or pupil due to the incompatibility of his various roles

d. the tension experienced by the teacher, principal or pupil due to the fact that the school tends to mirror some of the features of organizational informality, organization complexity, and cultural diversity characteristic of the larger society.

6   Roles in a formal organization differ from those in a less formally organized social system in that in the former:

a. it is essential that they be well coordinated

b. they tend to be more precisely delineated and defined prior to their assumption by the incumbent of the position

c. they tend to be more static and difficult to alter

d. it is necessary for all members to be aware of and committed to the goals of the association, as they interact in their roles

e. all of the above

f. none of the above

g. all but d, e and f.

7   Which of the following is not a good explanation of the sociological concept of role?

a. the various parts one performs (as an actor in a play) as one consciously tries to gauge each situation and react in accordance with the momentary expectations of the participants

b. the complex "set" of all the expectations that others have of how one in your position should behave, plus your perception of these expectations, plus your perceptions of how you as an individual should carry out your duties, all this being influenced by the regularities established by your own past actions as an incumbent of that position, as well as the past performance of other incumbents

c. a dynamic, evolving part of the entire structure and process of interaction in which one is involved; the part that results from the tension between the individual's value system and the expectations held by all concerned regarding how he is likely to behave

d. the sum total of all the responsibilities and duties attached to a position, continually mediated and altered by the personality and values of the current incumbent as he makes his daily choices and as he responds intuitively to situations and people.

Roles in a formal organization tend to become rigid and bureaucratized nd the organizational change process is stifled when:

a. role prescriptions are established prior to the assumption of the position by the member

b. role prescriptions are formalized

c. members perceive the boundaries established by the formal role definitions as maximal rather than minimal limits, and refuse to go beyond them in any way

d. a degree of consensus on goals is required

e. all of the above

f. none of the above.

An advantage of the presence of informal organization within the formal ssociation is that:

a. it is likely to contribute to greater integration of the association as a whole

b. it is likely to result in more open and effective communication among all the members on the subject of organizational goals and priorities

c. it provides opportunity for the person-to-person or primary type of interaction often lacking in the formal organization

d. it promotes a friendship pattern within the organization that tends to reflect the racial, religious and socio-economic divisions in the larger society.

0 According to the division of responsibilities generally accepted in anadian education today, the role of the individual teacher chiefly involves:

a. determining societal goals for education (the type of society to be achieved through education)

b. structuring the pattern of social interaction (communication and activities) and utilizing resources in his classroom most conducive to the achievement of the learning outcomes set out in the curriculum

c. determining the learning outcomes for his class

d. determining the subjects to be taught and how they should be sequenced.

nswers: 1 (a); 2 (c); 3 (d); 4 (a); 5 (c); 6 (c); 7 (a); 8 (e); 9 (c); 10 (b)

4 Authority

The Concept Explained

Probably no idea in the field of education today has been so subject to attack and so prone to confused emotional and ideological response as the concept of authority, whether it be authority within the formal organization or throughout society as a whole.

This is most unfortunate, for the educator more than most people requires clarity of vision as to the relationship of authority to power, to freedom, and to responsibility in the larger society: to leadership and decision-making in the formal organization and to teacher-control of the learning environment in the classroom.

John Dewey had a great deal to say about the relationship between authority and freedom. He felt that our philosophical tradition, especially since Rousseau, had set up a false and dangerous dichotomy between these two. It had established a tendency for us to see authority as the enemy of freedom, and the two as mutually exclusive, so that a gain in one must of necessity be at the expense of the other. He felt that this was understandable, because the greatest obstacle to individual freedom prior to the twentieth century had indeed been the authority vested in certain individuals and in institutions like the church. Because these groups had held a monopoly on social power for so many centuries, authority had also become vested in them as a matter of tradition, to be transmitted but not questioned. It was therefore natural that the freedom fighters of the period would see authority and power as one and the same thing, and would conclude that the maximal decentralization of both was necessary for democracy. In this way the democratic ideal became confused with anarchism in the minds of many nineteenth-century liberals. This has tended to lead to that rebellion against all forms of authority (and the resulting social chaos in which raw physical power or violence reigns) which has prepared the ground for a return to that extreme centralization of both power and authority that we have come to know as the phenomenon of twentieth-century totalitarianism.

It may well be that this inability to distinguish between the concepts of power and authority, and to clarify the relation of each to the freedom of the individual, will bring about the failure of the democratic experiment wherever it is being attempted today. Certainly, if the teachers of the young are confused about these matters, it is unlikely that they will be able to contribute to the development of freedom-respecting, democratic individuals rather than to the production of anarchists or totalitarians.

The following diagram may be helpful at this point:

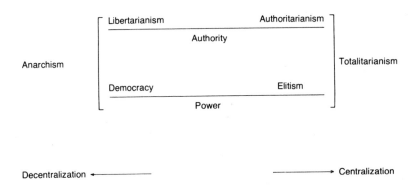

How can we justify making this sort of distinction between power and authority? Obviously there exists a close relationship between the two; authority clearly is one of the sources of power. (The official position of the teacher gives him some power to start with, regardless of any deficiency in personality and performance which might result in his subsequent loss of this power.) Also, power manifested over time will invariably produce the authority structures to legitimize and maintain it. (As in the case of a military junta, a new constitution and governmental organization is soon established.)

None the less, a crucial difference exists between these two phenomena. First, let us examine the concept of power in the social context. It means the ability to limit or control the alternatives for action available to others. It is a relative thing, in that one member of the group can only gain power to the degree that someone else loses it. Authority, on the other hand, stems from a set of rules which impose limits on the power wielded by individuals: rules which cannot be arbitrarily altered by the person wielding the authority. Where authority is absent, the source of social power will be physical force (and the control of resources which this makes possible) or certain personality attributes which endow one with charisma (and the control of masses of people which follows from this). The fact of biological variability guarantees that people will not be equally endowed with either of these qualities necessary for the acquisition of power. To make for even more inequality, control of the group's resources (resulting from the possession of a disproportionate amount of physical strength and/or charisma) is likely to give the children of the most powerful of one generation an unfair advantage over other contenders. This advantage will be cumulative, so that where raw power reigns it tends to become increasingly centralized into fewer and fewer hands from generation to generation, and to be increasingly associated with the control of resources. The only means by which it can be redistributed is by a counter physical force in the form of large numbers of people aroused to action by the charisma of one or more leaders. This redistribution may result in no more than a change in leadership, or it may result in greater decentralization for a while, with the cycle then beginning all over again.

This picture of social change will by now have a familiar ring to it. This particular pattern of competition for the sources and rewards of social power has been more often the rule than the exception throughout the history of mankind. Indeed, it was so much the rule that Karl Marx (writing in the mid-nineteenth century) assumed that the pattern was inevitable, unless and until a system of authority was established which would make the accumulation by individuals and elites of a disproportionate share of the group's resources impossible. Perhaps if Marx had made a clear distinction between the power of the aroused proletariat which would achieve this redistribution and the authority structure which they would subsequently establish in order to limit their own further accumulation of power, his ideas would not have been so distorted and misused during the succeeding century. But it is too much to expect that he would have made this

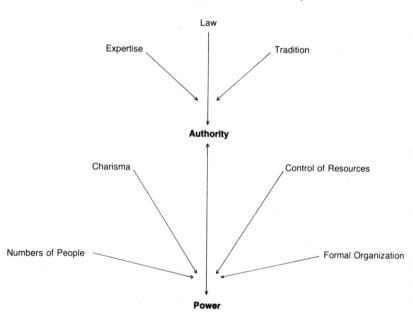

The Relationship Between Power and Authority

distinction; the cultural climate of his day was not conducive to an analysis of authority as a direct product of man's collective intelligence, rather than as a by-product of his physical and emotional prowess, frozen into tradition by the passage of time.

It was Max Weber who contributed a major plank in the construction of the twentieth-century concept of authority as distinct from power. Unlike power, which is an element in social interaction, authority was to Weber a cultural product. True, the possession of authority gives an individual power to act in a specific social setting, but its source is not momentary physical or psychological advantage, but is culturally defined. Weber identified three types of authority: that which is derived from custom or the tradition of the group; that which is based on the system of laws in which the group has codified its norms and sanctions; and that which has its source in the expertise or knowledge of the individual.

Weber saw society (especially the Germany of his day) as moving from a condition of control by traditional authority (mirroring a balance of social power favourable to an hereditary elite) to control by a type of bureaucratic authority based upon the legal system and individual expertise. His description of the bureaucratic formal organization is still apt and useful today. Some of the characteristics of bureaucracy which he discussed are: (1) an hierarchical arrangement of offices (or positions) with each having clearly specified spheres of jurisdiction (boundaries of authority) and each being responsible to the one above and responsible for the performance of those directly below in the line of command; (2) precise rules governing range and quality of performance; (3) clearly defined channels of communication with the memo and the file being emphasized; (4) hiring and promotion based on expertise and tenure rather than on personality or family connections; and (5) the office perceived as a lifetime career rather than a job.

Although Weber expressed some reservations about the future of individual freedom in bureaucratic social systems, he concluded that, in sum, this was probably a gain for humanity. For the transition was from a traditional authority, likely to reflect habitual, mindless responses to a highly centralized system of social power, to a structure of rules and laws devised by men through conscious application of intelligence. Bertrand Russell likewise expressed a preference for bureaucratic types of social arrangements over aristocratic or democratic ones. (He defined aristocratic arrangements as those based on authority or power derived from the accident of birth and custom. In the case of democratic structures, he seemed to equate authority, power and "sameness," so that what he was actually objecting to may have been anarchism and mediocrity.)

The significance of this change from a traditional authority structure to one based upon a system of law and the body of scientific knowledge constructed by the collective intelligence of the human group was not lost on John Dewey. In fact, he considered that an understanding of this was imperative if we were to continue to move in the direction of that maximal sharing of social power that we associate with the democratic ideal and with individual freedom. Weber's second and third categories of authority (that based upon law and that derived from expertise) were seen by Dewey as originating from one and the same source: the body of scientific knowledge which provides us with "warrantable assertions" about experienced regularities. Authority can thus be seen as that power which is derived from a set of rules for human behaviour, originating either with blind habit or with the ability of humans to discern relationships between cause and effect in their environment. The latter type of rule is the basis not only of functional laws, but of all knowledge and responsible human behaviour. If we did not acquiesce to the authority contained in highly verified rule-like statements of regularities among phenomena (scientific knowledge), we would be unable to anticipate the consequences of alternative actions, and would be reduced to non-reflective, random behaviour.

According to Dewey it is this knowledge and the process of systematic and publicly verified inquiry which produces it that should be recognized by human beings as the ultimate source of all authority. The legal system evolving within society should be based upon the knowledge (about social as well as physical relationships) constructed by this method, and laws should be continuously tested and altered on these terms. To Dewey, the scientific method of inquiry, used by all members of society as a tool for solving the problems of the human condition, is a prerequisite for a democratic and free culture. It provides for the continuity necessary for predictable social interaction as well as the source of constant change required for human adaptation to an evolving environment. For scientific knowledge changes only from within, by a process of incorporating the old with the new in a different and more comprehensive and useful set of explanations. In addition, it is both a uniquely individual task and a collective endeavour. Dewey maintained that only in the scientific approach to reality do we achieve this reconciliation of freedom with authority, and of individual creativity with the requirements for collective action.

Merely because traditional authority in certain times and places has been an obstacle to democratic progress, it is clearly illogical to conclude that authority *per se* is the enemy of freedom. Even Marx's projected system of authority—the dictatorship of the proletariat, designed to equalize economically derived power and be indoctrinated into the group members so that laws would be internally rather than externally applied—was intended to increase individual freedom of choice. Indeed, most of the laws passed in representative democracies since Marx's time have functioned to expand rather than restrict the number of choices available to the common man. Certainly, the authority of scientific knowledge has greatly extended the possibilities open to mankind. To rebel blindly against all authority is to cry for a system where physical force and charisma establish the limits of individual freedom.

In applying these ideas to the school as a formal organization, we can readily recognize the need for an authority structure of some kind, if we are to maximize freedom of choice for all its members, in the future as well as the present. Also, it is difficult to imagine how group goals could be achieved, or any complex set of activities carried out without authority and responsibility for specific tasks being delegated to certain people.

Furthermore, the school cannot be viewed in isolation from the societal authority structure in which it is embedded. Teachers and administrators in Canada hold positions which have been endowed with legal authority as spelled out by the School Act of each province. With this official authority goes responsibility to the public whose law it is, and whose children are being educated according to the provisions of that law, and presumably with the results planned for by those who passed (and continue to support) the regulations concerned. The typical hierarchical pattern of authority provides the public with the means to maintain control of this very vital institution. The principal knows that he is accountable for what goes on in his school, both to the parents and trustees directly at the local level, and indirectly through the line officials above him in the urban Board of Education or rural district, division, or unit office, the Department of Education, the Minister, and the Cabinet to the Legislative Assembly elected by the people of the province at regular intervals. Each teacher knows that in his professional capacity he is responsible to the parents and pupils and to the principal for what goes on in his classroom.

One way of understanding this legally based authority structure is to see it as the arm of the people reaching right down into the classroom to protect the present and future welfare of their children and of the society that these children will be shaping thirty years hence. One could argue that this type of authority might come into conflict with the authority wielded by the professional teacher as a result of his specialized expertise. However, it is still not clear that the teacher does possess a reliable body of *educational* knowledge which guides his practice; nor has the distinction between the determination of educational goals by the public and their implementation by the practitioner always been clearly demarcated. These are problems which teacher, trustee and government representatives must face up to in the near future.

All those positions in the direct line of command from the Minister through the Deputy Minister, branch head, or director, superintendent, principal and teacher we call *line* positions. Others such as subject area consultants and department heads within a school are considered to be *staff* positions. The person in the line position is responsible to his superior (the individual directly above him in the chain of command) and is responsible for the performance of his subordinates (those positioned below him and within his fan-shaped sphere of jurisdiction). The staff person is responsible to his superior for his performance, but is not responsible for that of his subordinates. This means that he has no official authority over the teachers. His authority with them stems from his expert knowledge, and it is on that basis that he coordinates and advises, but does not direct.

The concept of centralization versus decentralization of power and authority can apply within a school, or to the provincial schooling system, or to the political organization of the entire society. Because our schools are not autonomous entities, free from public control, it is difficult to imagine a single school in which power as well as authority was so centralized that we could classify it as totalitarian. No principal could ever centralize all power into his own hands as long as the society in which the school operated was sufficiently democratic that the people had the right to either refuse the school's services and opt for an available alternative, or to influence the shaping of those services.

However, one could easily imagine a school being extremely authoritarian, with authority highly centralized in the position of the principal. Failure of the administration to delegate authority and responsibility to teachers is a fairly common cause of staff dissatisfaction and ineffective performance. If only the principal can exercise authority, the parents and pupils soon realize it, and refuse to grant the teachers the respect that their position has traditionally commanded. Also, the less one is allowed to make decisions and is held accountable for them, the more irresponsible and incapable of handling authority one becomes. This applies to pupils as well. It may be desirable to arrange the authority structure so that pupils are gradually delegated small amounts of authority in designated areas of behaviour, from grade one on—a delegation which is increased from level to level as the students demonstrate developing responsibility. All members of the school organization should be made aware, however, that it is the principal who, in the final analysis, is answerable to the public for the efficiency and effectiveness of his school, and it is his prerogative to assign authority or to remove it if it is abused.

But what about the sharing of *power* within the formal organization? What about democracy in the school? It is at this point that the distinction between power and authority is particularly helpful. Authority has to do with the implementation or execution of policy resulting from decisions made about educational priorities. Power is the ability to determine what policy is allowed to be executed. Because a school is usually only one component in the complex of organizations that comprise a society's schooling system, it is hardly likely that it will be given carte blance to set its own policy in isolation from the other units of the system. The system could not operate as a system if this were so. Even more important, the members of the society would never risk losing control of an institution so crucial to the future of the entire group, and to the survival of their culture.

This means that many of the decisions that establish school policy are made outside the school, in the Legislature, the Department or Ministry of Education, the curriculum committee, and the trustees' meeting. There is no way to avoid this, if we grant to the people the right to influence school policy previous to its implementation. The suggestion that a particular school should operate as a self-contained, miniature democratic society, with all its members (including its immediate clients, the pupils) assuming an equal share of the policy-making power, and with the community therefore losing its control is a rather startling one. It seems to be based on three unwarranted assumptions:

1   that all members share equally the information, knowledge, thinking strategies and judgment required for the making of wise decisions in the area of expertise for which the organization has been given a mandate by society;

2   that the policy of the school is the responsibility and concern of only those who are temporarily housed within it, as administrators, teachers or pupils;

3   that the techniques and routines associated with the practice of decision-making are what determine ability to operate in and maintain a democratic society, rather than the wisdom and morality which the individual brings to his decision-making practice, and which is the long-term objective of education.

The first of these assumptions denies the raison d'être of any educational system: the teacher-learner relationship which is the basis of the planned and directed socialization process which we call education. The very concept of education implies that those responsible for directing the process possess more reliable knowledge, wisdom, and strategies for constructing and testing knowledge, than do the learners. Where this is not, in fact, the case, the teacher is judged to be incompetent.

The second assumption denies the right of the immediate community and larger society to a degree of control over the total process by means of which that community and society will be shaped in the future.

The third assumption emphasizes the routines of democracy (such as voting and making decisions) at the expense of the prerequisites for democracy (an enlightened, well-informed, reasoning and responsible electorate). The latter state is not one which is acquired full-blown by human beings as they emerge from the womb, but is the result of a long and difficult, guided developmental process.

Besides the plea for internal democracy, some people argue that schools should be competitive organizations rather than publicly operated and monopolistic, and that power should be wielded by the public, after-the-fact, as consumers who refuse the services that do not satisfy. The "voucher system" is based on this premise. This is a proposal whereby a pupil, (or a parent, acting in his interest) is provided with a claim on the society's educational services equivalent to the probable total cost of his regular public schooling: a claim negotiable anywhere in the country, and over an extended time period. Others maintain that schools should be community-run, with only the immediate neighbourhood served by the school sharing in the policy-making, and with the teachers being accountable directly to the community, but not to the larger society of which the community forms a part.

The community school, free school, and voucher movements are contemporary forms of the old centralization versus decentralization issue in education. One could have decentralization of control at the system level, in that the individual school would be an autonomous entity, but still have great centralization of authority and/or power *within* the school, in the form of a dictatorial principal or a bullying chairman of the local educational council. Or one could visualize extreme centralization of control at the provincial level, with no mechanism such as a board of trustees or educational council to allow for parent participation at the local level, but a decentralized authority structure existing within the individual school, to the extent that informal education prevailed in every classroom. Or any combination of these possibilities.

Arguments in favour of decentralization of control hinge on the desire of parents for a more direct say in the daily operation of their children's classrooms and in the determination of educational objectives for the school. They also hinge on the desire of teachers and pupils for greater autonomy. The potential for conflict among these three demands, however, is seldom adequately recognized; yet any one of the three groups can gain more power only at the expense of the power possessed by one or both of the other two.

Arguments for centralization are based on the need for provision of equality of opportunity for the children of the less vocal and powerful, the need to reduce sub-cultural prejudices and rivalries, the need to teach a common core of symbols and concepts representative of the national society and world community, and the need to protect the right of the teacher as a professional to make decisions within his area of competence without the interference of parents.

In the midst of all this confusion and competition for the power to make school policy and the authority to implement it stands the principal. Because of the authority vested in him by the local community and by the Legislature representing the public at large, his role is most appropriately one of leadership. Leadership requires more than this official authority, however. It requires the intellectual power to influence policy and executive decisions as well as the charismatic power to arouse commitment to those decisions on the part of the front-line members—the teachers and pupils—whose cooperation is necessary for their implementation. Along with this must go the judgment needed for delegating and withdrawing authority, and the intellectual and professional ability to evaluate performance.

One of the dilemmas of leadership faced by principals is that of member-participation in decision-making versus efficient operation of the organization. For instance, teacher involvement is desirable for effective performance, and to ensure their commitment to school goals; but at some point this involvement becomes an end in itself, and the entire organization becomes impotent. Where the principal lacks leadership some other member of the staff will invariably assume power, and operate behind the scenes. And in any formal organization where the authority and power structures do not coincide morale plummets and conflict tends to erupt among factions.

The teacher is also a leader of sorts. To be successful he must structure his classroom learning environment so that his authority is not questioned and his power never felt. It means that his pupils do have the freedom to select from among alternatives, but that these alternatives have been carefully planned by him, with their consequences for learning in mind. The teacher uses his authority to see that the pupils live with the consequences of their choices, so that they become increasingly responsible for their own learning as their schooling progresses. Some sociologists feel that this provision of planned alternatives within the classroom is not sufficient, however, in that pupils have not been previously exposed to the choice of classrooms and even of schools. Where the pupil feels that he has been forcibly recruited into the learner role in a particular classroom, he may see his tenure only as an ongoing power struggle with the teacher, to whom he refuses to grant authority over him.

What we term discipline problems are symptoms of such loss of authority by the teacher. There can be a number of causes of this, besides the one already mentioned. The teacher may be operating his class in an authoritarian manner, demanding total submission to his dictates and providing no opportunity to the pupil for the experience of choosing. This encourages irresponsibility and dependence on the part of pupils, as well as a generalized attitude of rebellion against all authority. Or else the teacher may be permissive, seeking the approbation and friendship, rather than the learning, of his pupils. Because this teacher has abdicated all authority and responsibility for leadership the pupils take him at his word and control of the classroom learning environment passes to the most powerful members of the group.

He may be inconsistent in his expectations and rewards, either from pupil to pupil or from day to day; or inflexible, compulsively repeating techniques and responses which do not work. Or he may not be sufficiently authoritative (as opposed to authoritarian) due to deficiencies in personality or knowledge background.

All too often, however, discipline problems are caused by factors beyond the control of the teacher. In these cases, if he is sociologically aware, he can sometimes salvage the situation by enlisting the cooperation of the school staff and community in attacking the problem at its roots. For instance, the individual pupil with severe behavioural problems can be removed from the classroom and not allowed to experience the rewards gained from disturbing the class. However, this practice cannot be followed consistently without the knowledge and help of the parents, other teachers willing to take him into their classes temporarily, and the principal, who may have to be ready with special arrangements.

Sometimes the problems are even more difficult for the individual teacher to identify and cope with, in that they are created and nourished by aspects of the formal organization of the school itself and by the relation of the school to the larger society. For example, we should not underestimate the potential for destructive conflict in today's large comprehensive high schools, where a bureaucratic organization is often operating in the pursuit of learning objectives which are repudiated by most of the pupils.

In too many cases these learning objectives have been couched in terms of coverage of subject content rather than the ideas to be attained by means of the content, and on that ground are rejected by many of the most committed learners among the pupils. These potential scholars resent being so submerged in information that they have no time to acquire the conceptual structures which lead to knowledge. To another group of pupils—those who have been academically crippled by previous failure in school—both the learning objectives and the alternative means for achieving them offered by the teacher are incomprehensible and threatening. To a third group—the rebellious students, impatient for direct experience in the world outside the school—the teacher's learning objectives are unrelated to current human problems, and the means of achieving them seem contrived and useless. A fourth group, the ambitious status seekers, see the high school solely as a channel of upward mobility; to them the learning objectives are merely perceived as distasteful obstacles to be overcome on the way to that desired success goal beckoning beyond the university.

If pupils repudiate the school's learning objectives they are unlikely to acknowledge or respect that natural authority which a good teacher can claim on the basis of his superior knowledge and wisdom. They are even less likely to grant the teacher authority based on his official position in the organization, as defined by tradition and law. With no authority in the eyes of his pupils, the teacher is reduced to manipulating their behaviour through the force of his personality, by inducing fear of corporal punishment or expulsion, by his control over grades, or by providing titillating entertainment in the guise of lessons.

In such a power struggle the teacher is bound to lose. Even grades are rapidly losing their force as rewards. The academically crippled have been overpunished by grades already. To the rebellious they are the symbol of conformity. To the extent that they have been used to manipulate pupil behaviour, they have been rendered meaningless to the serious scholars. Until recently the success-oriented pupils valued them highly as symbols of progress toward their future goals. However, a sudden change has occurred here, as the news is filtering down that once a university degree is available to everybody it can no longer be the magic key to power and affluence. At the same time and for the same reasons a high school diploma is now being viewed by employers as a doubtful indicator of competence. So it follows that if the name of the game is merely to get that diploma, with that high average, maybe the game is no longer worthwhile.

In these circumstances, what is the individual teacher to do? Perhaps an understanding that the crises of authority in the Canadian school today are the problems of society as a whole, and must be tackled on those terms, will at least give the teacher some perspective and emotional support. And this necessary awareness should also ensure that what he does in his classroom meanwhile is contributing to an eventual resolution, rather than an aggravation, of the problem for society.

The Concept Demonstrated

The little immigrant community in southeastern British Columbia was the latest in a series of pioneer settlements in that area. Wandering gold-seekers had come first, then a few early farmers, ranchers, and lumbermen, followed by a group of Doukhobor people from Saskatchewan. Now the latest settlers were chiefly Americans, refugees from urbanization, pollution, and a senseless war.

The Doukhobors, members of the militant Sons of Freedom sect, at first watched the newcomers warily. Their initial impulse was to distrust any strangers, especially a group so obviously city-bred and unfamiliar with the rugged British Columbian interior. But the Americans minded their own affairs and the Freedomites appreciated this. The neighbourhood re-established itself and soon it was business as usual throughout the valley.

All was calm, that is, except for the school problem. Among the new settlers were several people with teaching certificates and even Master's degrees. Many more were qualified in particular specializations. Most had special interests in and strong opinions on how to educate their young. It became apparent very early that public school in the valley simply would not do. The children of the newcomers were different from the native British Columbians: they wore their hair long; they wore jeans to town instead of for work; and they wanted to study what interested them instead of what interested the teacher or the Department of Education. They began to come home from school tense and unhappy, with stories of being "hassled" by the other children.

The new community set to work to plan their own free school. The organizers met with enthusiasm from both children and parents, and eventually managed to gain the approval of the school board for their enterprise. In the new school policy was to be made by pupils as well as parents and teachers; attendance was to be non-compulsory; there would be no time tables, set curriculum nor established classes; and the children were to be free to come and go as they wished.

At about the time that the free school was getting under way the school board made the decision to close down one or two of the public schools in the valley because of a shortage of pupils. The Freedomites, along with other residents, protested this move, arguing that their children should not be transported long distances to central points for schooling. The move seemed especially unjust to the protesters, in view of the fact that the newcomers had been allowed to withdraw their children from the public school system, thus increasing the board's financial problems. A few of the Freedomites even began to wonder aloud why one minority group should be permitted to set up its own school while a second, much longer-established minority group, was allowed no such privilege. The situation in the valley became tense, with the members of the school board feeling themselves to be caught on the horns of a dilemma. As Ralph Brown, one of the local officials phrased it, how could they ensure that the children of the Freedomites received some kind of choice without seeming to discriminate against their parents?

QUESTIONS FOR GROUP DISCUSSION

1   Try to explain this situation in terms of centralization versus decentralization of authority and power. In the case of the free school, how are power and authority distributed among the people of the province, the total valley community, the parents of the free school pupils, pupils, teachers and administrators?

2   Why are school board officials likely to be concerned about the effect of this development on the Freedomites? Explain in terms of the history of the relationship between the authority of church and state in B.C. education.

3   What did the school board official mean when he stated that they had to ensure that the children of the Freedomites received some kind of choice? Are any of the other arguments for centralization mentioned in this chapter relevant here?

4   It would seem that this type of free school offers the ultimate in decentralization of authority and power. How has this worked in practice in Canada? Discuss the history of free school experiments with which you are familiar.

5   Parents who opt for community control of schools claim that, although the provincial school system has an authority structure which makes it theoretically accountable to the public, parents nevertheless often feel themselves to be powerless to influence policy. Discuss the dimensions of this problem in Canada. Are there possible solutions other than that proposed by the newcomers to the valley?

CASE STUDY TWO

The Director of Education in an eastern Canadian city died suddenly three years ago after having filled the top position in the public school system for thirty years. His successor was an educator of some repute who had immigrated from the United States a few years previously. This former American began to make a number of changes soon after assuming office, changes which culminated in a major restructuring of the entire organization of the city system.

Under the new structure the old city textbook store was replaced by a large instructional resources centre. Budgets for individual school libraries were cut back drastically, while the resource centre received the major portion of the system's library allocation.

Supervisory staff were named to newly created "consultant" positions. They were attached to the resource centre and made available on call to schools and individual teachers.

Principals and teachers were requested to move from the single-year grade system to a non-ranking system of levels, with the expectation that this would ultimately evolve into the non-graded, individualized system proposed by the Hall-Dennis Commission. Curriculum developers were asked to move in the same direction, concentrating on the provision of numerous area studies, biographies, statistical and informational materials and in-depth studies of all kinds rather than of standardized curricula and textbook surveys.

The reaction of staff members was to a large extent one of widespread confusion and resentment. The former director had given his principals and teachers a relatively free hand and the relations among these people were based on long-standing intimacy and agreement on general aims of academic excellence in education. Now a network of highly paid supervisory positions had been created over them, and the change which was demanded of them in terms of school organization and teaching philosophy and procedures was a major one, and little understood by most of those expected to implement it.

The bookstore staff, although offered clerical positions in the new resource centre, felt betrayed and unappreciated by the new director. Union leaders and supporters in the city rallied behind their cause. Many of the parents joined forces with the teachers and principal in their disagreement with the radical changes being proposed. The local of the teachers' professional association began to describe the director's moves as an interference with the professional autonomy of the school personnel. A minority of staff members, on the other hand, supported the director and those members of the local and educational community who backed them.

The controversy eventually became so serious that the director was forced to resign. He went back to the United States convinced that the time was not yet ripe for significant organizational change in Canadian education.

QUESTIONS FOR GROUP DISCUSSION

1   Is organizational change engineered from the top down by the person at the apex of the authority structure likely to be successful? Discuss in terms of this case study.

2   In most school systems in Canada during the last decade there has been a rapid expansion in the ratio of non-teaching personnel to classroom teachers. Discuss some of the causes and consequences of this in terms of teacher authority.

3   The all-important question of *direction* of organizational change is too often sacrificed to the question of *how to effect* such change. Who, in education, have the authority and power to demand that all innovations be rigorously and reliably evaluated in terms of their contribution to pupil learning? Who have the authority and power to do this necessary evaluating, as well as the actual implementing of any specific change? Discuss.

4   Discuss the advantages and/or disadvantages of paying staff people like consultants higher salaries than classroom teachers with equivalent qualifications.

5   Was the problem here that the teachers and parents were too traditional and resistant to change, as the director concluded, or are there other possible explanations for what happened?

CASE STUDY THREE

Sylvia Ashley had taught in the Canadian Maritime provinces for seven years. Now, for the first time in her teaching career she had encountered what seemed to her to be an intolerable situation. She had been warned about Southern High School before being assigned to a teaching position there. Some schools gain a reputation for having a conflict-ridden climate. Southern High was one of these. Because Sylvia had always gotten along well at her other schools, however, she had not anticipated any problems.

The first warning of trouble came in the ladies' staff room. It seemed that this little cubby hole was dominated by a clique of "old timers"—elderly ladies who had spent almost a lifetime in this same school. Sylvia, as a newcomer, was told that smoking was definitely not allowed. She was shown her appointed place at the lunch table, and even graciously assigned her own special cup. She learned that there, tea was the order of the day. Instant coffee, or any coffee, for that matter, was definitely frowned on. A little dismayed, and somewhat amused by this obvious anachronism in a twentieth-century school, Sylvia decided to let matters ride. She could smoke downstairs in the janitor's room, she decided, and have the odd cup of coffee there too. As Sylvia taught Physical Education and stored her equipment in the basement, this seemed the easiest solution.

For the first two months of school Sylvia was so busy with her Physical Education activities that she saw little of the matriarchy who ruled the ladies' staff room. One morning early in November, however, she suddenly encountered the leader of the group, Mrs. Evans, in the gymnasium (which doubled as an auditorium). She was informed that for the next four months, Mrs. Evans and her music classes would require the use of the auditorium almost continuously. This was the period in which they prepared for the annual school concert and the Spring Music Festival. The male Physical Education instructor had always cooperated, Mrs. Evans told her, by postponing many of his Physical Education activities until spring.

Mystified and angry, Sylvia went immediately to the principal. The latter told her that things had always been this way, and that furthermore, Mrs. Evans, through her achievements in music, had brought a great deal of honour to the school. Sylvia decided to give up the battle for the time being. She felt that her best recourse was to wait for a staff meeting, at which time the entire issue could be examined by all the teachers.

As weeks went by, however, Sylvia began to realize that there would be no staff meeting. The principal seemed satisfied merely to send out directives to his staff, and to encourage each of them to come in to talk to him personally when the need arose. As a result, Sylvia seldom saw the man, but Mrs. Evans visited with him frequently, both at school and on a social basis.

Sylvia would have begun to feel completely alienated, if it hadn't been for the majority of the men, who treated her as a respected colleague. Interestingly enough, they seemed to have divided themselves into several groups too, competing, rather intensely at times, for the principal's favour. All this seemed strange and unhealthy to Sylvia. The situation began to worry her even more when she noticed that this atmosphere of conflict was being reflected in the behaviour of the pupils. For the first time in her teaching experience, Sylvia was encountering severe problems with discipline, and she couldn't help suspecting that these problems could be related to the general climate of antagonism and distrust which was so prevalent in the school.

She had been advised by the other teachers to "show the pupils who's boss" from the very beginning, or else "they'll think you're scared and weak, and you won't stand a chance with them!" She had considered this advice very carefully, but had determined to use her own approach. After all, this was the approach that had produced favourable results in her last two schools. She was sure that she could win these pupils over to her side if she offered them affection and friendship, as well as decisive leadership.

As time passed, however, and the conflict among the staff members intensified, Sylvia realized that order in her Physical Education classes was becoming increasingly difficult to maintain. Her home-room pupils were not coming to her for help and advice as she had imagined they would by now. Instead, they began carrying on strange games among themselves as she was trying to teach, shouting slogans back and forth, and laughing raucously at obscure jokes.

Was it possible to remedy the situation, she wondered at the end of a particularly bad day during which Mrs. Evans had reduced her to tears, and her pupils had reduced her to screaming for less noise? Or should she leave before she became totally ineffective as a teacher?

QUESTIONS FOR GROUP DISCUSSION

2   Did the power structure in this school coincide with the authority structure? Explain your answer.

2   Are regular and frequent staff meetings likely to contribute to the clarification of the spheres of jurisdiction and responsibility for each member? Or is it better for the person in charge to deal with his teachers on an individual, person-to-person basis?

3   Did the informal organization of this school and the particular type of network of communication that existed contribute to the conflict? Was bureaucratization a factor? Explain.

4   Discuss the possible causes of the crisis of authority which Sylvia faced in her classes. What advice would you give her about her discipline problems?

The Concept Applied
To Relevant Canadian Research

Black, Errol, "Regional Comprehensive Secondary Schools: A Comment on their Origin," *Manitoba Journal of Education*, 8, no. 1 (1972); 19-22.
The author discusses the Manitoba government commitment to the building of federally financed comprehensive schools during the late 1960s and early 1970s.

Byrne, T. C. "Urban-Provincial Relations in Canadian Education." *Education Canada* 9 no. 1 (1969): 35-43.
The article notes that in Canada the province is the major administrative unit in education and that large urban units define their role within the limits of the province. A social systems perspective is introduced by the author as a basis for making normative suggestions relating to easing strains arising from centralization and decentralization of control.

Cistine, Peter J. "Municipal Political Structure and Role Allocation in Educational Decision-Making." *Urban Education* 6, no. 2-3 (1971); 147-165.

It was hypothesized that, in specifying the division of responsibility between the school board and the superintendent, school board members in municipalities with a professional administrator (council-manager) would assign more responsibility to the superintendent than would school board members without a professional administrator. The sample consisted of all the school board members in twenty-two council-manager municipalities (182 respondents in all) in the Province of Ontario. The hypothesis was supported.

Downey, Lawrence W. *The Small High School in Alberta: A Report of the Investigation*, Edmonton, Alberta School Trustees' Association, 1965.
This report discusses the consolidation and reorganization of rural high schools, suggesting the concept of a "multi-campus" high school as preferable to the geographical centralization that has occurred.

Ems, Frederick, and H. T. Sparby, "The Legal Status of the Canadian Public School Board," *Alberta Journal of Educational Research* 7, no. 2 (1962): 71-84.
This is a documentary study, reporting the following major findings: (1) the courts of Canada have stated clearly that the primary concern of school boards must be the education of children, (2) the school board is to a great extent an agency of the Legislature in the community, and (3) it has the duty of providing equality of opportunity for access to schooling for all children in its jurisdiction.

Friesen, D. "A Semantic Differential Study of Attitudes Held by University Students Toward Educational Administration". *Alberta Journal of Educational Research* 15, no. 2 (1969): 103-115.
The sample used in this study comprised eighty-one first-year university students, twenty-nine elementary and secondary teachers (in graduate school) and fifty-nine graduate students in educational administration at the university of Alberta. Teachers tended to rate educational administration lower than did the two groups of students.

Hickcox, E. S., and D. J. Ducharme, "Administrative Staffing Patterns in Ontario School Districts." *Alberta Journal of Educational Research* 18, no. 2, (1972): 100-110.
The characteristics of organizational structure, administrator to student ratios, program integration and accountability flow were studied in sixty-three Ontario public school districts. Four categories of structure based on fuctions assigned to superintendents were identified: *pure area, tiered, combination* and *functional*. Almost one-third of the boards in the sample have not reflected integration of elementary and secondary programs in their organizational charts. In tiered organiza-

tions the principal reported to area superintendents, while in functional, to the central office. Information about administrative councils, where these existed, indicated that in no case were principals, teachers or students a part of the central decision-making process. It was also found that the ratio of senior central office personnel to student population was inversely related to the size of the district.

Holdaway, E. A. and R. A. Duboyce, "Development of Some Non-Instructional Components of a School System." *Alberta Journal of Education,* 17, no. 3 (1971): 155-164.
The administrative, auxiliary, and support components of the Edmonton Public School District were examined from 1944-1969. A series of ratios were established comparing these components with various measures of the size of the school district for this time period. The ratios showing the relative growth of the central office administrative staff, central office auxiliary staff and central office support staff all indicated that the growth of these components has been more rapid than has been the growth of the entire district.

Kind, Alan J. C. and R. A. Ripton, *The School in Transition: A Profile of a Secondary School Undergoing Innovation,* Ontario Institute for Studies in Education, 1970.
This study presents a comparative picture of a secondary school undergoing major innovation. A credit system and a student-centred approach to discipline were introduced in this Ontario school in 1968/69 while it was still reacting to the implementation of a subject promotion system and student timetabling. A preliminary analysis of the implications of these changes for student achievement and adjustment to school is presented. An attempt is made to identify resultant areas of strain for teachers, students, guidance personnel and administrators.

Loken, G. "Perspectives on change in Educational Structure in Alberta," *Alberta Journal of Educational Research* 15, no. 4 (1969): 207-223.
The author traces major structural changes in the organization of schooling in Alberta from its missionary beginnings in 1840 through the implementation of large school divisions from 1936 to 1957 to the gradual emergence of the county system in the 1960s.

Loubser, Jan J. et al. "The York County Board of Education: A Study in Innovation." *Profiles in Practical Education,* No. 5, Ontario Institute for Studies in Education, 1972.

This is a descriptive analysis of a board of education which has been undergoing a process of relatively rapid change.

Marshall, Leo. "The Saskatchewan Classroom as Seen Through Superintendents' Reports." *Saskatchewan Journal of Educational Research and Development* 2, no. 1 (1971): 44-52.
This study appears to indicate that Saskatchewan school superintendents place a greater stress on characteristics which typify the consistent and organized teacher than on characteristics of the empathetic and original teacher.

Quarter, J. J. et al. "A Study of Behaviour-Problem Students in a Suburban Junior High School," *Ontario Journal of Educational Research* 9, no. 2 (1966-67): 139-148.
This is a study designed to investigate differences between students who exhibit and those who do not exhibit conduct problems. Two categories were discerned: the "passive behaviour problem student" and the "active behaviour problem student." The most prominent difference between students who were identified as behaviour problems and those not, was found to be grades. The "active problem" student was found to be rebellious toward authority while the "passive problem" student was usually punished for untidy work and for inattention.

Sisco, N.A. "Canada's Manpower Training and Education: A View From Ontario." *Canadian Education and Research Digest* 7, no. 4 (1967): 299-304.
This is an examination of the problems and adjustments necessitated in the industrialized province of Ontario when the Canadian federal government began developing manpower policies in 1966 on the assumption that schooling was a provincial responsibility while the training of adult workers was a federal responsibility.

INDEPENDENT STUDY

Select one example of what might be termed "experimental" research and one of what we might call "documentary" research; locate them in the appropriate journal and read them carefully.

1   Compare and contrast these two studies regarding their possible contribution to the development of understanding of the sociology of Canadian education.

2   Analyse the conclusions of these studies in terms of the concept of authority as presented in this chapter.

The Concept Amplified
By Further Reading

Atlantic Development Board, *Profiles of Education in the Atlantic Provinces: Background Study, No. 5, Ottawa, 1969.* Cited in *Education Canada:* pp. 250-251.
This study discusses school consolidation in Alberta and presents recommendations for the procedure in the Atlantic provinces.

Bierstedt, Robert, "An Analysis of Social Power." *American Sociological Review* 15, no. 6 (1950): 730-738.
A discussion of social power as having its source in resources, organization and numbers.

Blau, Peter, "Formal Organization: Dimensions of Analysis." *The American Journal of Sociology* 63, no. 1 (1957): 58-69.
This article describes a method of analysing "formal organizational" behaviour that takes into account its (1) *structural* (patterns of interaction), (2) *organizational* (rules for conduct within the organization, such as personnel policy and supervisory policy) and (3) *developmental* (changes resulting from this complex interdependence) dimensions.

Campbell, Gordon. "The Community College in Canada," in R. A. Cavan, ed., *Universities and Colleges in Canada,* pp. 27-29. Ottawa: Queens Printer 1970.
A description of Quebec's community college system with its community involvement in governance and its two-year programs prior to university or employment. Seventy-five per cent follow the university preparation route although it had been anticipated that 70 per cent would elect to take occupational training.

Clavell, James. *King Rat.* Boston: Little, Brown and Co., 1962.
This is a novel set in a World War II prison camp, operated by the Japanese, which illustrates better than most sociological works, the inevitability of authority in human groups. The author compellingly and terrifyingly pictures the process by which the informal grouping (based on the prisoner-power structure) gradually undermined and replaced the original formal structure of authority, until it assumed its own formality of organization based on a new authority structure in the service of the arbitrary, self-serving goals of "King Rat."

Coleman, James S. "The Struggle for Control of Education," in Haughurst, Robert, et al. eds. *Society and Education: A Book of Readings,* pp. 62-72. Boston: Allyn and Bacon, 1971.
An excellent discussion of the advantages and disadvantages of centralized versus decentralized control of schooling.

Dalton, Gene, et al. *The Distribution of Authority in Formal Organizations.* Boston: Harvard University Press, 1968.
A study of the relationship between the authority structure in formal organizations and the process of organizational change.

Elboim-Dror, R. "The Management System in Education and Staff Relations." *Journal of Educational Administration and History* 4, no. 1 (1971): 37-45.
This article focuses on the bases of authority of educational managers. It emphasizes the relatively "flat" nature of educational hierarchies and the resultant lack of social mobility within the profession.

Etzioni, Amitai. *Modern Organizations.* Englewood Cliffs, N.J.: Prentice-Hall, 1964.
On page 59 we find the author's well-known classification of the means of control in organizations: (1) that based on physical means (coercive), (2) that based on the promise of material gain (utilitarian), and (3) that based on internalized commitment to symbols (normative).

Gouldner, Alvin, "Organizational Analysis," in Merton, Robert K., et al. eds. *Sociology Today.* pp. 400-428. 2nd ed. New York: Harper and Row, 1965.
The author discusses Weber's view of bureaucracy as involving two sources of authority: that based on sheer incumbence in office, and that based on expertise. He develops the idea of organizational tensions as a source of change.

Hamilton, Ian. *The Children's Crusade: The Story of the Company of Young Canadians,* Toronto: Peter Martin Assoc., 1970.
This book makes enlightening reading as a study of the trials and tribulations of an association of people committed to an "anti-formal organization" ideology, and burdened by a lack of understanding of the concepts of authority and power, who were attempting to bring about group action in the pursuit of ill-clarified goals.

Lortie, Dan C. "The Balance of Control and Autonomy in Elementary School Teaching," in Etzioni, Amitai, ed., *The Semi-Professions and their Organization,* pp. 1-53. New York: The Free Press: Collier-Macmillan, 1969.
The author is mainly concerned with the analysis of control over people at work and the sources from which it comes, an issue he relates specifically to the position of the elementary school teacher. He examines organizational, professional, and individualistic aspects of the teacher's role, emphasizing the various bases of authority and control.

Macdonald, J. B. "Report of Higher Education in British Columbia." *The B.C. Teacher* (February 1963): 207-211.
This is the proposal for new two-year colleges to be established at major centres throughout B.C.: a decentralization designed to equalize opportunities for higher education which has been implemented to a large degree in the subsequent decade.

Mills, Theodore M., *The Sociology of Small Groups*, Englewood Cliffs, N.J.: Prentice-Hall, 1967.
On pages 123 and 124 the author identifies types of authority relations as follows: (1) dependent-nurturant, (2) insurgent-coercive, (3) bureaucratic, or rule-determined, (4) idealistic (based on mutual commitment to symbols or ends) and (5) democratic (granted by the group).

Mouw, J. T. "Effects of Dogmatism on Levels of Cognitive Processes," *Journal of Educational Psychology* 60, no. 5 (1969): 365-369.
The researcher's purpose was to investigate the effect of dogmatism as defined by Rokeach's scale on five levels of cognitive processes as described in Bloom's taxonomy: (1) recall, (2) comprehension, (3) application, (4) analysis, (5) synthesis. Eighty-four education students were studied. The findings support Rocheach's notion that "closed-minded" (or dogmatic) subjects tend to rely on authority for direction and support more than do the "open-minded."

Ontario Department of Education, *Colleges of Applied Arts and Technology: Basic Documents* (June 1966), cited in *Educating Canadians: A Documentary History of Public Education*. Scarborough: Van Nostrand Reinhold, 1973: 244-245.
This section describes the proposal of May 1965, for the establishment of a new system of community colleges for Ontario.

Piaget, Jean. *Science of Education and the Psychology of the Child*. New York: Orion Press, 1970; 43-80.
This section of the book deals with changes in authority relationships in education and resultant changes in teaching procedures which are implied by the author's model of the nature of the learning process.

Saskatchewan Education Minister's Advisory Committee Report on Community Colleges, Department of Continuing Education, 1972.
This report recommends the establishment of a decentralized network of non-certifying community colleges to provide for local adult education needs and to be defined and governed by local boards.

Seeley, John, et al. "The School" and "Parent Education" in *Crestwood Heights*. 2nd ed. Toronto: University of Toronto Press, 1963: 224-276 and 271-291.
These sections contain a good description of a particular Ontario school as a formal organization, and the tensions pertaining in the area of authority.

Smith, Louis, H., and Pat Keith. *Anatomy of Educational Innovation*. New York: John Wiley and Sons, Inc., 1970.
The authors reveal, through the documentation of the process in one particular elementary school over a period of three years, how innovation can bring unanticipated problems. They cite conflicts between the "institutional plan" and democratic participation by teachers; and between pupil freedom and teacher authority, which, if unplanned for, can destroy the innovation before it can be evaluated.

Udy, Stanley Jr. "'Bureaucracy' and 'Rationality' in Weber's Organizational Theory: An Empirical Study." *American Sociological Review* 24 (December 1959): 791-795.
Seven of Max Weber's "ideal-typical" specifications for rational bureaucracy are reformulated as a system of three "bureaucratic" and four "rational" variables. The author discusses the uselessness of the formal-informal dichotomy, and recommends, instead, the idea of accommodation between the two, which must be achieved by any functioning organization.

Weber, Max. "Bureaucracy," in Gerth, H. H., and C. W. Mills, *From Max Weber: Essays in Sociology*, pp. 196-244. New York: Oxford University Press, 1958.
An elaboration of the concept.

Weiss, R. L., et al. "Student Authoritarianism and Teacher Authoritarianism as Factors in the Determination of Student performance and Attitudes." *Journal of Experimental Education* 38, no. 4 (1970): 83-87.
This study found that high authoritarian pupils exposed to low authoritarian teachers showed particularly negative attitudes toward their teachers, as well as particularly low grades.

Zentner, Henry. "Perspectives on Income, Aspirations and Values Among Native Peoples," unpublished paper presented at a School of Public Administration seminar at Queen's University, April 1972.
The author discusses the need for the acceptance and use of authority structures by Indians.

Zentner, Henry, *Prelude to Administrative Theory*. Calgary: Strayer Publications, 1973.
A collection of essays which develops a model of social organization envisaging a structurally differentiated although functionally interrelated series of levels of socio-politico-spatial organization ranging from the household group at the lowest extremity to the nation as a whole at the apex of the structural hierarchy.

The Concept Reviewed

1   Which of the following is a source of social power rather than a direct source of authority, according to the explanations of the concepts given in this chapter?
   a.   tradition
   b.   law
   c.   charisma
   d.   expertise.

2   The statement, "Schools should be operated as self-contained democracies, with all members—including pupils—sharing power equally," implies all but which of the following?

a. what we need in order to ensure the survival of democracy is a population which has practised the associated rituals and techniques from childhood on

b. it is the wisdom and morality (developed gradually throughout the entire schooling process if it is effective) that the voter brings to the practice of democracy which determines whether or not a democratic polity will survive.

c. the policy of the school is the concern only of those pupils, teachers and administrators who are members of it at any one time.

d. all the current members of a school (pupils, teachers or principal) are equally capable of contributing to the school's policy decisions.

3 Which one of the following is closest to Dewey's position on the relationship between "authority" and "freedom"?

a. authority and freedom are mutually exclusive

b. the more decentralized the authority the more freedom there will be for the individual

c. the authority which resides in the scientific process is the best guarantee of the freedom of the individual

d. rules and laws are always arbitrary limitations upon individual freedom imposed by those in authority.

4 Which of the following responses accounts for possible sources of discipline problems in the school?

a. pupils sometimes feel that they have been recruited against their will into the learner role in a particular classroom

b. the teacher may be authoritarian

c. the teacher may be libertarian or permissive

d. the teacher may be inconsistent in his expectations and rewards

e. the teacher may be inflexible, repeating responses that do not work

f. pupils may refuse to grant the teacher authority because they reject the school's learning goals

g. there may be a number of children with emotional problems in the class

h. all of the above

i. all but (b) and (h)

j. none of the above.

5 Leadership in a formal organization such as a school would seem to require:

a. the quality of judgment which enables one to achieve a balance between the need for decisiveness and direction derived from the overall view and the need for member-participation in decision-making

b. the official authority granted to the one who is held accountable to the public for the welfare of the client

c. the ability to acquire and remember relevant information

d. the ability to apply information and knowledge to specific situations and to convince others of the logic of this application

e. a measure of charisma to arouse commitment and allegiance in others

f. all of the above
g. none of the above
h. all but (b), (f) and (g).

6   Extreme decentralization of control in education might be undesirable because:
   a. it would be difficult to ensure that all children throughout the national society had equality of opportunity to benefit from schooling
   b. control inevitably would be solely in the hands of the principal
   c. no society could be maintained as an integrated social system if certain common concepts and beliefs were not taught in all schools
   d. the teacher might well find that he has lost his autonomy in the making of professional decisions concerning how best to achieve educational objectives
   e. regional differences, prejudices, and hatreds might be perpetuated at the expense of a universalism that binds all human beings together
   f. all of the above
   g. none of the above
   h. all but (b), (f) and (g).

7   The schooling system in Canada has tended to comprise more staff than line positions, a situation supposedly resulting in a relatively "flat" authority structure. However, the structure may in many cases, in fact, be rather steeply hierarchical because of:
   a. the assumption that staff positions such as that of subject area consultant is more meritorious and responsible than is that of the classroom teacher, and therefore deserving of more salary (along with the corresponding differential in authority and status which this implies)
   b. the fact that Canadian school systems have been increasing the size of their administrative and special service superstructure at a faster rate than they have been increasing the size of their teaching staffs
   c. the fact that teachers tend to see a move out of the classroom as career advancement
   d. the fact that the majority of educators with masters and doctoral degrees are in roles other than that of classroom teacher
   e. all of the above
   f. none of the above
   g. all but (b), (e) and (f).

8   It seems that authority structures of some kind (whether "flat" or "steep") are necessary in every institutional arena so that:
   a. group action in the pursuit of agreed-upon group goals can be achieved
   b. people will be motivated to climb in the structure and therefore to work hard
   c. superior people will be able to make decisions for those not capable of making responsible choices for themselves
   d. a group can react immediately and efficiently to environmental challenges, without any time being wasted in persuasion and argument

e. all of the above
f. none of the above
g. all but (b), (e) and (f).

9 Three of the following were reasons why Max Weber believed that the change from reliance upon traditional to reliance upon bureaucratic authority indicated a net progress for man. Select the argument which he would *not* likely have used.

a. traditional authority is likely to reflect a power structure highly centralized in the person of one man, or one institution such as property or the church

b. bureaucratic authority is based upon man-made rules and laws which are likely to have stemmed from the results of the organized intelligence of men, or what Weber termed rationality

c. traditional authority is more difficult than bureaucratic authority to change with changing conditions

d. bureaucratic authority is inevitably democratic.

10 This chapter implies that a teacher who held a libertarian philosophical position would likely tend to:

a. believe that freedom and authority are in inevitable conflict

b. behave in an authoritarian manner within the classroom

c. believe that there are only two possible alternatives for teacher-pupil interaction: authoritarianism and permissiveness

d. feel uncomfortable about viewing his responsibility as that of structuring the socialization-enculturation into more desirable directions that would occur by chance alone

e. believe that democracy requires the maximal decentralization of authority as well as power

f. all of the above

g. none of the above

h. all but (b), (f) and (g).

Answers: 1. (c); 2. (b); 3. (c); 4. (h); 5. (g); 6. (f); 7. (e); 8. (a); 9. (d); 10. (h).

Part Three
The Schooling System In The Urban Society

In the last two chapters references were made to the fact that the role relationships within the school, and the school's authority structure, are inevitably affected by the complex and interrelated web of relationships in the larger society which encompasses it. Just as the classroom can be perceived as a sub-system of the school, so too the school can be understood as a sub-system of a vast network of schools and provincial education departments and professional associations that we call the Canadian system of schooling. It is to this large complex of formal organizations and its relations with all the other complexes of organizations comprising Canadian society that we now turn our attention.

One problem that immediately becomes apparent is the "non-systematic" character of our schooling practices at the national level. Because the British North America Act assigned the functions of formal education to the provincial governments, what we have at the national level is an informal grouping of ten provincial (plus territorial) schooling systems, rather than one integrated system as is found in countries like Britain and France. The Canadian system can be characterized as decentralization to the point where the "parts" are so autonomous that they almost become "wholes" in themselves. Each provincial schooling system is a sub-system of the provincial society in which it is embedded and, therefore, indirectly of the entire Canadian society. But we cannot easily speak of the relation of the Canadian schooling system as a whole to the Canadian society.

A few decades ago we would have had to describe the Canadian arrangement for formal education as an aggregate of isolated provincial schooling systems. However, a number of developments have begun to provide at least a minimum of communication and mutual sense of belonging at the national level. The Canadian Teachers' Federation and Canadian Association of University Teachers attempt to speak for the country's teachers, just as the Canadian Education Association and the Association of Universities and Colleges of Canada seek to represent various academic and administrative interests in all areas of the schooling enterprise. Recently the new Canadian Society for the Study of Education was formed as an umbrella organization for a number of specialist groupings of educational scholars that had been meeting separately in conjunction with the annual Conference of Learned Societies. The Canadian College of Teachers has been an attempt to pull together the nation's professional educators, but it has had difficulty in competing with American-based groups such as Phi Delta Kappa. The federal Department of Manpower and the Indian Affairs Branch have both operated educational programs in the various provinces and in the Yukon and Northwest Territories, but the lack of liaison with regular schooling systems has often decreased their overall effectiveness. Probably the most effective integrating device to date has been the practice, adopted during the last decade, of provincial Ministers and Deputy Ministers of Education meeting regularly to discuss common concerns. However, all this is still very much at the level of informal organization, with no really effective coordinating roles having emerged at the national level.

In viewing the schooling system in its relation to the urban society, then, we will try to understand how it serves and is served by other organizational complexes such as those of government, business, recreation, the courts and the church, noting the problems inherent in the fact that many of these complexes are national in scope, while the schooling system is provincial. We will examine, as well, changes in the reward or distributive system in the society as it becomes less rural, and the ways in which these changes have affected, or been affected by, the schooling system.

It will be seen that the factor of organization is the most important characteristic of an industrial, urban society like ours. Members are located on power, prestige and privilege hierarchies: not primarily on the basis of property ownership, as is the case for rural societies, but in terms of organizational role and possession of expert knowledge. Those who manage to "make it into the mainstream" are members of one or more of the complexes of organizations structured around specialized functions such as education, science, government or industry. It is this factor of organization, and the power, privilege and prestige that it enables the group to demand for its members, that determines the individual's place in our societal system. Membership in these overlapping and interdependent specialist groupings is largely achieved by means of the schooling system's certifying process.

When we think of this service relationship of the schooling system to other organizational complexes and to the class structure of the society in which it operates, we begin to think in terms of the emergence of another set of roles: those of the *professional* as educator, as lawyer, as doctor, business executive, or civil servant. At this level people are perceived as members of society, rather than of their particular institutional sub-system, and in terms of what it is believed that they are contributing to the sustenance and enhancement of the life of the group as a whole. Everyone tends to aspire to those roles traditionally defined as professional, roles assumed to require a lengthy period of formal schooling as preparation. Schooling therefore becomes the crucial vehicle by which societal roles are allocated so that the social system of the society as a whole can keep functioning. And usually without any conscious intent on the part of the decision-makers involved, schooling tends to become the sole channel or means by which ambitious individuals are fitted for the most powerful, prestigious, and privileged of these roles.

5 Professionalization

The Concept Explained

For more than a century human societies throughout the world, at different rates and according to various economic patterns, have been undergoing a revolution in role relationships. This revolution involves a change from the simple rural (tribal or feudal) type of society to the complex industrialized urban one: a change resulting in turn from the two technological revolutions precipitated by the invention first of the heat engine and later, of the computer. Of all the role changes comprising this major social revolution, the evolution of the professional is perhaps the most significant. Just how certain fundamental alterations in the nature of society have affected the concept of professionalism, and the importance of these changes for teachers now struggling as a group for professional status, is the topic of this chapter.

Social scientists measure urbanization in terms of the proportion of the adult population making their living from other than primary food production, rather than merely by the proportion of the population actually living in cities. This means that even though an individual in a modern industrialized society happens to be located geographically in a rural environment, he may still be "urbanized," for he is still likely to be subject to the complexity of role relationships and the expansion of community which together distinguish the urban society from the rural one.

For instance, in Canada today only 6.6 per cent of the working population is employed in agriculture as compared to 9.6 per cent in 1966, with even the least urban areas, such as Saskatchewan, now having only about 25 per cent of their population in farming. This is why we classify the Canadian society as a whole as an urban, industrial one. When the proportion of urban to rural is so great, even the farmers, trappers and fishermen are exposed to an urban life-style and have little choice but to participate in the urban culture. Degree of affluence or poverty becomes the distinguishing feature that dictates the quality and characterisitcs of this life-style, regardless of whether one's family is rural or urban in occupation and location. Attempts to identify a distinctively rural Canadian society and culture—whether in the prairies, the Maritimes, or the far north—are singularly fruitless if not misleading, for they may even prevent social scientists from perceiving the rate that social change in the direction of urbanization is actually occurring in our country today. (Try asking the daughter of an Alberta farmer who has attended a consolidated school and taken weekly music lessons in the city seventy-five miles distant, and who gets a trip to Europe for her eighteenth birthday, to describe the "rural culture" of the Western prairies! It would make much better sense to ask an Indian sugarbeet picker's daughter and a Montreal slum-dweller's daughter to talk about the "culture of poverty." What the latter have in common is something more significant sociologically than geographical location: their relative status in a complex urban society.)

Complexity of role relationships is obviously a characteristic of the urban society. This is due to the number and diversity of formal organizations, social systems and informal groupings that comprise it. People belong to many of these at the same time, and move often from one to another. A Canadian today may perform roles in many occupational groupings during his lifetime, and may even change vocations three or four times. And each job usually involves a role within a specific formal organization such as a business enterprise or a school, as well as a role in the relevant union or professional association. In addition to occupational groupings there are organizations associated with the various institutions of the culture: the family itself, the church, political parties, community development associations, and home and school organizations. And there are special interest associations such as sports clubs, hobby clubs, bridge clubs, drama, art or music associations, singles clubs, boys' and girls' groups such as Scouts, Guides and CGIT, national and international academic associations, and so on. Sociologists often refer to urban society as "organizational"—a term descriptive of this great diversity and rapid shifting of roles in occupational, institutional and special interest associations.

The individual's membership and relative status and authority position in an occupational grouping assumes great importance in an urban society. It takes precedence over his institutional roles, and his special interest roles tend to follow from it. It becomes imperative in this type of society to get into an occupation of some kind, for the work role has become a major source of self-identity as well as of status in adulthood. Once in, the individual tends to seek status and privilege by fighting for the relative power and prestige of his occupational group. In a stratified society where the struggle for power among competitive occupational groupings is unregulated, the more powerful the organization the higher the income it can demand for its members. In this struggle those occupational groupings known as professional have typically wielded the greatest power, due to tradition, the intellectual resources at their command, and a general feeling on the part of the public that their services are indispensable.

In the rural society, the distribution of power, prestige and privilege is relatively stable from generation to generation and is determined by the institutional structure, mainly the family and the church. In the urban society, however, this distribution is flexible and dynamic and fraught with both opportunity and peril for the individual. If he doesn't "make good" in his work role he can plummet to the bottom, regardless of family connections. If he doesn't manage to achieve a work role he may find himself left out of the web of interaction making up society, alienated from the interest groupings which are so closely tied to occupational position. Eventually he may even become alienated from institutional groupings, for he may come to see himself as unworthy of being a father, husband or voter.

In the urban society the school, as almost the sole means by which the individual achieves an occupational role, becomes extremely important. This is true even though the family (because of its crucial function in early socialization) still carries considerable weight as either a help or a hindrance to the success in schooling which leads to occupational success. The professional grouping in such a society has remained as the culmination of progress up the schooling ladder.

One of the most significant consequences of the complexity of social organization in the urban society is that the individual's "reference group" has expanded and multiplied drastically. In the rural society the family or the tribe is the chief point of reference for the individual and the source of his self-concept and subsequent status and role in life. As urbanization develops it tends to be the occupational grouping which determines his major contribution to society, as well as his prestige and income. Another type of organization which the individual uses as a reference group is the social system which we commonly refer to as the community. In a rural society the individual's relevant community is his immediate neighbourhood only. In the urban society, because of his access to rapid transportation and communications media, the individual's relevant community becomes his municipal region, his province, Canada, the entire world—depending upon the particular interest or function being dealt with. Because of his traditional privileged position and access to education, the professional has the advantage of more exposure to this widening of the boundaries of community than does the average member of society.

In the "ideal type" rural society, the boundaries of all the groupings to which an individual belongs (occupational, institutional, special interest and communal) tend to coincide. The residents of the neighbourhood are his kin, either literally or emotionally. His occupation is known from birth and provides for the needs of the immediate community only. All the adults cooperate in teaching the young, although a few may be designated as particularly responsible. There is one schooling system, one church, one system of authority and rules, one interest group. The individual's total role is established firmly early in life, and is not subject to much alteration. Nor is there much likelihood that he can change roles, for everything that gives him his identity is attached to the one. If he was an outcast as a child, or if he displayed any personality characteristics considered deviant by the group, his entire adult role is likely to be shaped accordingly. The self-fulfilling prophecy operates extremely effectively in the close-knit rural type of community. However, the individual does have a role in the web of interaction of his community, even though his role may be that of village scapegoat.

In the urban society, on the other hand, an individual is likely to achieve roles in many organizations whose boundaries and membership do not coincide. The following diagram illustrates this:

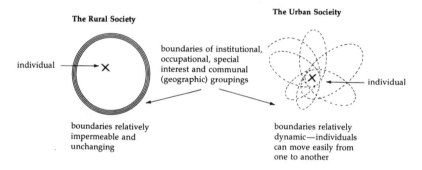

In the rural society the professionals are those who have acquired high status in one or another of the institutional groupings which exist within the immediate community. The position attained is usually *ascribed* rather than *achieved* (due to family connections rather than performance, although often there is a strong relationship between the two). The status of the professional (like his authority) is based largely on tradition. Along with this tradition of superiority and right to a large share of the group's surplus production goes an aura of mystery surrounding the "revealed" and transmitted knowledge assumed to be in the professional's possession. From the witch doctor to the priest to the philosopher to the technologist, doctor and lawyer, the tradition of high status, exclusiveness, authority, power and privilege has been so much associated with the concept of professionalism that even today, in a vastly different urban type of society, it is sometimes assumed to be implicit in the natural order of things.

Other characteristics of professionals in the rural society are their autonomy and commitment to excellence in the pursuit of the welfare of the group, as they perceive it. And long after the rural society was a thing of the past in Canada these features of the professional ideal remained; sometimes, however, more present in the rhetoric of professionalism than in the reality.

With the onset of industrialization came the need for professional elites to achieve expertise in the new scientific knowledge as well as in the classical tradition. This led to the development of lengthy training programs at the most prestigious schools. The cost and difficulty of the training ensured that still only a relative few of the offspring of the most privileged families would gain a professional position. At the opening of this century the earlier strong positive correlation between family status and entry into the professions in Canada still held, even though the relationship was now dependent upon an intervening variable: success in schooling. Professionals remained relatively few in number, and for the most part, made excellent contributions to society as autonomous and highly committed individuals. They became the pioneers of the emerging culture of humanity as opposed to ethnic and national cultures, and continued to demand and receive great power, privilege and prestige.

The rapid expansion of elementary schooling near the end of the nineteenth century was associated with an increase in urbanization in societies like Canada. Suddenly there was a demand for large numbers of teachers. Unlike the professionals of the period, these were people who were required to have achieved numeracy and literacy, but not much else. In no way was it considered that they could lay claim to a body of reliable knowledge about their occupation based on systematic theory. Furthermore, they lost out on the claim to exclusiveness immediately, as their numbers had to be large to fill the sudden societal demand.

From the beginning of public schooling in Canada teachers were not autonomous, for the education of the young was seen as the business of the parents and the immediate neighbourhood. Teachers were parental and community surrogates, the servants of these groups rather than their elites. The development of teacher commitment and excellence was increasingly sacrificed after the turn of the century for the objective of placing large numbers of bodies in the classrooms of the nation, at a price that the society could afford to pay. In spite of these pressures, however, a considerable number of Canadian teachers of this period *were* scholarly and dedicated. These were often the highly educated daughters of upper middle-class families to whom little else in the form of a career was open. Or the members of church orders who devoted their lives to the schooling of western and northern Canadian native peoples and the children of pioneers. Nevertheless, one would have to say that, for the most part, teachers in the late nineteenth and early twentieth centuries in

Canada were low-grade technicians rather than professionals, concerned with teaching basic skills and a minimum of information about the classics, from textbooks which they often had trouble comprehending.

This sad state of schooling led scholars like John Dewey in the United States to the conclusion that in order to attract higher calibre people into the classrooms, teaching should be raised to the status of a profession. The problem, of course, was how to accomplish this feat.

An analysis of those occupations that did have professional status at the time revealed a number of essential characteristics. If one studied the individual professional, two features emerged as definitive:

1   *a unique attitude toward one's work,* involving
    a.   insistence on reliance upon the authority derived from the scientific exploration and testing of the nature of things, rather than that claimed by individuals on the basis of administrative position or political power.

    b.   a striving for excellence

    c.   a concern for the welfare of the client and for humanity as a whole;

2   *a theoretical rather than a technical orientation,* consisting of the ability to apply theory to specific situations — to analyse, interpret and make judgements as to which procedure is appropriate where, and why.

In looking at doctors, lawyers, and engineers, as professional associations or organizations, five criteria seemed most significant:

1   possession of a body of systematic theory and the reliable knowledge that had been constructed in terms of it: specific knowledge about the nature of things, not possessed by the general public, which defined the role of the individual member of the profession and provided the justification for his authority to carry out that role without outside interference;

2   rigorous selection, so that only a relative few of the most excellent of the candidates were accepted into the organization and thereby classed as professionals;

3   acceptance and continued expansion of as many

para-professional categories as there were technical (as opposed to interpretive and judgmental) services to be provided;

4   self-employment, which allowed services to be offered to the public on an individual, competitive basis, and withheld at the will of the professional organization as a whole. (However this threat was implicit rather than explicit, and seldom, if ever, acted upon); and

5   a lengthy period of formal training in a prestigious university setting, a token part of the cost of which was paid by the individual as tuition. (The payment of tuition, and the lengthy period of income-deferment was important in that it allowed the professional to justify his claim to a disproportionately large share of his society's resources for the rest of his life—a claim so hallowed by tradition, however, that it seldom required conscious justification).

It is unfortunate that those who were most influential in teachers' movements in Canada during the first few decades of this century chose to focus on the last two of these characteristics of professionalism and to ignore all the others. For already there were signs that the autonomy resulting from self-employment was to become an anachronism left over from a more simply organized, rural past, as more and more doctors and lawyers were spending their working lives either in the context or the employ of large formal organizations. At any rate, the option of a privately operated, competitive system of schools was never even remotely available in Canada, where a sparsely settled population and extreme regional disparities even within provinces (coupled with a growing commitment to equality of educational opportunity) necessitated formally organized public schooling from the start. Encouraging teachers to ignore sociological reality and to behave as if they were self-employed and offering the public a service which the latter was free to reject if it were not satisfactory could only lead to frustration for teacher, parent and student alike, and a lack of responsiveness to societal demands on the part of the schools.

The ever-present but seldom-used threat of withdrawal of services by professionals was seen by teachers' organizations as the tool by which they could eventually achieve for their members salaries approximating what doctors and lawyers were receiving. A favourite argument of the period was that, as this was a money-based society, money was the source of status. It should follow, therefore, that the higher the salary the more status the group would have. The lengthy period of training in a university setting was immediately recognized as an excellent justification for these high salaries, as well as a direct source of the desired status itself.

With the wisdom of hindsight, it is easy to see that the argument was based on a well-known logical fallacy. (If A, then B; therefore, if B, then A.) The antecedent conditions for the type of professionalism for teachers that obtained for doctors and lawyers would seem to be contained in the requirements mentioned earlier, and in the order cited below:

1   a theoretical consensus and body of knowledge (a science of education?);

2   rigorous selection of candidates, prior to and throughout the training period;

3   identification of a majority of para-professional categories within the occupation, so that the professionals would be relatively few in number as compared to the technicians, or operatives; and

4   the appropriate attitude and orientation on the part of the individuals selected as professionals.

Among the consequences of the above might be the following (again in the order listed):

1   a lengthy period of university training, necessitated by the body of knowledge to be achieved;

2   the granting (by the public receiving the service) of a high status to the group concerned, based on respect for and recognition of their specialized authority;

3   a willingness (on the part of the public) to allow the group to claim a disproportionately large share of social power and privilege; and

4   high salaries for individual members of the group.

The teachers assumed that if they could use the power of their numbers and organization to obtain the consequent conditions, then the antecedent ones would follow. Accordingly, they concentrated their battle for professionalism on two fronts. They attempted to get teacher training incorporated into universities; and they wielded the strike weapon in increasingly militant salary-negotiating operations. To date, they have succeeded reasonably well in both thrusts. Education colleges and faculties are now housed in all western Canadian universities and in many eastern ones. However, evidence is accumulating to indicate that the university preparation of teachers (if it does not involve the teaching of a reliable body of knowledge governing the practice of the occupation concerned; if it does not incorporate a rigorous selection of students on the basis of relevant criteria; and if it does not develop a professional attitude and orientation) may be but an empty form without substance. It may be the symbol of professionalism without even the reality of technical competence. At worst, it can amount to a fraud perpetrated upon a trusting public.

At best, it is a far cry from what Dewey pictured when, at the turn of the century, he and other leading educators fought to professionalize North American education. However, they must share some of the blame for putting the cart before the horse; that is, for pushing for the university training and certifying of teachers prior to the development of an adequate science of education upon which that theoretical training could be based. Others are to blame for the lack of standards and valid procedures for evaluation and selection within many of these faculties, for the failure to instil in future teachers the desire to excel, the commitment to scientific inquiry, the concern and sense of responsibility for the welfare of the child and humanity, and the theoretical orientation of the professional.

The attempt to negotiate for higher salaries for teachers was, until recently, very successful. Since the depression, when many teachers taught for room and board, the Canadian public has been extraordinarily willing to devote large sums to public schooling; and approximately 75 per cent of these increases in expenditure have consistently gone into teachers' salaries. However, with the recession that began in 1969, there was a sudden, sharp change in public attitude. The public is beginning to realize that the total share of society's rewards going to teachers has not only equalled but surpassed the total being claimed by any of the older professional groups. This is far from apparent to the individual teacher, because the number among whom the pie must be shared is so large compared to these other groups; for instance, there are over twenty times as many teachers as doctors in Canada. It is highly unlikely that any society will be willing or able to reward any member of an occupation involving so many people with a considerably higher-than-average income. When we realize that the average income per worker in Canada in 1973 was about $7,000, it becomes easier to understand why the struggle for the continual increase of teachers' salaries is beginning to encounter opposition. Again, the failure of teachers as an occupation to follow the lead of the older professions in distinguishing among categories of personnel, on the basis of the technical or judgmental requirements of the job, may be of significance here.

To many members of Canadian society today the claim of the teacher to higher-than-average income due to a professional status, based on the individual and organizational criteria listed previously, is manifestly ridiculous. However, because of the blinding power of tradition, it is not so apparent that it may also become increasingly difficult for doctors and lawyers to maintain their present privileged positions. For, as the demand for their services expands, and as the demand for more public control of these services surfaces, there is likely to be more and more pressure for professional and para-professional alike to operate as salaried personnel within an authority structure responsible to the people.

Along with this demand may go a questioning of the traditional assumption that the more the training costs the society, the more money the trainee should be paid for the rest of his life, by the members of that same society. It may even be that, with increased awareness that the professional has already been highly subsidized by society during his years of costly university education, he will be progressively taxed during his career until his financial debt to that society is paid. Or else the relatively minor remaining cost of his education which he now pays in the form of tuition will also be subsidized, thus removing any justification for a higher-than-average income throughout his working life. However, to the degree that professionals such as doctors and lawyers are willing to respond to public demand by greatly expanding para-professional training while at the same time maintaining a relatively small, highly skilled and socially committed cadre of professionals to oversee these operatives as they function within formal organizations, they will likely be able to maintain the respect and status, and some of the privilege which has been traditionally granted them.

What are the implications for teachers? Perhaps the first lesson to be learned is that the demand for professional status, as a means to power and privilege for the members of an occupational organization, is no longer feasible. It is especially not feasible if the group concerned has no elite tradition behind it and is unwilling or unable to keep its membership small and exclusive. Secondly, professional status, like respect, is something that is granted by society on the basis of the competent, wise and dedicated performance of individuals over time; it cannot be demanded and grasped by holding the public up to ransom year after year. Thirdly, perhaps it is time for educators to face up to the great diversity of performance within their occupation, both as regards the extreme variations in competence that exist and the variety of tasks performed by people called teachers. It has been suggested that distinctions be made on both of these dimensions. Merit rating and differentiated staffing (resulting in a large contingent of teacher aides per teacher and of teachers per professional educator) have been discussed as possibilities.

The accomplishment of a functional system of differentiated staffing in the schools would require fundamental changes in teacher training. Faculties of education would have to devise programs articulated so as to provide "career ladders" for candidates. One possibility is a program in which entrance could be open to any adult, regardless of level of formal schooling, who had at least two years of successful experience as a teacher's helper, and who could demonstrate a designated level of communicative and academic competence. The first step could be a probationary period of academic study and school involvement during which candidates would have the chance to demonstrate *technical* potential (ability to communicate well, to utilize and develop instructional materials, and to apply specific teaching techniques). In addition, they would be selected on the basis of *attitudinal* potential: do they show promise of developing a desire for excellence, the scientific temper, and a sense of social responsibility and concern? Those surviving the probationary year would complete a second year of extremely practical technical training, much of it in the schools, and most of it involving communication skills and instructional materials. They would then graduate as teacher aides.

Only people interested in and intellectually capable of handling the study of educational theory would be accepted into the third year of the program. Here, in addition to professional attitudes, a *theoretical orientation* would be looked for and subsequently developed. Candidates would be required to have successfully completed two years as teacher aides. The third and fourth years would concentrate upon the study of the emerging science of education from the perspective of a variety of academic disciplines on a pass-fail basis, with all candidates for the B.Ed. being required to write a battery of comprehensive exams during the final semester. Those who graduated would be classified as teachers, and certified by the Ministry or Department of Education after two years of successful teaching. The title of professional educator would be reserved for teachers who had qualified, after five years of teaching and a demonstration of superior scholarship and leadership ability, for acceptance as members of the professional association.

Many young people entering teaching today start out with a refreshingly critical approach to the type of professionalism based on the power and prestige of the organization. They are much more concerned with professionalism as it refers to the individual's attitude toward his work and to his ability to apply theory in the making of wise judgments in a variety of situations.

A major concern, as well, is the role of the professional in a complex, urban society. It is the opinion of many young people that, too often, professionals have betrayed the individual professional ideal in the process of seeking power and status for their organization. They feel that too many have willingly sold their services and expertise to the highest bidder, regardless of consequences for humanity. They say that too many have willingly bowed to the authority of those persons with control over their advancement within the formal organization that employs them, even though that authority demanded behaviour of them that conflicted with "the nature of things" as indicated by their professional knowledge.

What can be learned by this apparent failure of many professionals to exert responsible leadership in the urban society? The first requirement for honest professionalism would seem to be thorough grounding in a field of expertise based on a body of scientific knowledge: the second, an intellectually honest, committed and concerned attitude towards one's specialized function in society, accompanied by a theoretical rather than a merely technical orientation. All the others previously referred to are secondary features of professionalism that have held in certain times and places, but are subject to change with alterations in the role relationships of society as a whole.

For example, in today's urban society, the professional is increasingly likely to be found working within the formal organization rather than operating in an autonomous, one-to-one relationship with a client. He is likely to have had his education largely (if not totally) subsidized by government and/or industry. He is likely to find it increasingly difficult to demand and get a disproportionately large share of society's rewards for his services. In other words, in organizational respects he will become more and more like the educator. It may be that the educator will be able to lead the way in demonstrating how people can operate as professionals within a large formal organization controlled by the public. In time, the educator may even be able to show how prestige and respect can be earned by excellence of performance, judgment and social concern rather than by demanding privilege to the limit of the power wielded by one's professional association.

The Concept Demonstrated

CASE STUDY ONE

Bill Andrews was in his fifth year of teaching in the province of Manitoba in the fall of 1970 when he was nominated and elected to the salary-negotiating team of his professional association. He was surprised and flattered at being selected, for he had not been particularly interested in the politics of his profession, and had not in any way sought the post. However, Bill took his teaching and his professional responsibility seriously, and was persuaded by his friends that he could make a worthwhile contribution by taking on the job.

At the beginning the entire procedure was exciting and ego-satisfying. Matching wits with the school board members made Bill aware of abilities that he had not known that he possessed. But as the wrangling went on from month to month, with neither side budging an inch from the position that they had started from, a number of things began to bother Bill. He knew enough about the grain market situation at the time to have some sympathy with the position that the trustees (all farmers) were taking.

The trustees were maintaining that the total income awarded the teachers (including increment as well as across-the-board raise) should not exceed the 2 per cent increase in the cost of living for that particular year, due to the fact that the farmers as a group had suffered a serious overall decline in income. The teachers were standing by their demand for an 8 per cent increase (excluding increments) arguing that they were still considerably below the position of doctors, lawyers, engineers and professors on the income scale. In addition, they had not yet achieved parity with American teachers whose average income was slightly higher than the Canadian one. The increase in the Canadian GNP for the previous year had been 3 per cent. As the months of deadlock wore on, the teachers' negotiating committee began to plan for strike action. The problem really began to focus for Bill one day when he was talking to Mr. Wallace, the storekeeper in the village in which Bill's consolidated high school was located. Bill was sharing with Mr. Wallace something that he and his fellow teachers had been discussing in the staff room during lunch. It seemed that the teachers were disturbed by the change in the attitudes of the people towards them. Since the salary negotiations had begun, and as they wore on to the accompaniment of increasing publicity, the teachers were beginning to encounter hostility wherever they went. Some of the more sensitive had stopped dropping in at the beer parlour and were now sending their wives downtown to attend to all the family errands.

Mr. Wallace was not surprised. "If you could see my accounts receivable," he said, "and could realize how many of the farmers around here are having trouble paying for their groceries this year, you would begin to understand their attitude."

"Are you aware," he continued, "of the fact that the average farm family income in this particular area is less than 50 per cent of what it was last year?"

Bill suddenly remembered a series of films about teachers in Poland, Puerto Rico and Japan which he had seen at the Faculty of Education a few years previously. The Japanese teacher's income and standard of living had been the lowest, but it was obviously on a par with that of the families whose children he taught. The Puerto Rican teacher, on the other hand, was highly privileged in comparison to his pupils, and lived in an affluent suburb far from the rural community in which he made his living. It had seemed to Bill that the teacher with the most professional attitude, the one who was most respected by his pupils and parents, and the one who appeared to be by far the most effective, had been the Japanese teacher. The memory made him vaguely uncomfortable and he pushed it out of his mind.

When the next meeting of the salary-negotiating committee was called, Bill was present as usual. But he found himself anticipating what he feared to be an inevitable recommendation for strike action with growing dread. Could he go along with his fellow members, he wondered, or would he have to stand alone against them, branded as unprofessional and a traitor?

QUESTIONS FOR GROUP DISCUSSION

1   Is professional status the result of a gradual accumulation of respect, or of power? Or is respect granted only to the powerful? If power is the key, do teachers as a group possess a big enough stick? Discuss, referring to Bill's problem.

2   Can the idea of parity among teacher salaries be reconciled with the idea of the teacher as a bona fide member of the community: one who shares in its ups and downs? Which principle do you consider to be conducive to the best teacher-pupil relationships?

3   If Bill's teacher group had agreed not to push for salary increases in Manitoba in 1970, is it likely that the farmers would have agreed to let them share in their burst of affluence in 1973?

4   Comment on what would appear to be Bill's definition of "professionalism." Compare it to the explanation of the concept in this chapter.

CASE STUDY TWO

Mr. Preston came to the little town in New Brunswick from the United States in 1968, to teach history in the high school. Because he was known to be a draft avoider he was viewed favourably by the majority of his new colleagues who tended to be indignant about American foreign policy. And because he was bearded and claimed to be committed to left-wing social goals, and to individual freedom from authority and control, he was promptly hero-worshipped by many of the pupils.

As the term progressed, however, it became obvious that relations between Mr. Preston and the rest of the staff were deteriorating rapidly. Those whose classrooms were near his, or who taught with him on team efforts, began to have uneasy feelings about his background and competence. Although the principal held frequent staff meetings Mr. Preston never expressed disagreement with the school's policies or rules at these meetings, nor addressed himself to issues of principle. Nevertheless, he talked continually to pupils about such matters, often repeating scornfully to them the remarks of other teachers.

The principal had given Mr. Preston responsibility for student affairs, assuming that he would communicate well with young people. Under his leadership pupil relationships altered suddenly and drastically. A clique of loyal followers were given key positions in student politics, the student paper and social activities, and these met almost every evening with Mr. Preston at his house. The rest of the pupils found that they were out-manoeuvred by this tight little group on every question, and soon lost interest in participating in student activities.

Those pupils in Mr. Preston's classes who did not agree with his espoused anarchist position regarding societal and organizational authority soon found that he countenanced absolutely no questioning of his own authority and no challenge to his own power in the classroom. His colleagues, who had heard a great deal of talk about his supposed left-wing social and economic goals, were amused to note that the only meeting at which they had ever seen him vocal was the teachers' meeting on salary negotiations, when he urged the members to be more inflexible in their demands for more money. They noticed, too, that he was the only staff member who refused to give to the United Appeal and to the school fund for needy students.

During February the principal began receiving complaints from parents who were concerned about Mr. Preston's influence on their sons, as well as from pupils who claimed that they were doing very little history in his classes. Toward spring rumours of drug experimentation at Mr. Preston's house began floating around the school, but the principal could locate no concrete evidence concerning the charges. In May several student-teacher confrontations erupted, one against the very teacher who had worked himself to the point of exhaustion for several years trying to make the school curriculum more meaningful and the organization and teaching more democratic. Mr. Preston remained in the background during these troubles, but his little group of favourite pupils were obviously the instigators of the conflict in each instance.

The principal was convinced that Mr. Preston was "bad medicine" as a teacher and a human being, but he was sure too that because the new teacher had associated himself with popular radical causes it would be difficult to confront him without being classified as an "imperialistic reactionary" or a "wishy-washy liberal." After several weeks of agonizing with the rest of the staff over the problem, the principal decided merely to ask the board to transfer Mr. Preston to another school, without specifying a reason other than "incompatibility." Accordingly, the following September Mr. Preston was placed in a small high school in the extreme opposite corner of the district.

QUESTIONS FOR GROUP DISCUSSION

1   What aspect of professionalism is being dealt with here: individual or organizational? Compare and contrast it to the aspect emphasized in Case Study One.

2   Would you consider Mr. Preston's attitude and behaviour to be professional? Why or why not?

3   What about the professional responsibility of the other teachers and the principal? How do you think this should have been carried out?

4   Does lack of professionalism on the individual level have consequences for the achievement of professionalism on the organizational level? Discuss, citing elements of Mr. Preston's case.

CASE STUDY THREE

Marc Pelletier had taught in the Montreal Protestant School system for fifteen years. His secondary school was in a high-income district and served the children of professional and business people.

During all his years of teaching, Marc had been committed to the idea that his major responsibility as a teacher was to try to arouse pupil-interest and to develop pupil-skills in many areas. He saw his role as that of helping his pupils identify their own specific aptitudes and providing them with guidance in selecting the means by which these could be further developed.

He was particularly interested in the community college movement, and was anxious that his pupils have the opportunity to take the two-year post-secondary program most appropriate to their interests and abilities. As time passed, however, Marc was finding it more difficult to accomplish what he felt he had to do.

The trouble was that the parents in this particular school all assumed that their children would go on to university. Those exhibiting technical or vocational, rather than academic abilities and interests were discouraged by parents and most teachers from following those pursuits in high school, and from taking the two-year work preparation program in community college.

Although no order had ever been given, Marc was aware that what was expected of him was to bow to the inevitable, and to discourage his pupils from the consideration of anything but the university preparation route. He suspected that his recalcitrance in this matter had something to do with the fact that he had been passed over twice in the last few years for promotion to department head.

Now the position of head of math and science was open in his own school. More than ever Marc, with his competence and qualifications, was the logical person for the job. This time he felt confident that the position would be his. In fact, when the principal asked him to step into his office one day, he was sure that the object of the interview was to inform him that he was the new head. But the principal's first words dashed his hopes.

"Marc," he heard, "I wonder if you are aware that I've had one devil of a time for a good many years protecting you from the wrath of parents. You must surely know that this is a university-oriented district—that the people around here do not intend that their sons and daughters will be merely plumbers or salesmen, or secretaries or nurses. Why on earth must you make such a fetish of encouraging those who are having trouble with academic studies to look to the vocational route? These youngsters have got to get their university entrance by hook or by crook. That's what we're here for, as far as their parents are concerned—to cram enough information down their throats so that they'll swallow enough to get that precious ticket!"

The principal went on, somewhat ruefully, to tell Marc that he had received complaints about the overly practical orientation of his science and math classes; about the fact that motor mechanics and instalment buying were being emphasized at the expense of nuclear physics and calculus. Marc explained that it was only for those pupils who were getting nothing but failure and confusion from the theoretical math and physics that he was providing the immediately practical emphasis.

"The fact remains," responded the principal, "that too many of your pupils are refusing to go on to university. You can't convince me that that has nothing to do with your influence. You know as well as I do that our success as a school is judged by the number of university entrants we turn out. You're part of this team, Marc. You could be one of its leaders. But we've got to have you working with us, and with the parents of this school—not against us!"

To Marc, as he considered his options on the way home that night, the issue was clear. If he wanted to get ahead in his chosen field, to reap the organizational rewards that his years of hard work and experience had surely earned for him, it seemed that he would have to do a little compromising. But could he, feeling as he did about the welfare of his pupils and his own role as an educator?

QUESTIONS FOR GROUP DISCUSSION

1   Is there likely to be tension (amounting sometimes to conflict) between the ethic of the professional and the integration requirements of the formal organization? What form did this take in this particular case?

2   Discuss the possibility of conflict between the individual's professional attitude and commitment and the reward and promotion system of the formal

organization. What price had Marc paid in the past for his professional integrity?

3   Paul Goodman maintained that most professionals in today's urban society were "finks" who had sold their knowledge and skills to the highest bidder. Would you say that his accusation is justified where teachers are concerned? Support your opinion with reference to your own experience as well as to this case study.

4   What is the likely fate of a society in which betrayal by the professionals becomes commonplace? How might the professional schools and professional organizations work to prevent such a universal professional sell-out from occurring?

The Concept Applied
To Relevant Canadian Research

Clarke, S. C. T. and H. T. Coutts. "The Goals of Teacher Education."
Saskatchewan Journal of Educational Research and Development 3, no. 2 (1973): 34-39.
The authors present the results of an attempt to elicit preferred goals from the following: Alberta Federation of Home and Schools, Alberta School Trustees, Edmonton Public and Separate School Systems, superintendents and officials of the Alberta Department of Education, students in the University of Alberta Faculty of Education who had completed practice teaching, teachers in the field, officials of the Alberta Teachers' Association, full-time members of the faculty of the University of Alberta Faculty of Education. They found that "ability to think" and "selection" received top priority, and that "identity with the profession" and "the imparting of knowledge" placed at the bottom.

France, Norman, "Teachers in Canada, Supply and Demand for the 1970s." *Education Canada* 10, no. 1 (1970): 2-7.
This is a revision of the teacher supply and demand forecast made by the author three years previously, with new predictions based on a changing economic climate, falling birthrate, etc. Trends foreseen are a delay in reducing the pupil/teacher ratio, recruitment for replacement rather than expansion, lengthening of the teacher training period, and a growing need for more university flexibility in adapting to community and professional needs.

Hodgkins, B. J. and Arnold Parr. "Educational and Occupational Aspirations Among Rural and Urban Male Adolescents in Alberta." *Alberta Journal of Educational Research* 6, no. 4 (1965): 255-261.

The sample for this study included the entire male population in the tenth, eleventh, and twelfth grades in a rural and an urban high school in Southern Alberta (184 in all). No significant differences in aspirations were found between rural and urban students. Differences did obtain on the basis of SES, however.

Horowitz, Myer. "Student Teaching Experiences and Attitudes of Student Teachers." *Journal of Teacher Education* 19 (1968): 317-324.
This study attempted to investigate the relationship between student teachers and cooperating teachers. The findings did not permit the researcher to claim that the cooperating teacher is influential in bringing about changes in attitude toward teaching on the part of the student teacher. Such changes are more probably the result of acculturation, effected by the total experience of student teaching.

Jones, Frank E. "The Social Origins of the High School Teachers in a Canadian City," in Blishen, B. et al., eds. *Canadian Society*, pp. 474-481. 3rd. ed. Toronto: Macmillan of Canada, 1965.
This essay reports on a 1956 study of 173 teachers in four non-denominational high schools in Hamilton, Ontario. Low SES teachers were found to be more likely to have worked at other (lower prestige) occupations before teaching. There was a tendency for the sample to have urban backgrounds, to be at least second-generation Canadian, and to be male.

Kalbach, Warren E., and Wayne W. McVoy. *The Demographic Bases of Canadian Society*. Toronto: McGraw-Hill of Canada, 1971.
An excellent source of information on population trends in Canada, including age, sex, ethnic, religious, marital, geographical, occupational and educational characteristics.

Kerr, Donald. "Metropolitan Dominance in Canada," in Mann, W. E., ed., *A Sociological Profile*, pp. 225-243. Toronto: Copp Clark, 1968.
This article documents the urbanization process in Canada.

McKague, T. R. "Preparing Teachers for Innovative Schools." *Saskatchewan Journal of Educational Research and Development* 1, no. 1 (1970): 39-48.
Fourteen principals of "innovative" schools in Canada were questioned on modes of teacher-preparation. Teacher qualifications needed were found to be "knowledge of subject," "organizing skills," and "ability to involve students in the learning process."

Robinson, Norman. "A Study of the Professional Role of Teachers and Principals: Their Relationship to Bureaucratic Characteristics of

School Organization." Ph. D. dissertation, University of Alberta, Edmonton, 1966.

This is a report of an investigation into the relationship between the professional role orientation of teachers and principals and the bureaucratic dimensions of school organizations. The sample was drawn from twenty-nine B.C. schools. A comparison of the top and bottom quartiles revealed a significant difference in staff professional scores among schools as well as on all six bureaucratic dimensions, but staff professional scores were not related to the latter.

Scharf, Murray P. *A Report on the Declining Rural Population and the Implications for Rural Education.* Saskatchewan School Trustees Association, Research Center, Report No. 17, 1974.

Changes in the rural population of Saskatchewan are presented and related by the author to rates of natural increase and to regional and interprovincial migration trends as well as to changes in the agricultural industry. These population projections are, in turn, related to the current situation in rural education in Saskatchewan. The author presents evidence that (1) there are no significant differences in scholastic achievement among elementary school children when classified on the basis of urban-rural, size of school, size of class, single grade or multiple grade classroom, and on whether or not they were bused to school; and (2) there are no significant differences in first year university achievement between students classified as to rural or urban high school attendance. On the basis of a projected school population decline of almost 50 per cent in rural Saskatchewan by 1980, the author makes a number of recommendations for the maintenance of an adequate rural education program in non-city areas.

Trone, Keith and F. Enns. "Promotional Aspirations and Differential Role Perceptions." *Alberta Journal of Educational Research* 15, no. 3 (1969): 169-183.

The researchers questioned a sample of 1,069 teachers, 65 vice-principals, and 67 principals, stratified and randomly selected, from 75 schools in a western Canadian metropolitan area. They found a strong positive correlation between high promotional aspiration and deference to superior authority, and "initiating structure" behaviour or leader behaviour, and strong negative correlation between all of the former and "consideration of others," for principals and vice-principals (with a limited, similar relationship being observed for teachers). "Deference to superior authority" was most highly predictive of promotional aspiration.

Young, J. E. M. "A Survey of Teachers' Attitudes Toward Certain Aspects of Their Profession." *Canadian Education and Research Digest* 7, no. 2 (1967): 112-127.

This sample for this study comprised 629 teachers enrolled in summer session classes in Quebec between 1957 and 1963. They were given questionnaires asking what they liked most about teaching. Sixty per cent of the responses mentioned children. The most common dissatisfaction was "the impersonal and housekeeping aspects of the job." "Best principals" were thought to possess "generally good personality," "leadership qualities" and "supervisory skills," but did not interfere. "Best teachers" maintained good discipline, were kindly and helpful, and liked children.

INDEPENDENT STUDY

Locate as many of the studies as possible.

1   Scan the studies, documenting evidence of lack of consensus on the requirements for, and characteristics of, professionalism.

2   Plan a research study which would attempt to relate the process of professionalization in Canada to that of urbanization. Use the explanations of these concepts in this chapter as the sources of the criteria for each for which you would seek observable indicators.

The Concept Amplified
By Further Reading

Broudy, Harry S. "Can We Define Good Teaching?" The Record 70, no. 7 (1969): 583-592.
The author suggests that didactic teaching (after the model of programmed instruction) is the kind for which outcomes, means and criteria can be made explicit, and will therefore be the dominant mode for some time to come. Encounter teaching may become possible, but as yet neither outcomes, means or criteria can be specified for this.

Cohen, Louis. "Student Identification With a Profession." Educational Research 12, no. 1 (1969): 41-45.
A population of 802 first-year students who chose teaching as a career was compared to those who had selected other programs. The would-be teachers were found to be more "people-oriented," and more likely to be from a working-class background.

Corwin, R. G. Militant Professionalism: A Study of Organizational Conflict in High Schools. New York: Appleton-Century-Crofts, 1970.
The data for this study came from 1,500 lengthy questionnaire returns and 737 taped conversations with the teaching staff and administration of 28 U.S. high schools. A typology of belligerent professionals is developed, and their characteristics outlined. Organizational characteristics of schools are related to teacher-militancy.

Davis, T. N. and D. J. Satterly. "Personality Profiles of Student Teachers." *British Journal of Educational Psychology* 39, no. 2 (1969): 183-187.
A sample of 149 female Education students was presented with questionnaires at time of entry and 26 months later, before final teaching practice. Small groups of students of "high" and "low" teaching ability were identified and their personality profiles compared. The "poor" teachers were found to be less conscientious and persistent, more tender-minded and sensitive, more prone to feelings of insecurity and timidity, and more liable to be tense, excitable and restless than were the "successes".

Etzioni, Amitai, ed. *The Semi-Professions and their Organization.* New York: The Free Press, Collier Macmillan, 1969.
This book deals with a group of so-called new professions (elementary school-teaching, social work and nursing) whose claim to the status of doctors and lawyers is debatable. The editor notes that their period of preparation is shorter, their status less legitimated, and their right to privileged communication less established.

Featherstone, Joseph. "Who's Fit to Teach?" *New Republic*, December 13, 1969: 19-21.
A thoughtful discussion of unsuccessful legislative attempts in California to "deprofessionalize" education (to remove the control of graduate schools of education over schooling).

Flanders, Ned A., and Amita Simon. "Teacher Effectiveness," in Abel, R.L., ed., *Encyclopedia of Educational Research*, pp. 1423-1436 4th ed. Toronto: Collier-Macmillan, 1969.
This is a useful review of research on the topic.

Freidson, Eliot. "The Impurity of Professional Authority," in Becker, H.S., et al., eds. *Institutions and the Person*, pp. 25-34. Chicago: Aldine, 1968.
This article presents the argument that professional "authority" is a logically mixed case, containing some of the elements of the authority of technical competence and some of the authority of legal or bureaucratic office.

Goodman, Paul. "Professionals vs. Professionalism," New York: Living Library (audiotape), 1971.
Here we have a good argument for the return of the professional attitude (responsibility for the welfare of the social group and accountability to man's most reliable conclusions about "the nature of things") in place of what the speaker considers to be the prevailing unionism, opportunism, and grasping for power, status, and privilege by organized professionals.

Graham, Per-Ake, and Bjorn Gustafsson. "What Do You Think Are the Characteristics of a Good Teacher?" *Pedagogisk Forsknong* 4 (1969): 183-198.
Results based on 17,414 answers given by Swedish grade eight pupils to the question were (rated in order) humanness and understanding, fairness, teaching ability, humour and pleasantness of manner, and ability to maintain discipline. Differences in rating emerged according to the type of school attended, sex, SES and IQ.

Hall, Richard H. "Professionalization and Bureaucratization." *American Sociological Review* 33 (February 1968): 92-104.
Analysis of structural and attitudinal aspects of professionalization, and of the organizational settings in which many professional occupations exist, suggests that there is generally an inverse relationship between professionalization and bureaucratization.

Illich, Ivan. *Deschooling Society*. New York: Harper and Row, 1970.
A sometimes-discerning attack on the certifying function of schooling.

Jencks, Christopher, and David Riesman. *The Academic Revolution*. New York: Doubleday, 1968: 199-256.
This chapter, entitled "The Professional Schools," includes a discussion of the meaning of professionalism.

Leggatt, Timothy. "The Use of Non-Professionals in Large City Systems," in Street, David, ed. *Innovation in Mass Education*. New York: John Wiley, 1969; 177-200.
The use made of the non-professional is examined in five American cities. Possible functions for the non-professional are outlined and explanations sought for their variations in different cities. Features of school systems such as degree of centralization, attitude of teacher unions, and role of the superintendent seem crucial.

Levin, Henry M. "A Cost-Effectiveness Analysis of Teacher Selection." *Journal of Human Resources* 5, no. 1 (1970): 24-33.
A report of some results of applying cost-effectiveness analytical techniques to decisions on teacher recruitment and retention. Data were derived from the U.S. Office of Education's Survey of Equal Opportunity for 1965-66. Evidence relating teacher characteristics to student achievement is combined with data on the cost of obtaining teachers with different characteristics. This evaluation suggests that recruiting and training teachers with higher verbal scores is five-to-ten times as effective per dollar of teacher expenditure in raising student achievement scores as is the strategy of obtaining teachers with more experience.

Lowery, Lawrence F. "A Study of the Attitudes of Parents Toward Teachers." *Journal of Educational Research* 62, no. 5 (1969): 227-230.
Two hundred and sixteen parents in a middle ses area were studied. The researcher's findings indicate that parents predominantly think of teachers as female: an image with negative connotations. When forced to think of teachers as male, the parental image of teachers became positive. This held for female as well as male respondents.

Moore, Wilbert E. *The Professions: Roles and Rules*. New York: Russell Sage Foundation, 1970.
Part I of this book deals with the nature of the professionalization of occupations and the socialization of the individual professional. Part II discusses a variety of aspects of the professional role, while Part III emphasizes the role of the professional as a man of knowledge in modern society.

Olmsted, Ann G. and Marianne A. Paget. "Some Theoretical Issues in Professional Socialization," *Journal of Medical Education* 44, no. 8 (1969): 663-669. This article raises two questions: (1) what kinds of relatively enduring, professionally relevant changes, if any, do students undergo under various social learning conditions? and (2) to what extent and in what ways is the professional school experience a significant part of professional socialization in contrast to general socialization into the role of university student? The authors conclude that to the extent that the structured demands of the school are congruent with the demands of practice, the professional school experience is an integral part of the professional socialization process, with the student role being incidental. Otherwise, any professionally relevant changes will tend to occur only after training is completed and in contexts in which the desirability of the changes may be open to question.

Pritchard, Keith W. "Social Class Origins of College Teachers of Education." *Teacher Education* 22, no. 2 (1971): 219-228.
A sample of 238 male and 29 female full-time professors of Education was used for this study. Findings indicated generally low SES origins, less so for females. The author concludes that the position of college teachers of Education becomes an upwardly mobile one for lower SES males and for women—one of the few professional level positions generally available.

The Concept Reviewed

1   The most meaningful measure of urbanization as a process is:
a. the proportion of the population involved in the primary production of food
b. the proportion of the population living in cities
c. the proportion of the population involved in the processing and distributing of food products
d. the proportion of the population favouring a return to a rural way of life.

2   Which of the following is not a characteristic of the urban society?
a. a structure comprising numerous and varied informal groupings as well as many social systems of the formally organized type
b. multiple group membership on the part of the individual
c. a great diversity of roles for any one individual during his lifetime, even within the occupational realm
d. occupational, institutional and special interest groupings whose boundaries coincide, so that membership in one automatically means membership in all the others.

3   Which of the following is most likely to be a feature of the rural society?
a. alienation
b. anomie
c. ostracism and/or scapegoating
d. anonymity

4 According to this chapter, which one of the following is least likely to be a characteristic of the professional in Canada at the present time?
   a. a greater exposure to the global community than is true of the average member of society
   b. a relatively low position in the stratification system
   c. a relatively high salary due to a consensus on the part of the group that he has a right to a larger share of their surplus production than does the unskilled labourer
   d. a commitment to excellence in the pursuit of the welfare of the group.

5 In the urban society the source of the professional's expertise and status is chiefly:
   a. certification based on schooling
   b. the immutable order of society based on natural law
   c. tradition
   d. the actual importance of the contribution which he is currently making to the group's survival.

6 Teachers were not granted the status of professionals in nineteenth and early twentieth century Canada for a number of reasons. Which one of the following does not apply?
   a. Almost from the beginning, the numbers required for the role were so great that little claim to exclusiveness could be made.
   b. The traditional role of the teacher in pioneer Canadian society was not a uniquely privileged nor high status one
   c. All Canadian teachers were poorly educated, of mediocre ability, and generally less deserving of respect than were our doctors, lawyers and engineers
   d. Teaching could not lay claim to a body of educational knowledge not readily available to any layman who had gone to school or raised a child.

7 According to the explanation of the professionalization process presented in this chapter, the most essential prerequisite for professionalism on the part of an occupation is:
   a. a rigorous selection of candidates
   b. possession of a body of systematic theory, and a fund of reliable knowledge that has been constructed on the basis of it
   c. a lengthy and costly period of university training
   d. self-employment, and the right to withhold services
   e. the existence of lower-status, technically-oriented, para-professional roles within the occupation.

8 In the struggle for professionalization in Canada to date, teachers have succeeded most in which one of the following endeavours?
   a. the achievement of wage parity with the members of the traditional professions
   b. the rigorous selection of candidates
   c. the incorporation of para-professional categories within the teaching career ladder

d. the push for lengthier and higher status training

e. the attainment of a theoretical consensus on the discipline of education which would conceivably lead to the production of a body of useful and reliable knowledge about teaching.

9 An emphasis on professionalism as a feature only of organized members of an occupation tends to downgrade:

a. the importance of the attitude of the individual toward his work

b. the importance of that elusive factor of status

c. the importance of the individual's sense of responsibility to the people whom he serves

d. the importance of the individual's ability to make judgments regarding the application of theory to specific situations

e. all of the above

f. none of the above

g. all but (b), (e) and (f).

10 The discussion of the concept in this chapter implies that as the process of professionalization continues in the urban society, it is likely to be characterized by:

a. an increase in the number of individual professionals working within the formal organization

b. greater insistence upon public control of the activities of professionals

c. much experimentation in the relationship between the professional and the society which he serves

d. much less disparity between the privileges (income, etc.) granted to the professionals and those granted to other workers

e. all of the above

f. none of the above

g. all but (b), (e) and (f).

Answers: 1. (a); 2. (d); 3. (c); 4. (b); 5. (a); 6. (c); 7. (b); 8. (d); 9. (g); 10. (e).

6 Social Mobility

The Concept Explained

As societies have become increasingly industrialized and urbanized, the structure of their social organization has altered in a number of ways. Not only has the horizontally demarcated pattern of role relationships greatly increased in complexity in Canada during the past century, but the vertical positioning of roles has changed drastically as well. In other words, urbanization has had significant consequences for the *social stratification* of groups. The movement of people up and down among the positions arranged vertically in status layers within groups, or movement from one group to another either above or below it in terms of the prestige associated with them, we call vertical social mobility. Horizontal social mobility is said to occur when people move from position to position along the same status layer. It is a consequence of the complexity of social organization rather than of stratification.

In terms of both these aspects of social organization, we could picture the urbanization continuum as follows:

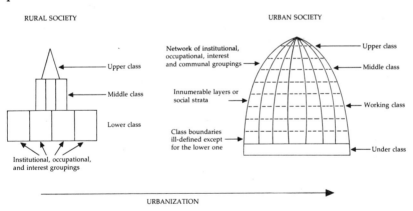

RURAL SOCIETY   URBAN SOCIETY

Upper class
Middle class
Lower class
Institutional, occupational, and interest groupings

Network of institutional, occupational, interest and communal groupings →
Innumerable layers or social strata →
Class boundaries ill-defined except for the lower one →

Upper class
Middle class
Working class
Under class

URBANIZATION

One way to describe this change in the pattern of social stratification is in terms of a change from a class society (of the type pertaining in Marx's time) to an organizational society. In the class society the individual's adult status is determined chiefly by that of his family. The status of the family is determined by its position vis-à-vis the relations of production: does it own or control these, or is it numbered among those who labour to produce?

In the organizational society, with the cooperative or the private or crown corporation dominating the function of production and distribution of resources, ownership is more diffused, control becomes somewhat obscure, and labour becomes highly managerial and technical. The result is that the distinction among these three categories becomes increasingly blurred. The individual is often on both sides of the relations of production, or on neither. It is sometimes difficult for us to realize that concepts for analysing societies must evolve at the same rate that social change occurs. Concepts such as "class conflict," appropriate for studying a rural, class society, may be utterly fruitless when applied to an urban, organizational one. For instance, in the conflict of interests between striking railway workers and Saskatchewan farmers, who are the "wronged proletariat" and who, the greedy owners of the means of production? When the Alberta government increases the cost of gas and oil to the eastern factory worker, where is the metropolis, where the hinterland?

Although the *pattern* has changed, it seems clear that the *fact* of social stratification, with its resulting inequality for individuals, is a feature of the urban society no less than of the rural. But whereas the structure of social stratification in the rural society is fairly stable from the standpoint of social mobility within it, in the urban society there is considerable movement of individuals upwards and downwards. In the rural society the individual's status is chiefly derived from family position, which is based on a tradition of ownership of either land or capital. In the urban society status is chiefly based on the occupational position which the individual manages to acquire. The major criterion by which occupations are arranged on the status dimension seems to be income, which in turn is highly dependent upon the tradition passed on from a more rural situation. Other criteria such as associated life style, privileges like opportunity for lifelong learning and travel, degree of responsibility, power over other people, length of training required, difficulty of the tasks involved, pleasantness of surroundings, danger to life and health, and perceived importance to the survival of the society are also associated with the prestige that the group assigns to a particular occupational position. In a stratified society the positions traditionally perceived by the group to have the greatest importance to the survival of the society, to require scarce abilities and a lengthy period of training, to demand a high degree of responsibility and to be associated with the most pleasant and healthful and least dangerous working conditions and most privileged and prestigious life style typically tend to be awarded the highest incomes as well. This explains the favoured position of the elite specialist professions. The occupational role ranking lowest on all these dimensions tends to have its undesirability compounded by being placed at the bottom of the income scale.

The following approximation of the Canadian stratification system today illustrates this traditional distribution of rewards and punishments rather clearly, although the upward surge of members of a few powerful unions during the last decade has altered the picture somewhat.

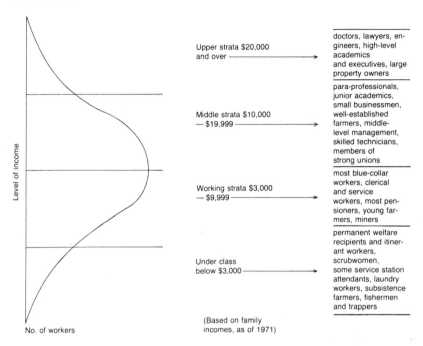

Upper strata $20,000 and over ⟶ doctors, lawyers, engineers, high-level academics and executives, large property owners

Middle strata $10,000 — $19,999 ⟶ para-professionals, junior academics, small businessmen, well-established farmers, middle-level management, skilled technicians, members of strong unions

Working strata $3,000 — $9,999 ⟶ most blue-collar workers, clerical and service workers, most pensioners, young farmers, miners

Under class below $3,000 ⟶ permanent welfare recipients and itinerant workers, scrubwomen, some service station attendants, laundry workers, subsistence farmers, fishermen and trappers

Level of income

No. of workers

(Based on family incomes, as of 1971)

With the advent of urbanization, occupations diversified and multiplied, and most came to require preparation not available in the family setting. Schooling became crucial, first because of what was learned there, and secondly, because of the avenue that it offered into the higher-status occupations which had hitherto been restricted to certain privileged individuals by birth. Now, the more schooling the individual was able to utilize successfully, the more likely he was to achieve high status. Family was still important, because both the genetic endowment and early childhood environment provided by the home greatly affected the subsequent intellectual development required for success in school. However, a favoured family background was no longer sufficient to guarantee success.

Sociologists of the first half of the twentieth century tended to underestimate the importance of family background in enabling children to utilize schooling and to overestimate the importance of opportunity for access to schooling. They shared the egalitarian ideals, widely espoused in the United States and Canada at the time, which seemed to indicate not equality in terms of the various rewards and punishments associated with societal roles, but something much easier to achieve: equality of opportunity to compete for the top positions. Most people assumed that the best and most just way to accomplish this was by means of public schooling. Everybody would be given an equal chance to enter the race. The race would be for positions in the same steeply hierarchical stratified structure that had prevailed in rural times, except that now there were many more positions at every level, and many more levels. The steps were closer together, but the gap between the bottom and top of the hierarchy remained immense; in addition, most of the traditional assumptions about those roles deserving of privilege and those rightfully to be condemned to poverty remained unchallenged.

It now seems clear that urbanization involved a trend toward meritocracy rather than egalitarianism, although the argument of reformers for equality of educational opportunity was invariably couched in terms of egalitarian goals. The meritocratic society is neither aristocratic (with positions in an inequitable reward structure based upon birth) nor egalitarian (with positions in an equitable reward structure acquired by achievement). It is instead a mixture of the two: a social system in which positions in an inequitable reward or stratification or "distributive" structure are acquired by achievement.

The diagram in chapter four illustrating centralization and decentralization of authority and power within organizations can now be enlarged to include social and economic rewards and generalized to apply to those larger social systems which we call societies.

Libertarianism		Authoritarianism
	Authority	

Democracy		Elitism
	Power	

Egalitarianism	**Meritocracy**	Aristocracy
	Social and Economic Rewards	

In a meritocracy the school is expected to operate as the sole channel of vertical social mobility, whereas in the egalitarian society it would provide for horizontal social mobility. (There would be no "up" and "down", only diversification of positions and role expectations, with the aggregate of rewards and punishments attached to each adding up to a more or less equal "desirability quotient.") The rural society is aristocratic, and exhibits very little social mobility of either type except in the case of pioneer societies, where the egalitarianism demanded by the hostile physical environment tends to weaken with the advance of urbanization.

Most examples of urban society (whether classified as capitalist or socialist) are neither very aristocratic nor very egalitarian, but are meritocratic in varying degrees. They are characterized by a considerable amount of both vertical and horizontal social mobility.

Educators in the United States and Canada tend to talk egalitarianism, but what we actually achieve seems instead to be an increasingly invalid and ineffective meritocratic function. Indications are that China is attempting to move to an egalitarian system, although there is insufficient evidence available yet as to the actual consequences of the attempt.

Only as a society moves away from aristocracy does the school become an agent of social mobility. However, it will operate differently as this agent in an egalitarian society than in a meritocratic one. In order to understand this difference, it might be well to first discuss the role of the school in a meritocracy, as that is what most urban societies seem to be moving toward. If a meritocracy is to operate effectively (so as to get the most able people into the top roles) the following conditions must hold:

1   a positive correlation between duration of schooling and educational results (intellectual and moral development of the individual);

2   a positive correlation between educational achievement and high status;

3   a high attrition rate throughout the schooling process so that the majority are selected out before they reach the top of the university ladder leading to high-status professional and executive positions; and

4   as many individuals moving down from the status of their parents as are moving up (except for periods of extremely rapid growth of the GNP and in situations where the birth rate of high and low socio-economic status families differs markedly).

If the educational selection has been valid and reliable, and has been going on for a few generations, the whole system will become increasingly stabilized (due to the factors of genetic endowment and early socialization) with a new aristocracy based on new families replacing the old, and social mobility through schooling occurring less and less. It appears, therefore, to the degree that a meritocracy operates effectively, it cannot avoid leading the society full circle, back to aristocracy: a revitalized aristocracy, certainly, in which the most privilege goes to the most able, and the incompetent, lazy, corrupt or just plain dull are continuously weeded out and condemned to poverty by the schooling system.[1]

Tremendous demands are made upon the school in an effectively functioning meritocracy. It must be staffed with teachers with an extremely high level of academic and intellectual competence: teachers capable of encouraging this development in others and of discriminating among students on the basis of academic ability and achievement at the crucial selection points in the schooling process. Evaluation must be valid and reliable, so that all and only top scholars get into and through university. Feedback to students must be continous and accurate, so that unrealistic expectations regarding adult roles are discouraged. Intervention programs, such as the 1968 Mickelson and Galloway study for young Indian children on Vancouver Island[2], are required to compensate for deficiencies in early socialization, so that actual equality of opportunity to utilize schooling is achieved as nearly as possible.

For the most part, Canadian educators have failed miserably in meeting these demands. A major source of this failure has been confusion in the minds of teachers and public as to the type of social stratification existing in their society, and the role of the school in maintaining or achieving it. It might help to clarify the problem if we understand that the school can determine social stratification only indirectly, by influencing the way individuals value high status and by shaping their expectations of rewards for role performance so that they are likely to take a political stand either for or against greater egalitarianism. The school cannot directly alter the social structure; it can only determine which individuals will climb to the top of it. The school, as only one of the components of an interdependent social system, cannot dictate egalitariansim by operating as if the society which it serves is not stratified, when it actually is. This amounts to a dangerous self-delusion on the part of educators and public alike. The consequence of failing to operate the school in a stratified society along meritocratic lines is either the inadvertent propping up of a

---

[1] See Michael Young, *The Rise of the Meritocracy*, in the Concept Amplified section of this chapter.

[2] This study is included in the Concept Applied section of chapter one.

corrupt old aristocracy based on property ownership and kinship, or the inadvertent creation of a corrupt new aristocracy based on certified quackery and power politics. "Romantic" critics of schooling, and conservatives who yearn for a return to education restricted to established elites are closer to one another than most people realize, if one is to judge by the consequences of their activities.

An attack on the degree of stratification existing in a society by the members of that society, must be made in the political rather than the educational arena. Do we really want to maintain a social structure in which the bottom fifth of Canadian families each live on approximately $2,500 (about 25 per cent of the average Canadian family income) while the families in the top fifth of the population each receive about 225 per cent of average (approximately $22,500)?[3] Do we really want to maintain a social structure in which the absolute difference between the income of the bottom fifth and that of the top fifth is widening, in spite of a steady increase in *average* family income? If we do, then let us be honest about it and start insisting that our schools no longer waste our physical and human resources, and at least succeed in bringing the most competent and hard-working (rather than the most crafty) to the top.

This confused situation is an excellent example of "cultural lag." There has been a change in cultural ideals or verbalized beliefs about a desirable social structure for Canada (most people espouse egalitarianism to some degree) and the schooling system is reflecting these newer ideals in a strange, distorted way in that evaluation, selection in terms of academic excellence, and compensatory programs are increasingly in disrepute. However, there has not been a corresponding change in the actual hierarchical nature of the social structure, nor in the values which determine the behavioural choices that individuals make. People still make choices in their daily lives, as they fight for their own group interests, which have the consequence of increasing income differentials and rendering the working poor and the unemployed underclass ever more powerless. Highly verified conclusions from the social sciences tell us that there is a direct relationship between the existence of extremes of poverty and privilege in a mobile urban society and the growth of violence. All of our accumulated wisdom in this area points to the long-term social advantages of egalitarianism. Yet we continue to behave so as to perpetuate a stratified society: a society that requires a meritocratic schooling system in order to ensure that the most demanding and crucial leadership positions are filled by the most competent people. But we are talking egalitarianism, and expecting our schools, by some

---

[3] These approximations are based on 1971 census data. The figures are increasing because of inflation but the relationships remain the same.

magic formula, to bring everyone to the top of the ladder. We want the schools to provide all comers, regardless of performance, with an exclusive, privileged position at the top, while at the same time keeping these top positions nine times as highly rewarded as those at the bottom. Who is to fill the bottom positions, one wonders?

The Canadian schooling system seems to have been operating under this ambiguous and contradictory mandate for several decades. After the Second World War the high schools were required to provide for an entirely new clientele, rather than the children of the aristocracy whom they had previously served. This altered mandate represented a political decision to move in the direction of meritocracy, although most educators (if not parents) interpreted it as a move to egalitarianism. But the appropriate system of schooling for a meritocracy—one which would have had to compensate for unequal starting points, and to select validly and reliably on the basis of academic performance—failed to materialize for a complex set of reasons.

Two of the assumptions underlying the new mandate for education were highly questionable but seldom questioned by either parents or teachers.

The first was that because the few who had in the past acquired expertise through extended schooling had been highly rewarded by society (a society that could afford to reward them this way only because they were few in number), therefore the many who were now being exposed to that extended schooling would similarly all end up far above average in terms of pay, prestige and power. (That this goal was mathematically impossible seemed to carry little weight with the dreamers who saw more schooling for everybody as the magic key to universal privilege.)

We are all too familiar with the exhortation posted in high school hallways to stay in school, because one can earn so many hundreds of thousands of dollars more in a lifetime than if one dropped out—figures based on the proportion of society's resources that had been awarded to the highly schooled in the past simply because there had been only a relatively small number of them. What these high school students were not told is that privilege is a relative thing in any society.

For example, the underprivileged in Canadian society today are the bottom 10 per cent on the income scale, regardless of the fact that the absolute level of their income has probably doubled in terms of real purchasing power since the Depression. What is considered poverty in Canada would be classed as privilege in some parts of Asia. Privilege is by definition only what the top-most few in a society achieve. Like an original painted by an old master, its value lies in its exclusiveness. This is why the attainment of privilege could be the goal of an aristocratic or even a meritocratic schooling system, but never of an egalitarian one.

Perhaps what we should have been concerning ourselves with was the flattening out of our societal reward structure so that it would be in keeping with the egalitarian role that we seemed to want our schools to perform, rather than with giving everyone the expectation that increased schooling would lead to privilege for them at the expense of the impoverishment of the less schooled. Of course the inevitable consequence of selling increased schooling on these terms was that the purchasers bought the product on exactly the same terms. Education became equated with officially certified schooling, and schooling became valuable to the individual only because of what it would subsequently buy for him in the way of a privileged life style.

The second premise of the promoters of extended schooling for all Canadians was that a one-to-one relationship was bound to exist between length of exposure to this schooling and degree of intellectual growth and competence. This, too, has become increasingly unwarranted.

It very soon became clear to Canadian high school teachers that "all of society's children" were coming to them not nearly so well-equipped with the basic concepts, skills and motivation for learning as had the few whom the high school had previously served. One reason for this was probably the fact that during this same period of rapid change the elementary school was being called upon to expose its students to an ever-widening range of experience. We were told that knowledge was increasing at an exponential rate, and without any clear consensus on what indeed constitutes reliable knowledge in any area, we were pressured into presenting more and more information on more and more subjects at an ever earlier age.

At the same time elementary teachers were told that an emphasis on skill development was somehow "anti-humanistic," and that children should be left free to choose when and even whether they should become proficient in certain communicative, arithmetical and conceptual skills. An individualistic approach to teaching, we were told, implied not only that teaching procedures and rate of learning must vary from child to child, but that the very concepts to be acquired must also be determined by the child's interests.

At the same time, however, the ideal of equality of opportunity for schooling seemed to dictate that every child should be brought to the door of the high school at precisely the same age, in that being "held back" had come to be defined as failure due to "unegalitarian" discrimination, whereas being propelled into an incomprehensible situation in which one was doomed to perpetual failure came to be defined as success, and egalitarian as well!

The result of all these contradictory platitudes being aimed at teachers and administrators has been a great confusion of objectives at the elementary level. In an attempt to be all things to all children the Canadian elementary school has too often exposed each child to more and more unrelated information while providing him with fewer and fewer of the necessary tools for handling it, and all the while pushing him through the system at the same rate as before. We have managed to achieve the illusion of equality of educational opportunity, while in practice what the children may be receiving is equality of tenure in a schooling situation in which learning has become increasingly random and haphazard. As a result, although children entering high school today may well be more widely informed than ever before, all too many are so lacking in the skills required for communication and figuring and in the basic concepts of science and logic that they are incapable of coping with the academic demands being placed upon them.

For many Canadian adolescents today the high school as a place of knowledge acquisition and moral development has no meaning. Intellectually crippled, and to some extent emotionally crippled without knowing it, they group together and cry for relevance. In this cry they are joined by many others who do possess the tools for learning but who are impatient for direct experience rather than what seems to them to be an endless preparation for some future role in society.

A steadily decreasing majority are still reasonably satisfied with what the high school has to offer. Some of these students are academically competent and very much involved as autonomous learners in the building of their skills and knowledge. They are the fortunate few who are able to turn every situation into a valuable learning experience: the few who often learn in spite of the social environment of the school rather than because of it. The remainder of this non-rebellious majority see their tenure in high school as a necessary (if somewhat boring and distasteful) step on the ladder leading to the kind of life style on which they have set their sights. If one cannot get into the highest salaried and most prestigious jobs without a university degree, and if one cannot get into university without good high school marks, then one perseveres and does what one must. Perhaps university will be better, but even if it represents only more years of drudgery and frustration, the prize (in the form of that upper-bracket income, and all that prestige and power that accompanies being a doctor or a lawyer or an engineer or a professor) will be worth the game.

So the high school is expected to serve them all: the educationally crippled, the bright and impatient would-be participants in the world outside, the little nucleus of budding scholars, and the ambitious status-seekers. In the name of equality of educational opportunity it is expected to retain and restrain all of them for a period of four or five years and at the end of that time to have brought them all to the level of academic competence required for university entrance.

We now have considerable evidence that, whatever we have been trying to accomplish by forcing everyone up the same schooling ladder at the same pace, it is not working.

If individual differences mean anything, they must surely mean that long hours of formal schooling are not appropriate for all young people. Some will be educated most effectively in other ways and places—on the job, or through travel, or in independent reading. And where it isn't appropriate, more and more schooling for the sake of the promise of privilege at the end of it does terrible things to people. It is bad both for the winners (who exact a high price from society forever after for their suffering and disillusionment) and for the losers, who live out lives of quiet desperation, and relative poverty, defined as failures by themselves and society.

And there are bound to be many losers and few winners in such a race. In a society like ours, where the average family income is $10,000, for every married couple that demands $20,000 because of advanced schooling, two families must be satisfied with $5,000 each. The only way that university graduation can guarantee a $20,000 income for one person, is for two out of every three to drop out in the early grades. Simply put, everybody cannot be above average, and there is no way that schooling can create privilege. It can only create the expectation of privilege in the minds of all, and a situation of fierce and prolonged competition for a prize which, by definition, must remain the preserve of an exclusive few.

⤟ It is only the members of society as a whole, through a change in their priorities, who can press for a redistribution of income in order to do away with the extremes of privilege and poverty which now operate as the ultimate rewards and punishments of the schooling experience, and which so restrict the choice of life roles now considered socially acceptable for the students.

It is clear that the problems of the schools in Canada today are the problems of society and must be tackled on those terms. Canadians have tried to maintain the high school as a pathway to privilege, while at the same time guaranteeing everyone equality of access to the pathway but not to an equal share of the prize at the end. Either the prize must be rendered sharable, by a flattening out of our reward structure, or we must narrow the pathway and institute an honest and effective meritocratic schooling system. To do otherwise is to continue contributing to the corruption of the high school and ultimately to the corruption of the entire society.

Granted that a schooling system can only become a source of corruption if it fails to perform a meritocratic role when the society that it serves is stratified, what about an egalitarian social structure as a viable alternative to what we have now? For a society to be egalitarian its occupational positions would have to be rewarded equitably. This does not simply mean income-equalization, although that would be a giant step in the desired direction. In a truly egalitarian society the total package of rewards and punishments associated with each role would approximate that of every other. The various components of the status of a role mentioned earlier would have to be balanced out, so that as a general principle, the job with the most dangerous and unpleasant working conditions, the fewest privileges, least power, and most anxiety-producing responsibility would demand the highest salary, and vice versa. There is no way that the most just mix of rewards could be established for all time, by government fiat, for social rewards such as income, power and prestige, are interrelated. The possession of a great deal of one of these is likely to attract a disproportionately large share of the others, and all may be associated with intellectual and personality attributes with which people are not equally endowed. In addition, technological advance means that working conditions and ways of life associated with occupational positions are undergoing constant change. The values which people attribute to things like material possessions and responsibility are also subject to change, as are group perceptions of the importance of a role to the national society, or to humanity.

If an equitable balance cannot be legislated and held constant, how is it possible for an egalitarian society to exist? Many sociologists argue that the very fact that some degree of stratification has been a feature of every human society, past and present, means that social inequality is the inevitable correlate of biological differences. Others argue that in no way does genetic variation necessitate social inequality; that this is due, instead, to social role relationships generalized from countless individual human encounters. They add that individual uniqueness would seem to necessitate differences in roles, but not inequality in the social rewards assigned to each. And sociologists readily acknowledge that there is nothing inherent or immutable (or even necessarily rational) in the pattern of reward distribution which has evolved in any particular society. Most would agree that what we are dealing with is another continuum: that reflecting the degree of centralization or decentralization of social and economic rewards among the society's members. Perhaps rather than argue about whether an aristocracy, meritocracy or egalitarian society is best for mankind in general, we should be posing the following questions:

1   How much of a reduction in social inequality can and should a specific society attempt?

2   How could this be achieved politically?

3   What would be the role of the school in a society politically committed to moving in the direction of increased
egalitarianism?

The responses to the first and second questions depend very
much upon the type of political system obtaining. In a totalitarian
polity a political commitment to increased egalitarianism requires
only that the leadership finds it desirable. This is why dictators like
Mussolini, Stalin, Castro and Mao accomplished a reduction of social
and economic inequality much more rapidly than the representative
democracies have been able to. Politics in a representative democracy, however, is very much the art of the possible. While this makes
change relatively slow in our system, it makes it possible for the consequences of any change to be evaluated continuously by the recipients (or victims) of the change. And it guarantees that these same
recipients retain the power to alter the rate and direction of the
change process according to their assessment of subsequent experience.
     Twentieth-century history has shown, rather clearly, the cost to
humanity of short-term gains in social and economic equality at the
price of the loss of this shared power to control the society's political
process over the long term. However, the time may be rapidly approaching in Canada when continued refusal of the privileged to
reform our obsolete economic institutions in the face of increased
relative deprivation of the underprivileged may spark a social holo-
caust that will destroy our precious but fragile political and legal
institutions.
     No Canadian government is likely to make the necessary moves
to reduce social inequality, nor even to prevent the gap between the
privileged and the poor from widening, as long as there exists a de-
monstrable consensus that a highly stratified social structure is a good
thing. In Canada today most people have been socialized to desire
privilege and to expect to achieve it sooner or later, at the expense of
the less fortunate or less able. This means that there is not at present
even a vocal minority who are committed to a flattening-out of the
reward structure. Most of the underprivileged and their spokesmen
are committed, instead, to a wholesale displacement of "top dogs" by
"underdogs": an attack on our political and legal institutions that
might well leave the social stratification system intact. "The first shall
be last" is still the cry of the reformers, rather than "There shall be no
first nor last, in terms of privilege"!
     Our third question, which asks about the hypothetical role of the
school in a society which was (in deed as well as ideology) politically
committed to moving in the direction of greater egalitarianism, is an
interesting one to speculate upon. Certainly this role would vary con-

siderably, depending upon whether the increased egalitarianism had been achieved by totalitarian or democratic means. If the polity tended toward totalitarianism, the school's priority would likely be the most efficient possible allocation of people to positions. If income were totally equalized (now the goal of most Communist polities) it is likely that far more of the students capable of doing both would select judging ahead of mining. This means that in order to guarantee enough miners the government would have to set quotas for all of the more desirable positions and those losing out in the competition would have to accept a second or third choice. Intensive "re-education" (indoctrinating) programs within occupations would be designed to develop the appropriate skills and commitment to the job, for these people.

If, on the other hand, the relatively egalitarian structure had been achieved by democratic means, the school's allocation function would be more complex. We would have to at least match the performance of the more meritocratic social systems in obtaining the best possible fit between personality and physical attributes and role demands and of the more totalitarian political systems in ensuring that all necessary societal roles are filled. In addition, our political ideals require that, in accomplishing these two feats, we also manage to maximize occupational choice for the individual. It is precisely because we seem to be failing so miserably in all of these tasks at present that we should be willing to consider a more egalitarian social structure as a possible solution to our problems.

If we are serious about our democratic ideal of maximizing individual choice of occupation, while at the same time achieving the best possible fit between ability and role requirements and ensuring that all necessary societal positions are indeed filled by the most willing and able people (rather than by frustrated, economically-coerced misfits), then we have no choice. We must attempt a greater equalization of the total package of rewards and punishments associated with each role. Income is only one component in the aggregate, but because it is the one most amenable to manipulation by government it would have to be used as the controlling factor. Income would have to be subject to alteration to restore the balance whenever certain positions were being over or under-selected. But because income includes gains from rents and investments as well as wages, the necessarily continuous process of adjustment would not be easily accomplished. To some extent this objective could be achieved by taxation. To some extent government might have to remove institutional supports such as the closed shop and the right to strike from the most sought-after occupations, so that as certain positions became too attractive, the resulting oversupply of qualified entrants would force salaries down.

If, for example, all the grade nine students in Canada each year were provided with adequate information about all the occupations available, with accurate descriptions of the reward and punishment characteristics of each, and with government assurance of financial support for the training required for each, and then asked to make a temporary choice, we would have a significant annual indicator of the relative desirability of the roles currently required by society. If, out of a class of thirty, twenty-five chose to be doctors, lawyers and professors and nobody chose the job of garbage man, housekeeper or laundry worker, then it would be obvious that an extensive readjustment of salaries would be needed in order to get the latter positions filled by means of free choice. Of course, not all those who chose a particular role would have the appropriate abilities, but a valid and reliable evaluation process would soon indicate this to all concerned. And of course any particular set of grade nine students could be expected to change their minds about future occupations several times in the years following. The point is that the distribution of choices arrived at in this way would be a regular indication of the degree and nature of the income adjustment required if the allocation process were to function without economic or political coercion.

It might be that the salary of the laundry worker would have to be high enough so that he or she would only have to work at the job three or four hours a day, and could devote the rest of the time to outdoor recreation or the arts. In this way all the roles necessary for the survival of the society would be performed by people who had freely chosen the positions and no one would be unemployed. The professor who felt dissatisfied because a coal miner was getting a higher salary than he, would always have the choice of returning to school on a government stipend, to retrain as a miner.

At the present time, however, there are few signs in Canada that a movement to increased egalitarianism is in the offing. It is likely that the destructive consequences, for rich and poor alike, of an inequitable social structure in an industrialized urban society will have to become much more apparent to all of us before the values by which we actually live will begin to approximate our espoused ideals. The currently popular practice among sociologists of labelling our schooling system as "class-ridden" and indicting it as the major cause of the injustices within our society stems from a failure to define the problem clearly. It is the society that is "class-ridden." To demand that the schooling system in such a society function in other than a meritocratic role is to guarantee the disruption and corruption of the educational endeavour.

For the schools can only service a social structure; they cannot (except indirectly, through individual value-change) create a different one. The American and Canadian attempt to "put the cart before the horse" has encouraged a corruption of the schooling system and the evolution of a pseudo-meritocracy in which it is possible for the power-broker, the incompetent, and the anti-intellectual to occupy positions of professional authority and privilege, while many young people with integrity, intelligence and leadership potential drop out.

This is not to suggest that the school is without influence. It contributes indirectly to the degree of social stratification and social mobility in the society through its role in the shaping of the expectations, values and abilities of the individuals who pass through it. Concerned educators who would like to help move their society in the direction of increased egalitarianism would be well advised, however, not to attempt to render their school "classless" by refusing to evaluate performance and by pushing all comers to the top of the university ladder. As long as the positions at the top of the hierarchy are few (and they must be few to be at the top) the competition will be the more ferocious for having been postponed and for having to be fought in the absence of individual awareness of levels of personal competence.

Those educators who are serious about contributing to the achievement of increased egalitarianism could do this, instead, in a number of ways:

1   by reducing inequalities in rewards among teachers. This means that the highest paid must stand still until the most poorly paid of their colleagues catch up to them. (Christopher Jencks, the Harvard sociologist, claims that there is more income inequality *within* occupational groupings than *between* them.) It means also that working conditions, responsibilities and additional privileges must be taken into account in the resulting income adjustment;

2   by doing an honest job of providing equality of opportunity for all children to utilize schooling in order to develop the intellectual and moral competence necessary to achieve the occupational role most suited to their aptitudes. This requires more than compensatory or intervention programs, for research indicates that these produce only temporary results if the regular schooling process and out-of-school environment remains the same. Teachers must build on the experience that the child brings to the classroom, rather than attempt to wipe it out and replace it with a set of foreign vicarious experiences. The teacher who insists on doing the latter is establishing a cultural discontinuity that only the exceptional child can bridge. If a child comes from a hunting

and fishing culture, then every concept and every symbol taught must be taught in terms of hunting and fishing and not in the context of Dick and Jane. This seems so obvious that one can only be appalled at the apparent refusal or inability of teachers and administrators to comprehend the tragic crippling that they are engaged in, when they do otherwise;

3   by doing a valid and reliable job of evaluating the progress of pupils, in terms of a variety of lines of endeavour, and of communicating the results accurately by means of percentiles, or other ranking systems, so that they and their parents will develop a realistic picture of their abilities; by attempting to remain with the same group of pupils for a number of years (perhaps as a member of a teaching team) so that each child moves along continuously at his own rate; and by refusing to label students as "passes" or "failures" at various hurdles, thereby forcing them to repeat some work that they have already mastered or to be propelled into new work which demands the use of concepts which they have not yet developed;

4   by refusing, as a professional group, to select for organizations of continuing education or employers. This implies the doing away with high school diplomas or any symbol that receiving agencies can substitute for their own carefully constructed assessment of candidates at the point of entry;

5   by making students aware of the consequences of extremes of social inequality in the urban world, and by refraining from encouraging the more intelligent (or more athletic) to expect that their success will buy them privilege.

In the event that such procedures (along with efforts in the political arena) did succeed in causing the social structure gradually to flatten out, most educators would probably be relieved to note that the role of the school had changed accordingly from that of a ladder of vertical social mobility based on selection (often in terms of irrelevant criteria) to a many-spoked wheel of horizontal social mobility based on informed individual choice and rigorous training.

The Concept Demonstrated

CASE STUDY ONE

Mary Canjo had attended the Indian residential school in the northern Ontario town for six years when the decision was made to do away with the system of segregated, church-operated schooling for the Indian children of that community. She had come under the care of the nuns and priests of the residential school at the age of nine, having been sent there along with some hundred or so others from homes on reserves anywhere within a four-hundred mile radius of the town.

The move to the newly integrated school system proved to be a difficult experience for Mary, as it was for most of her friends. The Catholic residential school to which they returned at night seemed a refuge from the strangeness of the public school and the apparent unfriendliness of their more urban and urbane classmates. Mary felt particularly alone because she was the only senior high school student among the Indian group. Although she had learned to speak English fluently and had loved her studies with the sisters, she felt inadequate and somewhat disoriented during her first year of public school. Until then her ambition had been to become a nun, and everything she had studied had seemed to confirm her in the rightness of that choice. But in the new school she began to wonder about her ability. Whereas previously she had been the most successful student in the residential school, now it seemed that no one expected her to do well. She was treated with compassion by her teachers and some of her fellow students, ignored by most of her classmates, and (it seemed to her) respected and liked by nobody.

After the first few months at the new school Mary began to realize that the non-Indian students were not all as intelligent as they had at first appeared to be. True, they knew much more about many things than she did, but they didn't all listen to the teacher as carefully as she, nor do their assignments as thoroughly, nor explore the magnificent library as eagerly. And with her growing self-confidence came a growing anger; at the teachers who expressed startled surprise when she answered a question; at the girls who moved away when she entered the washroom at noon; and at the boys who sometimes pushed against her with a strange boldness not present in their advances to the other girls.

With the passing of time Mary's goals began to change, so that by the time she graduated from high school she had decided to become a teacher. This decision had been the culmination of a gradual recognition that only through schooling could her people acquire the positions and standard of living that would force other Canadians to grant them respect. With financial help from the Indian Affairs Branch she studied for a B.A. in history. After graduating she took a year of teacher training. During these years Mary made many non-Indian friends, and the hard blade of her anger gradually diffused, as she learned to focus it on the general problems of prejudice and injustice rather than upon non-Indians as individuals or as a group.

One spring day Mary went home to the reserve as a teacher, with the intention of devoting her life to discovering other little potential Marys and making sure that they were given the opportunity to learn what too many of her former companions had missed. But she found the life lonely, for she had little in common with her parents and other members of the community. She missed the city that she had come to know: the food, the travel, and, most of all, the conversation. Most shocking of all was her discovery that, although the residents of the reserve granted non-Indian teachers an almost exaggerated respect, the prevailing attitude towards herself seemed closer to a resentment bordering on hostility.

By the end of her first year of teaching Mary had begun to suspect that her future would have to lie elsewhere. But the thought of betraying her people by leaving them when their need for leadership was so great saddened and dismayed her.

QUESTIONS FOR GROUP DISCUSSION

1   Could the Indian reserve be classified as a miniature rural society? Why or why not?

2   Where would you place Mary's family in the Canadian stratification system? Why? Where would you place the adult Mary?

3   What would an effectively functioning meritocracy provide for youngsters like Mary and the companions of her childhood? Why do you suppose the process worked differently for Mary than for most of the others?

4   Discuss the necessity for compensatory education in this type of situation. What form should it take? What about rigorous and reliable evaluation?

5   Analyse Mary's failure as a teacher on the reserve in terms of (a) socialization, (b) role, and (c) authority.

CASE STUDY TWO
Rosemary Cullen had received all of her education in the Halifax-Dartmouth metropolitan area. She was the oldest girl in a Negro family of nine children whose parents had never quite managed to keep their

brood adequately fed, clothed and sheltered. In spite of hardship at home, however, Rosemary had exhibited average achievement during her first six years in school, and was even beginning to read widely in her spare time when she entered grade seven.

Suddenly, everything changed. Rosemary was caught several times smoking in the washroom. She began to be disruptive in class, especially when sitting near boys. Her grades fell markedly and at the beginning of the next term she was placed in a low ability class. This particular class was assigned no outside reading or homework, and was expected to accomplish little during school hours. The behaviour of the group was so bad that it required all of the teacher's energy merely to contain their noise and vandalism. Rosemary stopped reading entirely and began to play hooky frequently.

By the time she had been moved along into grade ten, Rosemary was being provided with remedial classes in reading, language and math. When she left school in grade twelve her reading level had sunk to a grade four standard, and her puzzling encounters with the mysteries of algebra and geometry had almost entirely obliterated arithmetical concepts and skills acquired in elementary school.

Rosemary, now nineteen, discovered that she could not read nor figure well enough to hold a job as a waitress or a sales clerk. But even if she had succeeded in one of these jobs, it was not really what she wanted to do with her life. For she was discovering that what she really had a talent for and enjoyed doing was teaching little children. Little ones in the slum district in which she still lived congregated on her doorstep, hanging on her words as, with seemingly infinite patience she told them stories and shared with them her meagre fund of skills and knowledge.

She became captivated by the idea of helping other underprivileged children so that they would not work themselves further and further into a trap as she had done. But she could not ever become a teacher, Rosemary decided. Without being able to articulate her problem precisely she was aware of the fact that too many doors would have to be opened. And these were doors for which the keys had been long since lost to her: embedded forever somewhere back there in those wasted years of schooling.

As she tells her story to the Nova Scotia Newstart researcher, Rosemary weeps. The researcher has worked for several years in this experimental adult education program, sponsored by the federal Department of Regional Economic Expansion, so he is not surprised. He is saddened, nonetheless, not because the situation is so unique and startling in Canada in the 1970s, but rather because it is so commonplace.

QUESTIONS FOR GROUP DISCUSSION

1   Rosemary had obviously been provided with equality of opportunity of access to schooling, having been kept in school for twelve years or so. What is the problem here, if any?

2   Compare and contrast the cases of Rosemary and Mary Canjo, in terms of equality of opportunity to utilize schooling as a means of vertical social mobility.

3   Are there other reasons, besides inappropriateness in terms of ability and current interest, that might be rendering the role of waitress or sales clerk unacceptable to Rosemary?

4   Is there a loss to society as well as to the individual implied here? Might this situation be avoided in a more meritocratic society? In a more egalitarian one? How?

CASE STUDY THREE

It seemed that Dr. Joseph Krewski and his son Ted had come to an irrevocable parting of the ways. May, the wife and mother, was being pulled between the two as, more and more, they communicated only through her. Joseph was interpreting his son's refusal to complete his university education as the repudiation of everything that he, his father, stood for. All those years of working his way through high school and college, in order to escape the harsh poverty of his childhood in a northern Ontario mining town, seemed to mean nothing to Ted. That gruelling period of study in medical school, and the hard years of practice since, working at a job that even long familiarity did not seem to render easier or more pleasant to someone who felt comfortable only in the outdoors, had been totally unappreciated by Ted, Joseph now realized.

The boy had enjoyed the affluence that his father's labour and sacrifice had made possible (the home in the exclusive Toronto suburb, the private school, the sports car on his eighteenth birthday) while scoffing at the very values and way of life that had provided it. Joseph's bitterness at what he saw as his son's betrayal was now affecting his relationship with May as well, for he was beginning to wonder whether she too judged the privileged life style with which he had provided her, and the prestige of his position, to be of so little worth.

May reflected that for a long time now, her two men had been travelling in opposite directions. Ted had chosen the social rather than the physical sciences when he entered university, and had been increasingly critical of his father's conservative political stance ever since. Their arguments over the Carter Commission recommendations for tax reform, for instance, had seemed never-ending. After that period Ted had begun to bring home research studies which he encountered in his sociology classes. One of these which his father had found particularly objectionable was a 1971 study undertaken by Systems Research Group, Inc. for the Commission on Post-secondary Education in Ontario. The study found that the above-average-income families (those earning $10,000 or more) were providing 34 per cent of the students for higher education but paying only 28 per cent of the costs, while the lowest income groups (those earning less than $7,000) were contributing more to these costs than they were getting back.

Ted also quoted at length from another 1971 study, a survey of 10,000 Ontario university students conducted by the sociologists Bernard Blishen and John Porter. These researchers had concluded that the best way to achieve equality of educational opportunity would be to abolish tuition fees, give maintenance grants to students, and finance education through a much more progressive tax system. However, because they saw little chance of this happening, Blishen and Porter had recommended higher tuition fees for the offspring of financially able parents and grants to needy students.

Another study which had infuriated Joseph whenever Ted referred to it was the Alberta Worth report which recommended a new delivery system for adult education outside of formal schooling, and which was generally critical of current university programs.

Ted had often claimed that the expansion of the Canadian community college movement was a good thing, provided that the jobs that these colleges led to were at least as highly paid as that of doctor, lawyer or engineer. This opinion invariably had led to violent argument between the two men. It was in the midst of one of these shouting matches that Ted had informed his father of his decision to drop out of university and to work in the field of basic education in Toronto.

By now, May was reconciled to Ted's decision. But she wished, with all her heart, that he had refrained from his parting shot at Joseph. When, at his father's insistence, Ted had moved out of the house with all his belongings on his back, he had said, "I've got to find out what I'm *good* at, Dad. I don't want to spend my life as you have, fighting to get to the top and then finding that the prize is only a trap that I can't escape from!".

QUESTIONS FOR GROUP DISCUSSION

1   Analyse the generation gap between Ted and his father in terms of the concept of social mobility. Why did the top of the ladder not beckon as invitingly to Ted as it had to Joseph?

2   What does this case seem to indicate about our use of the Canadian schooling system as a ladder of vertical social mobility? How does this practice seem to have been working for the individual? For society?

3   Do any of the studies referred to by Ted indicate that change may be in the offing? If so, what seems to be the direction of these changes?

4   If the university should lose its position as the most prestigious and almost sole pathway to status and affluence, what might be the consequences for the structure of Canadian society? For the university? Would a multiplicity of pathways upwards be likely to increase or decrease the stratified nature of our society?

The Concept Applied
To Relevant Canadian Research

Bancroft, G. W. "Some Sociological Considerations on Education in Canada." *Canadian Educational and Research Digest* 4, no. 1 (March 1964): 26-28, 32.
The author produces data indicating that while there has been a marked expansion in opportunity for access to schooling in Canada, the capacity of the school system to provide for and retain the student is far from satisfactory.

Belanger, Pierce. *School Retention in the Province of Quebec.* Quebec Government Publication, 1962.
The researcher reports on a massive study on the problem of socioeconomic influences on success in schooling. Forty-two thousand families were surveyed. It was found that school retention rates were higher for youngsters from smaller families with both parents present, for those whose parents had been educated, and for children of white-collar workers. In all, less than 47% of those aged sixteen or more were being retained in school. The researcher concludes that, while theoretically the school system at that time was providing all the population with equal access to higher education, the opportunities were, in reality, far from equal.

Berger, A. "The Education of Canadian Indians: An In-Depth Study of Nine Families." *Alberta Journal of Educational Research* 19, no. 4 (December 1973): 334-342.
The author employed intensive interviewing and content analysis to reach the following conclusions regarding his sample of Hobbema (Alberta) reserve families: (1) the major concern of these Indians is education, which they see as a way to a better life for their children, (2) there is a general concern for greater involvement in their children's

education, and (3) there is little prejudice about ethnic differences between teachers and taught.

Blishen, Bernard R. "Social Class and Opportunity in Canada," *Canadian Review of Sociology and Anthropology* 7, no. 2 (1970): 110-127.
This study shows the extent to which regional and provincial differences exist in the class distribution of native-born and immigrants who arrived before 1946, and immigrants who arrived between 1946 and 1961. Using six classes from a socio-economic index (based on income and education) of 320 occupations, the author shows that in the Atlantic provinces and Quebec, the Canadian-born are slightly under-represented in the top three classes. In Ontario and the West, Canadian-born are over-represented. Postwar immigrants from the U.S. have a higher degree of over-representation in the higher strata throughout the society than do any other group.

Blishen, Bernard R. "A Socio-Economic Index of Occupations in Canada." *Canadian Review of Sociology and Anthropology* 4, no. 1 (February 1967): 41-53.
This is an attempt to update and revise the 1951 Blishen Scale, by relating those Pineo-Porter scores which correspond to the occupational categories in the Canadian census to the corresponding income and educational level indices from the old scale. The new scale places chemical engineers, dentists, doctors and college professors at the top and trappers and hunters at the bottom.

Card, B. Y. *Trends and Change in Canadian Society.* Toronto: Macmillan of Canada, 1968.
The comments on rural-urban migration in this useful little book (p. 22) are relevant here as is the section on social inequality (pp. 28-44).

Coleman, Peter. *Educational Opportunity in Manitoba: A Study of Equality of Opportunity and School Division Organization.* The Manitoba Association of School Trustees, 1973.
This is an in-depth documentation and analysis of the distribution of a variety of educational services by groups of school divisions (categorized by size of enrolment) across the province of Manitoba, for the year 1969-70.

Economic Council of Canada. "Education and Economic Growth," in Anand, Malik. *Social Foundations of Canadian Education,* pp. 98-121. Scarborough: Prentice-Hall, 1969.
This article contains a chart on p. 113, showing incomes of Canadians by age group and educational levels for 1961.

Ellis, Eleanor A. "Education of the Eskimo for Wage Employment." *Canadian Geographical Journal* (November 1966): 147-155.
The author documents the increase in access to schooling and vocational training for the Canadian Eskimo from 1955 to 1965.

Fisher, A. D. "Education and Social Progress." *Alberta Journal of Educational Research* 12, no. 4 (December 1966): 257-268.
The author attempts to document the "fallacy that the school is the crucial variable in programs directed toward the amelioration of social and economic injustice," by comparing steady improvements in the schooling attainments of Alberta's Indians with rising welfare costs and high unemployment among Indian youths.

Fleming, W. G. "Background and Personality Factors Associated with Educational and Occupational Careers of Ontario Grade 13 Students." Toronto, Ontario College of Education, 1957.
A report of the detailed Atkinson study on the utilization of student resources.

Fowler, William and Nasim Khan, et. al., "The Later Effects of Infant Group Care: A Follow up Study." Ontario Institute for Studies in Education, Toronto, June 1974.
This study sought to determine whether the developmental gains made in the infant day care programs reported on in chapter one would be maintained over later periods. Evidence was presented to show that this was indeed the case for the advantaged children. The disadvantaged group partly regressed over the longer follow-up period, however, with the result that the IQ gap between the two groups began to widen once the low-income families lost the support of the day care program. The researchers conclude that improved education alone, without a corresponding improvement in life circumstances, cannot solve the learning problems that stem from socioeconomic disadvantages.

Friesen, David. "Profile of the Potential Dropout." *Alberta Journal of Educational Research* 13, no. 4 (1967): 299-309.
In a population of 2,425 pupils in two urban composite Canadian high schools, a comparison was made of the attributes of those wishing to leave school and those wishing to remain. Significant differences were found in the areas of school experience satisfaction, plans for higher education, athletic, religious and academic orientations, nonconformity, parental influence and recreational activities. The largest proportion of potential leavers were found to have the lowest socio-economic backgrounds.

Harvey E., and L. Harvey. "Adolescence, Social Class and Occupational Expectations." *Canadian Review of Sociology and Anthropology* 7, no. 2 (1970): 138-147.

A questionnaire survey of 345 Toronto tenth-grade pupils in a socio-economically heterogenous, multi-program, urban high school attempted to measure congruence (1) between pupil occupational values and occupational choice, (2) between the pupil's financial expectations of his work and his actual likely earnings, and (3) between the pupil's occupational choice and his parents' choice for him. The findings showed that pupils from higher SES backgrounds demonstrated more congruence in all three dimensions than did those from lower SES. Sex differences emerged as important only among those of the lower class.

Holdaway, E. A. and J. E. Seger. "Socio-Economic Level and Some School Characteristics." *Alberta Journal of Educational Research* 13, no. 2 (1967): 111-120.

The researchers attempted to discover what differences exist between socio-economic level of school attendance area and educational variables related to the principal, the school building and program, and the teaching staff in forty attendance areas in a western Canadian urban school system. It was found that the principal tended to be more highly trained and teaching fewer hours per week in the higher SES schools. The school buildings tended to be larger, with better equipment and more teaching of oral French in the lower grades in the higher SES areas. The teachers also tended to have had more formal training in the latter areas.

Humphreys, Edward H. "Equality? The Rural-Urban Disparity in Ontario Elementary Schools." *Education Canada* 11, no. 1 (March 1971): 34-39.

A sample of 880 teachers was questioned in 1967, and 720 in 1969. The researcher presents evidence from this study indicating marked disparities in the provision of facilities, personnel and services in favour of urban schools.

Jocas, Yves, and Guy Rocher. "Inter-Generation Occupational Mobility in the Province of Quebec." *Canadian Journal of Economic and Political Science* 23 (February 1957): 58-66.

The authors used a 1954 sample of 1,045 cases drawn from marriage records. Their findings reveal differences between English and French groups, with mobility in general being greater for the English.

Kennett, K. F. "Measured Intelligence, Family Size, and Socio-Economic Status." *Alberta Journal of Educational Research* 19, no. 4 (December 1973): 314-320.

A sample of 144 Sydney, Nova Scotia junior high school children, divided into subgroups according to family size and SES, was tested on the Hennon-Nelson Intelligence Test. The results demonstrated a definite relationship between IQ and SES, and a significant negative correlation between family size and IQ except in the two upper SES groups.

Knill, W. "Occupational Aspirations of Northern Saskatchewan Students." *Alberta Journal of Educational Research* 11, no. 1 (March 1964): 3-16.
This study presents the results of a comparison between the aspirations of Métis-Indian and white students.

Linton, Thomas E. and Donald F. Swift. "Social Class and Ninth Grade Educational Achievement in Calgary." *Alberta Journal of Educational Research* 9, no. 3 (September 1963): 157-167.
This is a preliminary report on a major study of the total population of public school boys who wrote the grade nine departmental examinations in Calgary in June 1962. A significant relationship was found between socio-economic position of the family and the achievement level of the son.

Manning, W. G. "A Follow-up of High School Students Taking Vocational-Technical Courses." *Saskatchewan Journal of Educational Research and Development* 2, no. 1 (Fall 1971): 62-64.
The author reports on the results of a longitudinal study to determine the relative value to Saskatchewan students of secondary school programs involving technical courses, as compared with the value of traditional courses. Two hundred and eighteen matched pairs from twelve high schools were used. Over 50% of the technical group claimed to have chosen their courses because of interest. Only 12% of the academic group claimed this. Over 50% of the academic group admitted to having taken classes only so that they could get into university.

Marsden, L. and E. B. Harvey. "Equality of Educational Access Reconsidered: The Post-Secondary Case in Ontario." *Interchange* 2, no. 4 (1971): 11-26.
The first section of this article discusses a recent report of the Ontario Department of University Affairs which suggests that, in terms of combined family income, economic differentials in access to post-secondary education have been greatly reduced in the past few years. The second section reviews some recent studies concerned with equality of access and suggests that variables other than income may well be equally relevant in a definition of "access." The third section analyses an existing pool of data to test and evaluate hypotheses presented in

the second section. The last section develops conclusions from the findings.

New Brunswick Teachers Association. "Inequalities and Education." *The Educational Review* (November 1964).
This article reports on inequalities in educational opportunities in Canada, concluding that most are economically induced.

Nova Scotia Newstart, Inc. "A Sociographic Comparison of Two Neighbourhoods." Yarmouth, N.S., 1971.
This study indicates that, while the ideology of self-improvement through education is deeply rooted in both the advantaged and disadvantaged communities, parents in the latter report many more problems in providing their children with the level of schooling deemed desirable. In addition, the disadvantaged group expressed lower educational aspirations for their children, and reported considerably more learning difficulties on the part of these children.

O'Reilly, Robert R. "Northern Students Attending Post-Secondary Institutions in Canada, 1966-1967." Canadian Council for Research in Education, Ottawa, 1970.
The author studied a sample of sixty-seven students from the Northwest Territories enrolled in Canadian post-secondary institutions in 1966-67. He found (1) great diversification in fields of specialization, (2) a generally poor academic record (only 27% were qualified for university entrance), (3) 50% said that they would have preferred high school in the south, and (4) 86% had wanted to come south for higher education.

Ossenberg, Richard J. "The Social Integration and Adjustment of Post-War Immigrants in Montreal and Toronto," in W. E. Mann, *Canada: A Sociological Profile*, Toronto; Copp Clark, 1968; 49-57.
The author used a sample of 156 respondents to find that there was a higher rate of social mobility in Montreal for immigrants with little education, and a higher rate in Toronto for the more highly schooled.

Pavalko, Ronald H. "Socio-Economic Background, Ability and Allocation of Students." *Canadian Review of Sociology and Anthropology* 4, no. 4 (1967): 250-259.
In a sample of 889 grade nine and 379 grade thirteen pupils from seven high schools in Thunder Bay, Ontario, it was found that the likelihood of being in grade thirteen increases as IQ increases within each SES (as measured by father's occupation). Among those of comparable ability chances of reaching grade thirteen are better for the higher SES group.

Paterson, Ian W. "Determinants of Expenditures for Education."
   Canadian Education and Research Digest 7, no. 2 (1967): 155-169.
This is the report of an exploration of the socio-economic and educational characteristics of Canada's ten provinces as determinants in
expenditure level for public elementary and secondary education for
the years 1941, 1951 and 1961. Three variables were established as
significant "non policy" determinants: (1) personal income, (2) income
distribution, and (3) primary industry (with the former accounting for
the largest proportion of variance). Significant "policy" determinants
were found to be: (1) enrolments beyond compulsory school age, (2)
number of teachers per thousand pupils, (3) school size, and (4)
teachers' salaries.

Pike, Robert M. *Who Doesn't Get to University and Why: A Study of Access
   to Higher Education in Canada*, A.U.C.T. Ottawa: The Rounge
   Press, 1970.
This is a comprehensive documentation and analysis of enrolments in
institutions of higher education in relation to the population of possible candidates.

Pineo, Peter, and John Porter. "Occupational Prestige in Canada."
   Canadian Journal of Sociology and Anthropology 4, no. 1 (February
   1967): 24-40.
This study of occupational prestige was designed to make possible
rigorous U.S. – Canadian comparisons. Respondents were required to
rank 204 occupational titles. Also ranked were 72 industries and corporations, 36 ethnicities and 21 religions. The average evaluation made of
an occupational title by a national sampling was used to establish the
social standing of that title.

Porter, John. "Social Class and Education," in M. Oliver, ed., *Social
   Purpose for Canada*, pp. 114-127. Toronto: University of Toronto
   Press, 1961.
The author applies the Blishen Scale to 1951 Canadian census data to
show evidence of class bias in high school and university student
cohorts.

Porter, John. "The Economic Elite and the Social Structure of Canada,"
   in W. E. Mann, *Canada: A Sociological Profile*, pp. 126-136. Toronto:
   Copp Clark, 1968.
This is a study of the family, educational, and occupational backgrounds of 907 Canadian resident directors of 107 corporations dominant in the Canadian economy, plus 78 directors of 9 chartered banks
(985 business leaders in all). Of the 118 Canadian-born, 42 graduated

from McGill, 35 from Toronto, and 4 from Queen's; 58.3% had university education, while 34.2% had attended private schools.

Stafford, Jim. "Canadian School Life Tables." *Alberta Journal of Educational Research* 19, no. 1 (1973): 55-65.
School life tables, based on birth cohorts, school participation rates, and mortality rates are constructed for Canada as a whole. Dropout patterns are compared among Canada, the United States and India, showing that Canadian children begin their schooling at a later age than do those in India and the United States, and that their participation rate peaks a year earlier and declines more rapidly thereafter than does the American rate.

Ryan, Thomas J. *Poverty and the Child: A Canadian Study.* Toronto: McGraw Hill-Ryerson, 1972.
This is an extremely valuable source of information and understanding on the problem of poverty and its effect on the learning process of disadvantaged Canadian children.

Subcommittee on Research and Planning, Committee of Presidents of Universities of Ontario. *Towards 2000: The Future of Post-Secondary Education in Ontario.* Toronto: McClelland and Stewart, 1971.
This book includes a great deal of useful information on the present situation, although the authors' conclusions and recomendations are debatable.

Symington, D. F. "Poverty in Rural Canada." *Canadian Geographic Journal* 71, no. 6 (December 1967): 188-197.
The author provides a thought-provoking description of the problem of poverty in rural areas.

Tremblay, Marc-Adélard and Walton J. Anderson, eds. *Rural Canada in Transition,* pp. 9-26. Ottawa: Agricultural Economics Research Council of Canada (June 1966).
This section presents a description of rural-urban migration.

Tu, P.N.V. "Optimal Educational Investment Program in an Economic Planning Model." *Canadian Journal of Economics* 2 (February-November, 1969): 52-64.
A mathematical model is developed to deal with the problem of the proportion of the national product which should be expended on education, and the proportion of the working-age population which should be trained to maximum social utility. The model is only an illustration for one kind of education under assumed conditions, but it provides guidelines for establishing optimal schooling programs, tak-

ing into account relations among educational budgets, the present working-age population, birthrate, average cost per pupil, and other variables.

Vigod, Zena. "The Relationship Between Occupational Choice and Parental Occupation." *Alberta Journal of Educational Research* 18, no. 4 (December 1972): 287-294.

The author's findings indicate that parental socio-economic status is more highly correlated with the pupil's "expected" occupation than his "wished-for" occupation. Correlations between SES and occupational choices are found to be much smaller among girls than among boys.

Wilson, Lolita. "Canadian Indian Children Who Had Never Attended School." *Alberta Journal of Educational Research* 19, no. 4 (December 1973): 309-313.

Thirty Indian children, aged six to twelve years, with little or no formal education, achieved IQ test scores very similar to those of thirty non-Indian school children of the same age and similar socio-intellectual background. The test scores of a third group of school children from intellectually enriched home backgrounds were significantly higher than were those of either of the first two groups. Indian children in a residential school achieved IQ scores similar to those of Group 3.

Zentner, Henry and A. R. Parr. "Social Status in the High School: An Analysis of Some Related Variables." *Alberta Journal of Educational Research* 14, no. 4 (December 1968): 253-264.

The researchers are reporting on a comparison of "leading crowd" members and other students, to discover factors associated with high social status in Canadian high schools. The study involved 766 students from three Calgary high schools.

INDEPENDENT STUDY

Select the research study which most interests you, locate it, and read it carefully.

1   Determine whether the study is documenting:
     a.   an inadequacy in the way the schooling system is functioning as an agent of social mobility,
     b.   the degree and nature of social stratification in Canadian society.
Justify your decision.

2   Select a study exemplifying the other category in the previous question. Compare the findings of the two studies in terms of their significance for enlarging our understanding of the concepts developed in this chapter.

The Concept Amplified
By Further Reading

Broom, Leonard. "Social Differentiation and Stratification," in Merton, R. et al., *Sociology Today* pp. 429-441. New York: Harpers, 1965.
This writer assumes that stratification must follow differentiation, because "certain behaviors are deemed more appropriate in one stratum than another, and because positions in the various strata are not only differentially ordered, but differentially valued."

Coleman, James C. "The Concept of Equality of Educational Opportunity." *Harvard Educational Review* 38, no. 1 (1968): 7-22.
The author traces the evolution of the concept, from its initial meaning as similarity of exposure to a curriculum common to the whole country, through its coming to mean the provision of *different* curricula in order to accommodate differences between children's abilities and aptitudes and therefore differences in their future occupational requirements, to its present meaning of equality of *effectiveness* of schools (assuming necessarily unequal inputs other than physical equipment) in improving the pupil's performance. He suggests the following policy consequences:
1   educational provision is likely to be increasingly fitted to initial differences among entrants, and
2   the responsibility to create achievement will be with the school—not with the child or his family.

Collins R. "Functional and Conflict Theories of Educational Stratification." *American Sociological Review* 36, no. 6 (1971): 1002-1019.
The author examines two contrasting theories to account for the increased levels of schooling required for employment in advanced, industrial society: the technical-functional and the conflict approach. The former argues that technological change calls for new and improved skills. An increase in the educational level of the population is associated with growth in the economy. (Yet the author notes that changing job structure explains only 15% of the change in the levels of schooling required, with the remainder apparently due to increased formal requirements for the same jobs.) The conflict approach, on the other hand, underlines the key role of schooling as the path to membership in elite status groups. Popular demand for increased schooling is thereby explained, in part, by the status it confers. According to this explanation economic expansion, rather than necessitating more schooling for workers, merely leads elite groups to raise their entry levels.

Elder, Glen H. Jr. "Family Structure and Educational Attainment: A Cross-National Analysis." *American Sociological Review* (February 1965): 81-96.
This study found that, across nations, parental dominance was a factor in determining achievement in school. The expectations of significant others was found to be of importance as well.

Greenough, Richard. "Co-education as a World Trend." *School and Society* 98, no. 2322 (1970): 31-32.
This is a note on the UNESCO survey on the status of women, giving international figures on co-education. The report also notes the conflict for many countries between an egalitarian system of schooling and a discriminatory society and employment system.

Halsey, A. H. ed. *Ability and Educational Opportunity.* Organization of Economic Cooperation and Development, Paris, 1961.
A collection of papers delivered at an international meeting of educators and sociologists, all of which acknowledge that the crux of the problem lies in differences associated with social status.

Holt, John. *Freedom and Beyond.* New York: E. P. Dutton and Co., 1972.
This entire book is well worth reading, but the following quotation is particularly relevant: (p. 161) "As long as the overall shape of the job pyramid is not changed, as long as the numbers of good, fair and bad jobs remain about what they are, any poor person who moves up to a better job is going to move up at someone else's expense. He may make it. But that someone else is almost certain to be someone only slightly less poor than he is. When we try to apply on a large scale what works on a small; if we try, through schooling or otherwise, to move large numbers of people from the lower job boxes up into higher ones, the result is to put poor people and working class people . . . into competition for jobs that are scarce."

Jencks, Christopher, and David Riesman. "Social Stratification and Mass Higher Education," in *The Academic Revolution*, pp. 61-154. New York: Doubleday, 1968.
In this chapter the authors attempt to identify the nature and consequences of the relationship between the academic revolution and egalitarianism. They conclude that what America needs most is not more social mobility, even of the meritocratic variety, but more equality; that condemning a man to a lifetime of poverty and drudgery for having a low IQ is really not much better than condemning him for having a black skin or a working-class accent.

Jencks, Christopher, ed. *Inequality.* New York: Basic Books, 1972.
This is a masterly, in-depth documentation and analysis of inequality in America: inequality of opportunity for adequate schooling, of cognitive skills, status, and of income. The authors argue that income inequality must be attacked directly; that it cannot be accomplished merely by equalizing opportunity for schooling.

Kozakiewicz, Nicolaj. "Education and Social Mobility in Poland." *Revue Française de Pédagogie* 13 (1970): 23-37.
A description of how the Polish system of education works, and an analysis of the unequal rates of improvement of the various social classes. The researcher challenges the official ideology of the system with the facts of a survey about

attitudes of young people toward education. Data on inequalities between town and country are presented as well.

Lasswell, Thomas E. "Social Stratification: 1964-1968." *Annals* 384 (1969): 104-134.
A summary of current developments in this area of study. The author reviews the theories, terms and concepts, observational methods, problems and findings in current sociological literature. He concludes that, although no consensus on the theory of social stratification has emerged, there have been significant contributions towards one.

Lenski, Gerhard. *Power and Privilege: A Theory of Social Stratification.* Toronto: McGraw-Hill, 1969.
A comprehensive book which presents an integrated theory of social inequality—a synthesis of the older functionalist and conflict models. The theory postulates as constants, (1) man's social nature, (2) man's self-seeking propensity, (3) unequal endowments, (4) man's reliance on habit and custom, (5) a short supply of rewards, and (6) human societies as imperfect systems.

Lewis, Oscar. "The Culture of Poverty." *Scientific American* 215, no. 4 (October 1966): 19-25.
The author develops the idea that there is a culture produced by people who are members of the underclass in industrialized urban societies which is the result of their relationship to other strata in those societies, and which is probably much more determinative of their values and habits than are the variety of ethnic sub-cultures which they represent.

Lipset, S. M. and R. Bendix. *Social Mobility in Industrial Society.* Berkeley: University of California Press, 1967.
A carefully documented work which argues that social mobility is likely to increase with increases in industrialization.

Porter, John. *The Vertical Mosaic: An Analysis of Social Class and Power in Canada.* Toronto: University of Toronto Press, 1965.
The author analyses the Canadian stratification system at the beginning of the 1960s, in terms of the concepts of social power, elites, and classes.

Terrill, Ross. "The 800,000,000." *The Atlantic Monthly* (November and December 1971).
The author reveals that the top professors in Chinese universities, (even those temporarily involved in manual labour) earn about six times the salary of the lowest-ranking teacher, and over eight times that of the typical factory worker. The writer's data should be more trustworthy than most, as he is a respected scholar, is sympathetic to the Chinese regime, speaks Chinese fluently, and spent an extended period in China before writing the book from which these articles are taken.

Tumin, Melvin H. *Social Stratification: The Forms and Functions of Inequality.* Englewood Cliffs, N.J.: Prentice-Hall, 1967.
The author presents an overview, for the beginning student, of various

sociological explanations of the forms, functions and scope of social inequalities and of the features of social structure that seem to generate and sustain them. He proposes viewing the concept of social stratification as a continuum reaching from total equality to total inequality.

Turner, Ralph H. "Modes of Social Ascent Through Education," in A. H. Halsey, et al. eds., *Education, Economy and Society*, pp. 121-139. Glencoe: The Free Press, 1961.
This article presents a two-category classification system for vertical social mobility by means of schooling: that which differentiates children early and "sponsors" them in various directions assumed appropriate, and that which postpones the differentiation until high school graduation or even junior college, where the "contest" for the narrow upper pathways leading to high status jobs is sudden and fierce.

Wei, Tam T. D., et al. "Piaget's Concept of Classification: A Comparative Study of Socially Disadvantaged and Middle Class Children." *Child Development* 42, no. 3 (1971): 919-927.
Two deprived and two advantaged groups of white children were tested on four of Piaget's classification tests. It was found that the culturally deprived children were progressing at a slower pace than were the advantaged. Differences in reasoning process were also found.

Wrong, Dennis H. "Social Inequality Without Stratification." *Canadian Review of Sociology and Anthropology* 1 no. 1 (February 1964): 5-16.
A useful review of relevant literature, plus a discussion of the need to redevelop and redefine sociological concepts of social stratification, in the light of changing social relationships. He suggests that "social classes" are rapidly disappearing, but that pronounced status inequalities are surviving in modern societies. He advocates abandoning the obsolete "social class" concept and talking instead about "social inequality".

Young, Michael. *The Rise of the Meritocracy, 1870-2033: An Essay on Education and Equality.* (6th. ed.) Harmondsworth: Penguin Books, 1968.
This is a satire on the future evolution of British society from an aristocracy (by the provision of equality of educational opportunity) to a meritocracy and back full circle again to an aristocracy of birth.

The Concept Reviewed

1   "Social Stratification" as it is used in this chapter, stands for: (select the best definition)
  a.   a vertical layering of roles and positions in society, resulting from the inequality of the rewards (of power, prestige and privilege) attached to each
  b.   a horizontal partitioning of roles and positions in society, resulting from the complexity of social organization (or differentiation of social structure)
  c.   the division of society into at least two distinct, inevitably warring classes, easily recognizable by member and observer alike, and based only

on relationship to the means of production

d. the division of society into a number of rigid castes, determined by birth, and considered by the particular society's members to be the result of "natural law."

2 By "vertical social mobility" we mean:

a. the movement of people from one part of the community or country to another

b. the movement of people up or down among unequally rewarded positions in a stratified society

c. the horizontal movement of people from position to position among relatively equally rewarded positions in society

d. the movement of people from one organization to another, regardless of resulting gain or loss in power, authority, or social and economic rewards.

3 The "class" society and the "organizational" one are similar in that:

a. in both the status of the family is determined solely by its position vis a vis the relations of production

b. there is a high degree of vertical social mobility in both

c. in both, the individual's position is typically "ascribed" (assigned by birth) rather than "achieved" through demonstrated competence and/or ambition

d. social stratification (or inequality of rewards and punishments assigned to individuals) is a feature of both.

4 Positions seem to be arranged from top to bottom of the power, prestige and privilege dimensions in human societies in direct relationship to:

a. income

b. degree of safety and pleasantness of surroundings and work

c. associated life style

d. degree of influence over people and events

e. opportunity for lifelong learning

f. opportunity for subsidized travel

g. actual importance to the survival of society

h. degree of responsibility

i. difficulty of tasks involved

j. length of training required

k. all of the above

l. none of the above

m. all but (g), (k) and (l).

5 Which one of the following is not a major function of schooling in the urban society?

a. the socialization of individuals for ascribed roles

b. the allocation of individuals to positions

c. the provision of opportunity for education

d. the provision of opportunity for upward social mobility

6 In a stratified, urban society in which the schooling system performs the function of allocation of people to roles, but fails to evaluate individual learning

validly and reliably, we are likely to find a social structure that is:
   a.   increasingly egalitarian
   b.   increasingly meritocratic
   c.   increasingly corrupt and unstable
   d.   increasingly aristocratic.

7   In a stratified, urban society in which the school system performs the function of allocation, and succeeds in evaluating individual learning validly and reliably, we are likely to find a social structure that is:
   a.   increasingly egalitarian
   b.   increasingly meritocratic
   c.   increasingly corrupt and unstable
   d.   increasingly aristocratic.

8   In a differentiated, but non-stratified urban society in which the schooling system performs the function of allocation, and succeeds in evaluating individual learning validly and reliably, we are likely to find a social structure that is:
   a.   increasingly egalitarian
   b.   increasingly meritocratic
   c.   increasingly corrupt and unstable
   d.   increasingly aristocratic.

9   The assumption that extended schooling can create privilege for individuals implies:
   a.   that if a social group is willing to devote enough of its resources to schooling, all of its members can eventually be above average in power, prestige and privilege
   b.   that opportunity for access to the best schooling will continue to be restricted to a relative few
   c.   that privilege and poverty are absolute rather than relative phenomena
   d.   all of the above
   e.   none of the above.

10   The assumption that there are both rewards and punishments associated with positions in society implies:
   a.   that in order to reduce inequalities, a balance among the total packages of these associated with the various positions must be attempted, with income (as the most readily manipulated) being subjected to a degree of control
   b.   that we need only to equalize income in order to achieve an egalitarian society
   c.   that these will inevitably balance themselves out in any urban society because of the law of supply and demand
   d.   that only a totalitarian government, by applying the threat of force, will ever be able to get its less rewarding and more punishing roles performed.

Answers: 1.(a); 2.(b); 3.(d); 4.(m); 5.(a); 6.(c); 7.(b); 8.(a); 9.(d); 10.(a).

Part Four
Education As An Institution

In attempting to understand education as a process of directed growth or evolution—unique to, and carried out for and by the human species—we must enlarge our perspective even more. It is to the global community of humanity, seen as a social system in its entirety, that we must now look. We can thus begin to conceive of education as mankind's instrument for transmitting, selecting and reconstructing that core of beliefs about the real and the good that holds the human group together and enables them to adapt to their changing physical environment, and to changes in human civilization.

At the classroom level the roles of instructor and learner emerged. At the level of the school we referred to the roles of teacher, pupil, counsellor and administrator. Interaction at the schooling system level was seen to be based on the various roles of the professional educator vis-à-vis professionals representing other organizational complexes in the containing society. And at the final, most comprehensive level of analysis, we are able to see that *institutions* (long-established, yet continuously evolving group ways of doing things) become the interdependent units of interaction that make either the national or international community a social system.

At this particular moment in the history of mankind we find most institutions (such as the family, education, government, business, law and religion) interacting in regular ways only at the national level of community. The global community is still largely an aggregate of relatively isolated national social systems, each striving to maintain a stance of absolute autonomy, or national sovereignty. The various international arms of the United Nations (such as UNESCO and FAO) represent only fledgling attempts to organize, on a world-wide basis, the achievement of certain functions for mankind as a whole.

The concept of one world is still a strange and frightening one for many people. For countless centuries, the geographic boundaries of each human community have been, to its inhabitants, the boundaries of the world. One among other worlds, it is true, but discrete unto itself. With little regular movement or communication among nations, men could live as if social reality were a multiplicity of isolated systems, or social worlds. Some of these worlds could be at war while others were left at peace. Some could adhere to doctrines that others would find irrational or abhorrent. Some could live by a pattern of social organization that others would consider degrading to human beings. But because each social world was relatively independent, the consequences of its way of life would only impinge on other communities if its government made moves to encroach on these others by force.

The era of the nation-state, up to the watershed of the two world wars, was largely the era of a multiplicity of social worlds whose rapidly increasing interrelationships (some cooperative, some competitive) can only be described as informally organized at best, and at worst anarchical. Nations could survive in this potentially inflammable situation only because of their technological, sociological, and cultural isolation from one another. However, since the advent of the Bomb, with the accompanying cybernetic revolution, human beings no longer have the choice of whether or not to become members of one world-wide social system. Technological developments have forced the issue. The more complex our technological tools and their accompanying social organizations become, the more interdependent we necessarily become. Our production and distribution systems, our transportation and communication systems, our energy-transforming and information-processing systems are already world-wide. We have become one world technologically and therefore environmentally. And it now seems clear that we must adapt culturally and socially—by constructing a functioning world social system—or as a species we shall die.

It appears, then, that we are already living in one world. But we are without the values and knowledge concerning human social organization that would enable us to move from a state of world anarchy to a state of world order. (Or, in terms of our conceptual framework, to move from a warring aggregate of nationally sovereign social systems to a global system of interdependent but identifiable national social systems.)

What about the role of education in this adaptive process? When we think of education as an institution we think of its contribution to both continuity and change in human ways of believing and behaving. It is analogous to the vehicle of natural selection by which the species evolved biologically. Beliefs and behaviours that enable human groups to respond effectively to environmental challenges are constructed as well as transmitted through education. Old responses which have worked in the past sometimes become obsolete and must be selected out of the culture and replaced by new ones. This selection process requires people who have not only been deeply informed about the nature and varieties of the culture of all humanity, but who have also been imbued with the spirit of scientific inquiry. Old responses which may well be selected out as their destructive consequences become increasingly apparent to people so educated, may be certain beliefs about tribal superiorities, whether of the nationalist, racist, sexist, class, or cultist variety. Others may be certain beliefs about particular human beings or institutions as the ultimate sources of authority. Some, such as the belief in the efficacy of the reflective and systematic approach to problem-solving, may have to be developed in a much more consistent way than is presently the case in any educational system in the world.

What is selected by the social group to be taught to its young (or what is not selected, through neglect or ignorance of consequences) is the most significant set of choices that any group can make. For the beliefs developed in human beings through that aspect of the socialization-enculturation process which we term education are capable of both maintaining and subsequently reshaping their culture. And, as Julian Huxley claimed, clearly it is now cultural rather than biological evolution which will determine the future of man on planet earth.

7 Culture

The Concept Explained

Culture and *society* are two of the most important, and the most difficult to understand, of all the conceptual tools used by the behavioural scientist. This is probably because they are so all-inclusive. At first glance, each seems to take in everything associated with human beings in group settings. Yet we all know that a concept that includes everything can explain nothing about social phenomena. So our first task in attempting to clarify the concept of culture is to discriminate between those aspects of social reality which it makes sense out of and orders for us and those which the concept of society can best help us to understand. (In the next chapter a third set of aspects of social phenomena which are encompassed by a third all-inclusive concept—that of *personality*—will be dealt with.)

In order to clarify the distinction between culture and society, we can draw once more on the example of the beehive. The bees are involved in a continual process of social interaction based on communication: interaction in which patterns of social organization and even social stratification might become apparent to the observer if he watched long and carefully enough. In other words, there is a society here, but there is no culture. Bee societies do not, in the process of their interacting, produce a pool of beliefs about the good and the real which is shared by their members and passed on to the young by means of a socialization-enculturation process.

Why are humans culture-producers and transmitters and bees not? One explanation for the difference is that most bee behaviour is instinctive, while that of man is learned. Most of what the bee does throughout his life cycle is programmed previous to birth; most of what man does is programmed after birth, through experience. Man has both the need and the ability to adjust his behaviour on the basis of feedback from experience: to construct and reconstruct internalized pictures of his world and to act in accordance with these. Man is intelligent; he is a concept-builder and the bee is not. Is this, then, the key to culture?

But wait—what about a species of animal which is much closer to man in ability to communicate, to establish lasting social organization, and even to conceptualize? The ape does all these things, yet we

...y that although he is hovering on the very brink of culture, he has
...ot quite achieved it. What is the crucial component, missing from
...e societies, but present in those of humans, which allowed the lat-
...r to make that gigantic leap into culture or civilization, and which
...as, so far, restricted the ape to a simpler stage of evolution? The
...nthropologist, George Murdock, points to the missing link in the
...llowing passage:

> Four factors... have been advanced by various writers...
> as explanations of the fact that man alone of all living creatures
> possesses culture—namely, habit-forming capacity, social life,
> intelligence, and language. These factors may be likened to the
> four legs of a stool, raising human behaviour from the floor, the
> organic level or hereditary basis of all behaviour, to the super-
> organic level, represented by the seat of the stool. No other ani-
> mal is securely seated on such a four-legged stool. Many live in
> societies. Some manifest no mean intelligence and habit-forming
> capacity. None, however, possesses language. Just as no one or
> two of these factors alone can suffice to explain culture, so no
> animal can maintain an equilibrium on a stool with but one or
> two legs.

> ... the case of the anthropoid apes is particularly instruc-
> tive. They possess three comparatively well-developed legs
> of the cultural stool, lacking only language. Kohler has de-
> scribed the fads which occur with great frequency in groups
> of chimpanzees. From time to time one of these restless and
> curious animals makes an invention or discovery, e.g., suck-
> ing water through a straw, painting objects with white clay,
> catching ants on a twig moistened with saliva.... The rest
> of the group then takes up the innovation by imitation, and
> for days or weeks the new practice rages with all the vigor of
> a new fashion among humans, only to disappear after its
> novelty has worn off.

> While the fad lasts, it is certainly a group habit, an incipient
> element of culture. Only the absence of language, appar-
> ently, prevents the retention and accumulation of such ac-
> quisitions and their transmission to succeeding generations
> as a social heritage (by means of education and incidental
> socialization). Chimpanzee fads, in short, differ from human
> folkways only in their impermanency.... Little more than a
> time element differentiates the chimpanzee use of straws
> from the modern folkway observable in soft drink
> parlors.... The chimpanzee seems to be in the position of a man
> insecurely perched on a four-legged stool of which one of the

legs is wanting. He can preserve a precarious balance only for a short time before the stool overturns and plunges him and his incipient culture once more to the floor.[1]

We can conclude that the ability to manipulate symbols is the key to culture. Symbolic language frees the individual from the concrete time and place of a specific experience; he can store it in memory or book and retrieve it years after it occurred, to share it with others in far-removed territories. It allows for a socialization-enculturation process which goes beyond direct imitation. It allows for an accumulation of shared and tested beliefs which transcend concrete times and places. It means that individuals need not go back to the water or the caves and begin all over again with each generation. It means that we can learn not only from direct experience, but from the experience of all those generations who went before; that through education in literature, history and science we can stand on the shoulders of giants, and go on from where they left off.

The meaning of culture should now be becoming a bit more clear. Dewey defined it as " . . . a state of interaction of many factors, the chief of which are law and politics, industry and commerce, science and technology, the arts of expression and communication, and of morals, or the values men prize and the ways in which they evaluate them; and finally, though indirectly, the system of general ideas used by men to justify and to criticize the fundamental conditions under which they live—their social philosophy."[2] In other words, culture is the sum total of everything that man produces in the process of his social interaction: everything that is capable of transcending a particular time and place.

Society, on the other hand, is that network of ongoing social interaction, or the encompassing social system, participated in (and thereby continuously in the process of being formed) by the members of the social group located in the neighbourhood or country under consideration. If one can imagine crystallizing such an ongoing process at a particular moment in time, a society can conceivably be represented as a structure comprising horizontal partitions (social organization) and vertical layers (social stratification). A *social group,* in the process of living together in a given territory called a *community,* constructs a continuously evolving pattern of interaction which we call *society,* which, in time, results in the production of a pool of shared beliefs about the meaning, nature and purposes of that in-

[1] George Murdock, *Culture and Society* (Pittsburgh: University of Pittsburgh Press, 1965), pp. 76-77.

[2] John Dewey, *Freedom and Culture,* (New York: Capricorn Books, 1963), p. 23.

teraction among people (as well as their transactions with the physical environment) which we refer to as *culture.*

It is important to understand that culture is organically related to the behaviours of individuals in social systems or societies. Regularities in chosen responses to specific stimuli in the environment result in habit-formation for the individual. Regularities in the habits of a large number of interacting individuals result in group habits, or what we call *social norms.* These norms are the patterns of group interaction that could be identified by the man from Mars with his computer. Examples of norms in a school would be the teachers eating lunch in the staffroom while the students eat in the cafeteria, or teachers smoking only in the staffroom. Norms become established in the culture when they are recognized and believed to be appropriate by the members of the group: when they become shared beliefs about "good" ways of behaving. At this point we call them customs or folkways.

The propensity to form habits which eventually evolve into cultural customs is a characteristic of human beings. Another characteristic is their aptitude for constructing beliefs (or explanations) about the nature of "the real" in the process of their acting upon and experiencing their physical and social environment. As these beliefs are communicated to, shared with, and tested by others through the use of symbolic language (either formally, as with scientific experimentation, or informally, as with commonsense experiencing) they become more or less well verified components of the culture of the society concerned. To the degree that they are highly tested and reliable beliefs (more objective than subjective) we call them *knowledge.* Associated with knowledge is *technology*: beliefs about how to make the specific technical tools for coping with the environment.

Some beliefs that humans share have to do with good ends for men to strive for: desirable states of existence in some other world, or desirable social systems on this planet, or desirable personality characteristics or behaviours. When these are shared by the group to the degree that they are self-evident to the members, we call them the *ideals* of the culture.

This brings us to a rather straightforward definition of culture. It is the accumulated pool of explanations or beliefs shared by the members of the relevant society concerning:

1   appropriate ways of behaving (customs)

2   the nature of "the real" social and physical environment (knowledge)

3   how to apply knowledge in the making of specific tools (technology)

4   desirable end-states of human existence (ideals)

5   how to apply ideals, knowledge and technology in the making of objects of beauty (art and music).

Culture is created by human beings as they interact in societies, and aspects of it are selected, discarded, reconstructed and transmitted from generation to generation by means of the socialization–enculturation process.

Murdock lists seven fundamental characteristics of culture. He says that culture is *learned*. It is not instinctive, or innate, or transmitted biologically but is acquired by the individual in the form of predispositions to act (habits and values) gained, through his own life experience after birth.

Secondly, culture is *inculcated*. The factor of language is vital here. Beliefs are transmitted from parent to child over successive generations and, through repeated inculcation, there are produced customs, knowledge, technology, ideals and art that acquire that persistency over time and that relative independence of individual bearers, which justifies classifying them collectively as culture. Thirdly, culture is *social*. Beliefs are not only inculcated and thus transmitted over time; they are also shared by human beings living in organized societies, and kept relatively uniform by social pressures. Fourth, culture is *ideational*; in other words, more or less consciously conceptualized and verbalized by the group members. (This is why we say it is a pool of beliefs rather than a pool of habits and values, or objects and techniques). Fifth, culture is *gratifying*. Murdock maintains that it always, and necessarily, satisfies basic biological needs and secondary needs derived therefrom. Elements of a culture can continue to exist only when they yield to the individual members of the society a margin of satisfaction, a favourable balance of pleasure over pain.

Sixth, culture is *integrative*. The various elements tend to form a functioning whole (or system) based upon a core of beliefs considered by the members of the society in question to be self-evident. Lastly, Murdock says that culture is *adaptive*. It changes, and the process of change appears to be an adaptive one, comparable to evolution in the organic realm but of a different order. Cultures provide their bearers with the means for coping adequately with their geographic, technical and social environments. As general life conditions change, traditional ways of doing things cease to provide a margin of satisfaction and are eliminated; new needs arise or are perceived and new cultural adjustments are made to them.

The adaptive nature of culture implies a two-fold function for education. Not only is education the means by which the group deliberately structures its socialization process so as to transmit cultural beliefs as efficiently and effectively as possible, but it also has a role to play in the construction of more adequate and reliable beliefs and in the discarding of those which have become impediments to their bearers. Education can thus be seen as the instrument by which a culture is not only perpetuated, but is reconstructed and renewed. It can be the mechanism of cultural stagnation and obsolescence, or of cultural evolution and survival.

So far we have been discussing "culture" rather than "cultures" in the plural. When we refer to the concept in the singular we are usually thinking of the culture of all of humanity, or the phenomenon of culture in general, rather than that of a specific group. However, we must keep in mind that, wherever a number of people are interacting in a social system, a corresponding culture exists. Just as each society is both a sub-system of some larger social system, and the encompassing social system for some smaller micro-society, so too is each culture a sub-culture from the perspective of the larger unit of which it forms a part, and a containing culture for the sub-cultures within it. Each social system (from the school class to the world community) produces its corresponding culture. Each culture is a dynamic set of shared beliefs which shapes the members of the relevant group and at the same time is shaped by them, just as a stream both shapes and is shaped by the pebbles in its bed.

When two groups, representing different ethnicities, religions or classes, and having different societies and cultures, come into contact the inevitable result is *acculturation*. This term refers to the process of cultural change by which the beliefs of the members of each group are affected by those of the other, just as their ways of behaving are altered through mutual imitation. *Integration* in this context is the social process by which the members of the two groups begin to interact with one another to the point where a system of relatively permanent role relationships (leading to cooperation and interdependence) is established, so that ultimately, what were two social systems have, for some purposes at least, become one.

Assimilation, on the other hand, refers to a cultural process which may, or may not, result from integration. Acculturation, which is usually a culture-building process by means of which there is produced a more comprehensive and fruitful pool of beliefs than either of the groups possessed prior to contact, is the more likely consequence. Acculturation takes the form of assimilation only when there is a wholesale replacement by the members of one of the groups of their original pool of beliefs with that of the other group. It can happen because the assimilating culture provides a more effective and satisfying means of dealing with the social and physical environment, or because the members of the assimilating group are perceived by the others to have more status and power, or for a combination of these reasons. As long as the groups are in contact, the process of assimilation can seldom be checked by recrimination, exhortation, or even force. An educational program which succeeds in enhancing the status of the historical carriers of the weaker culture in the eyes of the members of both groups could possibly be effective. However, the most lasting solution to the problem in urban societies has proven to be the successful integration of the carriers of the weaker (or minority) culture into the larger society, to the point where they become relatively prestigious and powerful and then select and exhibit the more valuable components of their original culture, to be woven into the fabric of a new and better whole. The history and contribution of the Ukrainians in Canada is a case in point.

The building of a community (at the neighbourhood, national or global level) demands integration of the relevant social system. It results in a continuous process of acculturation, with a consequent evolution of culture. Only the carriers of static (and therefore already dying) cultures fear acculturation. However, the carriers of all cultures have reason to fear assimilation, for it implies the total loss of cultural identity.

In considering cultural change we can think of the culture of the family, the peer group, the classroom, the ethnic community, the nation or the world community. Each individual is contributing to and being influenced by a number of these "levels of culture" at once. Each level is undergoing rapid change as a result of the process of diffusion being accelerated by modern transportation and communication. Some people fear that urbanization will do away with cultural differences, that eventually we will arrive at one homogenized global culture. However, this would happen only if we all became members of one and only one social system: if the world community were to become the simple, monolithic rural society writ large, rather than the complex network of intricately interrelated variable social systems that seems to characterize the urban society.

One can conclude from Dewey's theories that, as long as the scientific temper is encouraged in human beings, they will be system builders. Experimentally oriented humans will continually form and re-form groups around different goals and functions in response to varying environmental demands and in the service of unique individual values and innovative beliefs. Many social systems will remain small enough to allow for primary, or fact-to-face interaction, for there are some functions such as that of procreation, and early socialization (and perhaps most education) that cannot be carried on effectively in large social settings. For other purposes, such as control of pollution and skyjacking, the relevant society must be world-wide.

Every social system (large or small) inevitably produces culture as a product of its ongoing interaction. Interaction inevitably varies with the objectives and functions of the group, which in turn depend upon differences in environmental demands and the values and habits of individual members. It seems, therefore, that both cultural diversity and cultural commonality are likely to be part of the human condition for a long time to come.

Education can contribute to both. In order to understand how this may occur, let us look at the Canadian situation. Here we have what is called a condition of cultural pluralism. At least three major levels of culture impinge upon many Canadians: that of the ethnic group (as mirrored by the family), that of the national society, and that of the world community. In nations with monolithic cultures, only the national level pertains, and the function of education is simply to inculcate the customs and ideals of the national culture. (Because knowledge and technology are universal, these aspects of culture inevitably belong to the global level and often present a problem for societies with monolithic cultures; sooner or later they tend to undermine unchallengeable cultural assumptions.)

A society such as the Canadian one, which is attempting to maintain a pluralistic culture, faces the difficult task of reconciling these three levels of culture. Education is expected to equip the individual to function at each level. It is expected to teach him enough of the customs, ideals and arts of his ethnic culture so that he can remain an "insider" in his home community, and can contribute elements of his family heritage to the evolving national culture. It is expected to give him the common core of customs, ideals and arts that define him as Canadian, and which provide the glue which holds the national society together. And it is expected to equip him with the scientific knowledge and technical tools which will enable him to cope effectively in the world community, and to move easily up and down among these three levels.

Education is considered to be one of the institutions in any society. We conceptualize institutions as components of both society and culture; they are the bridge between the two. They are the means by which societies produce and perpetuate culture. Just as individual roles develop in any simple social system such as a classroom (as interdependence is established among the members) so, too, do group roles evolve in a complicated social system such as a society. These group roles are performed not by one individual, but by large numbers of individuals interacting within informal groupings, social systems, or formal organizations. We could say that these group roles are carried out by organizations (or complexes of organizations) rather than by individuals, and that each of these complexes contributes to one aspect of the functioning of the society. At least five such group roles seem to be crucial to the functioning of any human society:

1   regulation of sex and procreation of the species
2   socialization and enculturation of the young
3   protection of the weaker members from arbitrary power wielded by the strong
4   production and distribution of the group's resources
5   determination of priorities for the group and the translation of these into action.

The major function to which all five of these contribute is the adaptation of the social group to changing environmental demands so as to provide for the group's long-term survival.

The complexes of organizations which surround these group roles provide the means by which group beliefs are perpetuated from generation to generation, and a degree of continuity and predictability is ensured for the society as a whole. We call these group roles, and the organizational structures encompassing them, institutions. The family is the institution which performs the first of the group roles listed above, and its structure may vary from the extended to the nuclear to the communal form. The second function is handled by education, religion, the communications media and, again, by the family. The third is the responsibility of the law; the fourth, the economy; and the fifth, government. As with the family, the organized structures by means of which the law, the economy, government and education function vary considerably over time and from society to society. In addition, institutions may expand their functions, or lose them and gradually wither away.

Although institutions transcend the life spans of the unique individuals who participate in them, at any particular time in a particular society, they are no more and no less than the products of complexes of individuals, behaving in accordance with their habits and values. One of the most serious mistakes of early sociologists (especially of the Durkheim school[3]) was to "reify" institutions: to attribute to them some sort of mysterious, unchanging social power and causal priority where human behaviour was concerned. Institutions are to society what role expectations are to the individual. They predispose the members of the society to cope with their crucial group functions according to certain established patterns. However, these patterns are

[3] Emile Durkheim, a French scholar who wrote during the latter part of the nineteenth century, is considered one of the founders of modern social science.

amenable to change in response to changing environmental circumstances, just as roles are. But if the habitual behaviour of any one individual and the roles of any one organization are difficult to change, how much more difficult is institutional change likely to be, when it is dependent upon the gradually changing habits, values and role expectations of countless participating individuals?

We could say that institutions provide the structure or framework of a group's culture. They are the enduring sets of responses to environmental conditions which have grown out of and are based upon the customs, ideals, knowledge, technology and arts produced by the members of the society in the ongoing process of their social interaction.

The following analogy may help to clarify this:

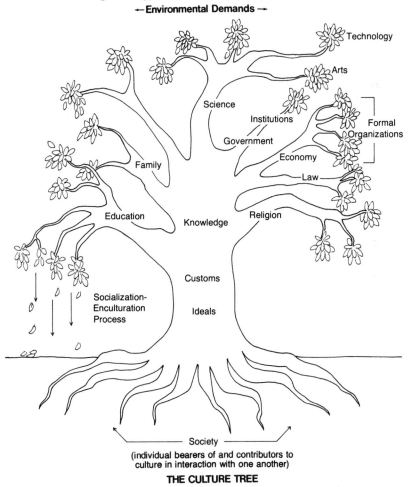

THE CULTURE TREE

The small branches of the tree are analogous to the various types of formal and informal organizations encompassing any one institution. Where culture is allowed to grow haphazardly, it is these organizational forms that tend to respond first to changing environmental demands (especially to changes resulting from the introduction of technology), gradually producing changed habits in the individuals operating within them. A cultural lag results from the slowness of corresponding changes, especially in the ideals. The more desirable sequence of cultural change would be from the surrounding environment to the knowledge component of the trunk to ideals to individual behavioural change to organizations to technology which in turn would alter the environment.

Society is pictured here as the root system out of which the culture tree grows. If the culture provides a way of life for its bearers which allows them to cope adequately with environmental demands, then they will maintain that culture. If it does not, its bearers will join another society (root system) with a more viable and gratifying culture, or will sprout new offshoots, or will dry up and die.

The analogy begins to break down when we try to picture the socialization-enculturation process by means of which the culture is perpetuated. However, we can think of the leaves as the beliefs of the culture which fall to nourish the roots, in combination with rain and other nutrients from the environment. If we could imagine the entire process (by which the branches are formed, and the leaves and fruits are produced and enrich the soil) being directed by the roots through the planned provision and application of the sap (knowledge) by means of the education branch, we could begin to appreciate what Dewey saw as the desirable relationship of education to human culture.

John Dewey's concern was that the culture of humanity is evolving continually, but not necessarily in a rational or systematic or humanly fulfilling way. It is evolving randomly and haphazardly, in the wake of uncontrolled technological drift. The problem would seem to be the divorce of organized intelligence (the scientific construction of knowledge) from the values of the individual and the ideals of the culture. Thus divorced from values and human goals, the process of knowledge-construction tends more and more to take its direction from technology. Technical advance creates problems which scientists subsequently pursue; the tools available determine what will be measured, and so on. At the same time, ideals and values become more and more incompatible with human experience: more and more unrealistic and irrational.

But this need not be so. Within the culture, the realm of scientific knowledge-construction need not be separated from that of ideals;

within the individual, beliefs about the good and beliefs about the real need not be rigidly compartmentalized. For the situation to be different, however, a change in our educational procedures and objectives is required.

Education is the means by which the members of a society deliberately renew or alter or perpetuate their culture. It is therefore a major potential source of either cultural change or cultural stagnation. If it is to provide for the transmission and continuous reconstruction of human culture, it will have to cause the scientific attitude to permeate every institution, just as the sap must be allowed to nourish every branch of the tree. It must encourage a continuous interplay between ideals and customs and scientific knowledge, allowing no institution to be based on beliefs which cannot withstand the light of reason and scientific inquiry.

A study of the sociology of education leads us to conclude that education for a democratic culture must be concerned, above all else, with the development of reasoning abilities, wisdom and morality in the individual. For by no other means will cultural evolution be guided collectively by all of the members of society in a rational way into directions conducive to the enrichment of life on this planet. And for such individual wisdom and morality everyone must become a scientist in the broad sense in which the sociologist views himself as a scientist: the sense of acting upon one's total environment in a systematic way, and utilizing the body of reliable knowledge already constructed, in predicting the consequences of action.

The Concept Demonstrated

CASE STUDY ONE

Mr. Larré, the principal of the French and English high school in the New Brunswick town, had been expecting trouble ever since the Quebec Legislative Assembly had passed its controversial Bill 22. To Mr. Larré, the bill seemed to spell the denial of the principle of bilingualism as far as Quebec was concerned. Because his school had a major investment in that principle, and because he himself had devoted most of his professional career to the goal of achieving bilingualism in fact as well as in law in his own province of New Brunswick, Mr. Larré was worried. He knew that many of his friends and neighbours, both English and French-Canadian, were worried also.

Trouble began in a minor way the following autumn. The town's only high school had been teaching many of the subjects in both English and French for several years. This experiment had been supported by a majority of the parents in both the English and French-speaking communities. Both sets of parents had encouraged their children to attempt some of their high school subjects in the second language. However, only a small number of the Anglophones were, as yet, taking their schooling in French, in contrast to the high proportion of the Francophones who were studying almost completely in English. This was understandable (although not excusable) in view of the fact that so few of the elementary schools were actually teaching in French. Mr. Larré and a group of concerned parents from both language groups had been trying, for some time, to correct this imbalance. But progress had been slow.

A minority of the parents from both linguistic communities seemed to have been aroused to considerable excitement by Bill 22. A vocal group comprising what Mr. Larré termed the French intellectual elite began a series of meetings, attended by numerous high school students, at which speakers attacked the very concept of an integrated school system. They argued that in spite of the fact that the town was rather evenly divided between the two ethnic groups, the schools were, in reality, operating so as to make "little Anglos" out of everybody. They maintained that the community's French-Canadian culture was being eroded rapidly as a result.

A group of English-speaking people, who for some time had opposed the teaching of French in the public schools, now began to rally anew to their cause. Argument waxed hot and heavy during the fall months, with the two small newspapers (one French and one English) entering the fray on opposite sides. The members of the school board (who were fairly evenly divided as to ethnic origin) were bombarded with demands for a parallel school system, beginning immediately with the opening of a second, all-French, high school.

Recognizing that such a move would spell the destruction of their tender experiment in biculturalism, the school board stood firm. The conflict in the community continued until, as Mr. Larré had feared, it began to spill over into the high school. Students began to carry placards in the hallways calling for an end to assimilation by the English. The situation worsened in spite of the efforts of Mr. Larré and his staff to keep the two groups talking to one another.

Before long classes had come to a standstill as students marched in the streets, or sat-in around entrances and offices. The student leaders on each side were now vehement in their demands for a school of their own. They were joined by most of the student body in their claim that the bilingual school was nothing but a farce and a façade, just as a bicultural Canada, under the present federal system, was nothing but a vain dream.

The time came when even Mr. Larré began to wonder if he, and the members of the community who had favoured one integrated, bilingual system of schooling for New Brunswick, had been mistaken in assuming that this was the way to build a strong and peaceful Canada. Perhaps it *was* just an impossible dream. Or worse, perhaps it was, as the student marchers claimed, merely a roundabout way of arriving at an American-style melting pot. Still, his reason and all that he knew of human social behaviour told him that if a bicultural federalism could not be maintained in Canada, a country so richly favoured in its resource base and its history of pluralism, tolerance and compromise, then all hope for human cooperation on a global scale might just as well be abandoned. And that pessimistic conclusion Mr. Larré refused to accept.

QUESTIONS FOR GROUP DISCUSSION

1   In your opinion, is it likely that an integrated educational system will contribute to the integration of a pluralistic community? Justify your response in terms of the concept of culture.

2   Was it acculturation or assimilation that the French-speaking intellectual elite feared? Explain by referring to the issue of Quebec separatism.

3   What do you predict would be the consequences of a successful student strike for the society and culture of the community in question?

4   Does it seem that the school board had been using educational means designed to accomplish a dynamic acculturation rather than an assimilation of the French-Canadian culture? Discuss. If you think that they were not, what should they have been doing?

CASE STUDY TWO

Carlotta Schmidt had always intended to go back to teaching after her children grew up and left home. The opportunity came when she heard that a Hutterite colony located not too far from her farm home was without a teacher for the English-language public school they were required by law to operate in addition to their own German-language, religious one. As Carlotta spoke almost fluent German as well as English, she was eagerly accepted and welcomed to the post by the members of the colony.

During the fall, Carlotta commuted to her school from the farm, a distance of some thirty miles. However, with the onslaught of winter, she decided to stay in the little teacherage on the colony from Monday to Friday, relying upon her husband to come for her on weekends. She felt that this would give her more time for getting to know her pupils, and to prepare lessons and provide extra help for those who needed it. Besides, the roads in the district frequently became impassable, making daily travel a constant source of worry.

With her extra time, Carlotta began to establish a few social relationships with her forty-seven pupils. The little ones were so shy that this was a slow process, but the grade seven and eight boys and girls responded readily to her offers of friendship. They loved to read the German books which she began to supply for them, although reading in English was obviously a distasteful chore which they suffered only when forced to struggle through a reader or arithmetic problem. They began to enjoy coming to her teacherage and admiring her possessions. To them, Mrs. Schmidt seemed to live in an exciting and almost magic world.

The youngsters especially loved to watch the TV and to listen to the radio and record player that Carlotta had brought over from the farm. Carlotta monitored their viewing and listening very carefully, however, as she was aware of their parents' and elders' objections to the obsession with violence, sex, and material possessions which was portrayed by the media as representative of the larger, Canadian culture. On the other hand, when a good educational, science, or public affairs program was available she encouraged these older pupils to watch or listen, for she was convinced that the lack of intellectual stimulation and cultural perspective provided by their daily experience was having a stultifying effect on their learning.

Not long after the New Year, the superintendent for the school division visited Carlotta. He had received an informal complaint from the head of the colony about the undesirable influence that the new teacher was having upon the colony's children.

"You have got to realize," he told Carlotta, "that the objective of schooling for these people is quite different from what it may be to you. All they want from the public school is the foundation of communication in the English language, and computational skills, that will enable their youth to engage in a trading or market relationship with the larger society. They definitely do not want the school to equip their children for a wide choice of future jobs in the Canadian society. They train their children for their own appropriate adult roles themselves: roles that include that of farm engineer, mechanic, electrician, plumber, and health-care specialist, as well as cook, laundry woman, seamstress, gardener, pig man and goose man. But most of all, they do not want the public school to interfere in value formation; this they see as the function of their own German school. Their ideals and customs are in most cases so dramatically opposed to ours, that only conflict and unhappiness would result from exposing their children to our ways."

Carlotta discussed the problem with her husband on the following weekend. How could any teacher teach, she wondered, under such strictures? But she understood, too, the point of view of the Hutterite people. How could they hope to keep their culture intact, and thereby maintain their colony, if she and her school, like the Trojan horse, subverted it from the inside?

QUESTIONS FOR GROUP DISCUSSION

1   What do you think Carlotta Schmidt considered the chief cultural function of education to be? Explain the basis for your opinion. How did this compare or contrast with the position of the Hutterite elders as to the major cultural function of education?

2   Which of the two schools attended by the Hutterite children do their parents and elders intend should provide them with an education? Which, with some necessary rudiments of training? Explain your answer in terms of their reaction to Carlotta's introduction of German-language books and media programs into her curriculum.

3   To what degree have the Hutterite colonies integrated successfully with the larger Canadian society? To what degree and by what means do they refuse to allow contact? How is this working in terms of the maintenance of their culture?

4   What consequences do you think would follow from the integration of Hutterite children into the schools of the surrounding community: for the children? for the Hutterite society and culture?

CASE STUDY THREE

The Indian residential school in the northern Alberta mixed-farming community had been closed for five years when the native people began to express considerable dissatisfaction with the results of the change. Their earlier expectations that the integrated school would provide their children with better opportunities for academic success seemed not to have materialized. In fact they were beginning to suspect that even fewer of their youth were completing high school than before. And of the few who had managed to get high school diplomas, none seemed to have found regular jobs either in the surrounding district or in the city.

The more discerning and thoughtful of the Cree and Métis parents in the district had begun to pose serious questions about the goals and procedures of the public school system. They were objecting to the quotas which placed arbitrary limits on the number of native children allowed in any one of the district's public schools. They were objecting to the curricula and the teaching materials that seemed so unrelated to their children's home experience. They were beginning to resent, also, the attitudes of many of the teachers and school board officials, who seemed to view the native children as problem cases which they would prefer not to have to bother with.

A few of the younger and more vocal of the Indian leaders were expressing other sorts of objections. They began to demand, not the return of the church-dominated residential school, nor even of the Indian Affairs–dominated reserve school system. Instead, their demands had to do with Indian control of all things involving Indians. Only when they determined their own curriculum and hired and fired their own teachers would they be satisfied. They viewed education as the crucial key to the welfare of their poverty-stricken people. They knew that it was somehow related to the ability to acquire funds and to make the reserves in the district into successful farming units, but they were not sure, as yet, just how this was to be accomplished.

They saw education, too, as the means of maintaining a separate Indian identity, as distinct from that of the white man. "In the past," they said, "education was used by the Whites to take our children into the cities and destroy them. It was used to take our culture from us and destroy it. Now we want an education that will keep our children on the reserves and will keep them Indian!"

The controversy came to a head when the members of the two reserves in the district suddenly withdrew all their children from the public schools. They set up two schools of their own, staffed by parents and a few young white graduates of the education faculty who volunteered to help them get established. The move came as a surprise to the white community, most of whom were convinced that their attempt at integration had been going well. To the school board and the Indian Affairs Branch, who had been cooperating in the effort, it was also unexpected. Many representatives of the white community expressed concern about the narrowness of the educational goals cited by the Indian dissenters, and the degree to which such schooling would limit the future life chances of the Indian children. Governments at all levels trod carefully, for no one wanted to see an inflammation of the racial prejudices smouldering on both sides.

QUESTIONS FOR GROUP DISCUSSION

1   Compare and contrast the Indian and Hutterite situations in terms of culture-contact between a minority and majority group. How do the histories of the experiences of the two groups differ? To what degree has each been successful in maintaining a distinct and viable culture? Explain the difference, applying concepts from this chapter.

2   At this point in time, what are the possible advantages of an integrated education for Canada's native people? For the rest of the Canadian citizens?

What are the possible disadvantages for each of these groups?

3   Discuss the possible advantages and disadvantages, for the Indian culture, of a segregated educational experience. What effect might this have on Canada as a society? On the future evolution of Canadian culture?

4   In your opinion, by what educational means might the Indian people achieve that balance of proficiency among levels of culture which would maximize their life choices in an urban society, while preserving the best parts of their culture as well as the unity and identity of Canada as a nation?

5   Might one aspect of this problem be the general ineffectiveness of the schools in providing for the optimal development of *all* pupils, with their failure to help the Indian children being merely more visible to all concerned? Discuss in terms of the concept of socialization.

The Concept Applied
To Relevant Canadian Research

Bowd, A. D. "Some Determinants of School Achievement in Several
     Indian Groups." *Alberta Journal of Educational Research* 18, no. 2
     (1972): 69-76.
This study examines the relative importance of vocabulary, general intelligence, language background and SES in determining the grade level achieved by Indian boys aged 12-14 in western Canada. Accepting the distinction between present ability and educability for peoples undergoing acculturation, it was anticipated that, while general intelligence would be a satisfactory predictor of achievement among white children, vocabulary and SES would be the most important for Indian groups. This hypothesis received general confirmation.

Chubb, Sally. "Toil and the Peaceful Life." *Arbos* (May-June 1966):
     15-23; 35.
This is a descriptive, historical type of study of the Doukhobors in Saskatchewan.

Elkin, F. *The Family in Canada.* Ottawa: Vanier Institute, 9th ed. 1971.
This book contains valuable data on variations in Canadian family life: for example, the degree to which the children of various ethnic groups attend school. The chapters on "The Rural Family," on "Ethnic and Immigrant Families in Canada" and "The Family in French Canada" are especially relevant.

Francis, E. K. "The Adjustment of a Peasant Group to a Capitalistic Economy: The Manitoba Mennonites." *Rural Sociology* 17 (1952): 218-228.

This is a historical study which indicates that the process of acculturation occurring when a minority subculture is confronted by the larger containing culture need not result in wholesale assimilation. "By developing new behavior patterns and institutions which are unlike both those of the parent culture and those of the host society, an ethnic group may be able to... continue to function as a distinctive social subsystem."

Havel, J.E. "Some Effects of the Introduction of a Policy of Bilingualism in the Polyglot Community of Sudbury." *Canadian Review of Sociology and Anthropology* 9, no. 1, (1972): 57-70.

The researcher is reporting on a survey of school children in grades four to nine in Sudbury, Ontario. His data indicate that the bilingual policy of the governments of Canada and Ontario has inspired optimism among French Ontarians concerning the future of their language. Parents who, ten years ago, would have sent their children to English schools now send them to French ones. French is now spoken more often in the home. English remains dominant, but its role is changing.

Hawthorne, H.B., ed. *A Survey of the Contemporary Indians of Canada.* Vol. 11, *Economical, Political, Educational Needs and Policies.* Ottawa: Queen's Printer, 1968.

This is an extremely comprehensive study of past ideologies, current practices and future needs in the education of the Indian people of Canada.

Hobart, C. W., and C. S. Brant. "Eskimo Education, Danish and Canadian: A Comparison." *Canadian Review of Sociology and Anthropology* 3, no. 2 (May 1966): 47-66.

The authors analyse data from six months of fieldwork in the Canadian Arctic during 1963 and 1964, plus one and a half months' research in Greenland in 1965. Over two hundred interviews were conducted during this process. It was concluded that, while the direction of change has been toward "cultural synthesis" in both cases, the magnitude of such change has been very great in the Danish case and very slight in the Canadian one. It is suggested that in Canada, so far, the main result of educational efforts has been "cultural displacement."

Hobart, Charles W. "Eskimo Education in the Canadian Arctic." *Canadian Review of Sociology and Anthropology* 7, no. 1 (1970): 49-69.

This paper reviews the literature on teacher characteristics, curriculum and classroom teaching techniques as these relate to effectiveness in teaching Indian and Eskimo children. There follows a consideration of the extent to which ideal teacher and curriculum characteristics and teaching techniques are found in northern classrooms, based on published literature and the author's research in the north in the spring of 1969. The author suggests that ill-trained Eskimo teachers might teach the early grades more effectively than white, formally qualified teachers. He refers to such an experimental program in Nouveau Quebec, where Eskimo teachers, using special material, employ Eskimo as the initial language of instruction.

Hostetler, John A., and Calvin Redekop. "Education and Assimilation in Three Ethnic Groups," *Alberta Journal of Educational Research* 7, no. 4 (December 1962): 189-203.

The authors present a classification of three minority groups: U.S. Amish, Old Colony Mennonites of Alberta, and the Alberta Hutterites, in terms of assimilation and dissolution. They also indicate some support for the hypothesis that "a group will resist dissolution to the degree that it can 'control' the educational offensive of the great society and exploit it to their own advantage."

Jaenen, C. J. "French Public Education in Manitoba." *Revue de l'Université d'Ottawa* 38, no. 1 (January-March 1968): 19-34.

This is a historical-sociological study of the status of French in Manitoba public schools, from Confederation to the passing of Bill 59 in 1967 which made French once more an official language of instruction in the province.

Jansen, Clifford J. "Assimilation in Theory and Practice: A Case Study of Italians in Toronto," in J. E. Gallagher and R. D. Lambert, eds., *Social Processes and Institutions: The Canadian Case*, pp. 466-474. Toronto: Holt, Rinehart and Winston, 1971.

This is an analytical study of previously gathered data on the Italian population of Toronto, with a view to assessing the degree of assimilation into the larger Canadian culture. The author concludes that the process is proceeding very slowly.

Johnson, Henry. "The Doukhobors of British Columbia: The History of a Sectarian Problem in Education." *Queen's Quarterly* 70, no. 4 (Winter 1964): 528-541.

This is a descriptive study of the history of the Doukhobors in Saskatchewan and British Columbia, and the long-term conflict of the orthodox group with the B.C. provincial government over the compulsory school attendance laws.

Lambert, W. and E. Anisfeld. "A Note on the Relationship of Bilingualism and Intelligence." *Canadian Journal of Behavioral Science* 1 (1969): 123-128.

This report re-examines the findings of an earlier (1962) study on the relationship of bilingualism and intelligence, in order to correct misunderstandings about how the original samples of students were selected and tested. Since an apparently positive relationship between intelligence and bilingualism is involved, the various possible interpretations of the findings are considered. For example, the possibility that bilingualism affects intelligence favourably has received considerable support in recent research, some of which is discussed.

Lambert, Ronald M., and James Curtis. "Nationality and Professional Activity Correlates Among Social Scientists: Data Bearing on Conventional Wisdoms." *Canadian Review of Sociology and Anthropology* 10, no. 1 (1973): 62-80.

The authors offer an analysis of data from a recent Canadian Sociological and Anthropological Association survey of members to provide perspective on propositions raised in current debates on the nature of Americanization of academe in Canada.

Lawton, S. B., and G. P. O'Neill, "Ethnic Segregation in Toronto's Elementary Schools." *Alberta Journal of Educational Research* 19, no. 39 (1973): 195-201.

This study examines the effect of incidental ethnic segregation on school achievement as it relates to the Toronto public elementary school system. Segregation indexes were calculated for each ethnic group and attempts were made to account for observed differences. The findings indicated that the Portuguese and Italian pupils were the most segregated while the Chinese and Greek pupils were the least. No conclusions could be drawn as to the effect of ethnic segregation on academic achievement.

Lee-Whiting, Brenda B. "First Polish Settlement in Canada." *Canadian Geographic Journal* (September 1967): 108-112.

This is a descriptive study of the history of the Polish immigrant group at Wilno and Barry's Bay, Ontario.

Lipset, S. M. "Canada and the U.S.: A Comparative View." *Canadian Review of Sociology and Anthropology* 1, no. 1 (1964): 173-185.

The author claims that institutional structures and values (cultural ideals) have been found to be clearly interrelated. The author found Canadians to be less egalitarian in education, more respectful of the law, more prone to grant civil liberties to minorities, less competitive or achievement oriented, and more pluralistic than Americans.

MacKay, R. A. *Newfoundland: Economic, Diplomatic and Strategic Studies.* Toronto: Oxford University Press, 1946; pp. 157-163.

This section contains a documentation of segregation along religious lines as perpetuated by the school system of the province of Newfoundland.

Millett, Don. "Religion as a Source of Perpetuation of Ethnic Identity," in D. I. Davies and K. Herman, eds. *Social Space: Canadian Perspectives,* pp. 174-176. Toronto: New Press, 1971.

This is a study of ethnic churches as perpetuators of diversity in the Canadian culture.

Nagler, Mark. "Patterns of Social Adjustment of Indians in the City," in Davies and Herman, *Social Space: Canadian Perspectives,* pp. 123-131. Toronto: New Press, 1971.

This is a study of the problems of adjustment encountered by Indians in Toronto.

Rattan, M. S. and R. S. MacArthur. "Longitudinal Prediction of School Achievement for Métis and Eskimo Pupils." *Alberta Journal of Educational Research* 14, no. 1 (1969): 37-41.

For three samples of Métis and Eskimo pupils, several culture-reduced measures of general intellectual ability are shown to have substantial validity in predicting school achievement over three-to-four year periods.

Saruk, Alec, and Metro Gulutson. "Academic Performance of Students and the Cultural Orientation of their Parents." *Alberta Journal of Educational Research* 16, no. 3 (1970): 189-195.

Pupils of Ukrainian descent in northeastern Alberta (N=587) were divided into four groups according to the cultural orientation of their parents: "bicultural," "English," "Ukrainian," and "apathetic." The groups were compared as to their performance on the grade nine departmental exams, on a standard reading test (STEP), and on school and college ability tests. No significant differences were found among the groups.

Schwartz, Mildred. "Barriers to Consensus on Canadian Identity," in
M. Schwartz, *Public Opinion and Canadian Identity*, pp. 146-171.
Berkeley: University of California Press, 1967.

This chapter contains an analysis of data from available Gallup polls
taken in Canada since 1940. Answers on specific issues—revealing
great diversity in values—are related to religion, region, ethnic origin,
etc.

Shimpo, Mitsuro and Robert Williamson. *Socio-Cultural Disintegration
among the Fringe Saulteaux.* Centre for Community Studies, University of Saskatchewan, April 1965.

A comprehensive report of a study probing the causes of the social
pathology of large numbers of Indians on the reserves near Kamsack,
Saskatchewan. The researchers identify the problem as the breakdown
of the traditional culture and society, while, at the same time an
inadequate education prevented the Indians from being able to comprehend the institutions of the larger Canadian society in which they
found themselves.

Thompson, Laura and John Hostetler. "The Hutterian Confession of
Faith: A Documentary Analysis." *Alberta Journal of Educational
Research* 16, no. 1 (March 1970): 29-45.

The authors present the results of an experimental attempt to formulate the traditional charter of the Hutterian Brethren from sixteenth
century source documents. Original texts are analysed in terms of five
categories developed for the purpose of cross-cultural comparison.
The purpose of the analysis is to provide a basis for illuminating the
problem of change in cultural belief systems, and to demonstrate a
scientifically valid method of charter analysis, using historical sources.

Thomson, Keith H. "Religious Institutions in Alberta Public Schools."
Alberta Journal of Educational Research 13, no. 1 (1967): 65-73.

A study of the extent to which public schools take advantage of existing
legal provisions for religious education. A sample of the Alberta
schools exclusive of those in Calgary and Edmonton was used. It was
found that 75% of the superintendents, principals, and teachers questioned favoured discontinuance of the provision. The same proportion
favoured retention of religious opening observances each morning.
Only 18.5% of the schools were currently offering religious instruction. The greatest concentration of these was in the northern half of the
province.

"In Search of a Sense of Community," *Time,* April 6, 1970, pp. 8-11.

The history of Negro settlers in Canada is briefly described. The essay comments on the lack of black ghettos, as well as lack of a sense of cohesion with others of similar skin colour, which is characteristic of Negroes in Canada.

Turner, G. H., and D. J. Penfold. "The Scholastic Aptitude of Indian Children of Caradoc Reserve." *Canadian Journal of Psychology*, 6 (1952): 31-44.

The authors compare Indian children of Muncey, Ontario with white children from the surrounding rural districts, on group tests of intelligence. The sample comprised about 240 Indian children and 215 white children, aged 6-13. The Indian children did as well as average whites on the performance scale of the individual Wechler Intelligence Scale for Children, but did more poorly on the verbal scale of the WISC, and on the three group intelligence tests employed. For any given school grade, the age of the Indian children was, on the average, greater by six months or more.

Turner, J. M. A. "The Common Campus Concept." *Education Canada* 9, no. 1 (1969): 44-47.

A descriptive case study of a new type of polyvalent secondary school complex in Lachute, Quebec, in which a Catholic, French-speaking school board and a Protestant, English-speaking school board have combined French-speaking and English-speaking schools on the same campus. A common day program with a common code of behaviour is carried on. The combined school is seen as a means of survival and cooperative growth of components of Canada's cultural mosaic.

Vernon, P. "Education and Intellectual Development Among Canadian Indians and Eskimos." *Educational Review* 18 (1966): 79-91, 186-195.

The sample for this study consisted of fifty Eskimo and forty Indian boys, aged about eleven years, interviewed and tested in northern schools. The author concludes that all aspects of the Indian culture tend to contribute to the deficiencies in language and conceptual development which he found to be more characteristic of the Indians than of the genetically similar Eskimos.

Wangenheim, Elizabeth. "The Ukrainians: A Case Study of the 'Third Force'," in Peter Russell, ed., *Nationalism in Canada*, pp. 72-91 Toronto: McGraw-Hill of Canada, 1966.

The author presents a descriptive analysis of the group as a Canadian sub-culture. Changes in their position regarding education are noted.

Winks, R. W. "Negro School Segregation in Ontario and Nova Scotia." *Canadian Historical Review* 50, no. 2 (June 1969): 164-191.

A descriptive study of the great diversity of sources from which Canadian Negro people have originated. The author describes how, in the two provinces in which they were most numerous, they were progressively restricted from access to the public schools until, by 1850, both Ontario and Nova Scotia had introduced segregated school systems. Only in 1965 was the last segregated school in Ontario closed, and the last four in Halifax County, N.S., soon after.

Yatsushiro, T. "The Changing Eskimo: A Study of Wage Employment and the Consequences Among the Eskimos of Frobisher Bay, Baffin Island." *Beaver* (Summer 1962): 19-25.

A report of field research conducted in 1958-59, in which the researcher examines the effect of socio-cultural change upon a nomadic hunting group, only a few steps removed from the stone age, when they were propelled suddenly into the urban, industrialized society.

Zentner, Henry. "Cultural Assimilation Between Indians and Non-Indians in Southern Alberta," in *The Indian Identity Crisis,* pp. 21-32. Calgary: Strayer Pub. Ltd., 1973.

The author reports on a study of changes in attitudes, and values of both groups—assumed to be indicative of cultural assimilation (or acculturation?). The sample comprised 115 Indian students and 335 non-Indians.

INDEPENDENT STUDY

Select two studies which are similar in research methodology or in the subject dealt with. Locate these and read them carefully.

Analyse the findings of both studies in terms of the conceptual framework developed in this chapter. To what extent does this provide either a more comprehensive and adequate explanation of the findings or a less comprehensive and adequate explanation than that provided by the author?

The Concept Amplified By Further Reading

Ahenakew, Edward (ed. by Ruth Buck). *Voices of the Plains Cree.* Toronto: McClelland and Stewart, 1973.

A valuable account of early Indian life on the Canadian plains—a rich storehouse of stories told by a great Indian, illustrating the culture of this group as it existed before the treaties were signed with the white man.

Barbeau, Marius. *Indian Days on the Western Prairies*. Information Canada: Ottawa, 1970.

An excellent source book of authentic tales about the experiences, beliefs and customs of Canada's native people. It would be a valuable teaching aid for all social studies teachers or for anyone teaching Indian and Métis children.

Beals, Alan R. (with George and Lousie Spindler). *Culture in Progress*. Toronto: Holt, Rinehart and Winston, 1967.

This book develops the concept of culture as a dynamic system, explaining it by means of specific examples of the way that various groups throughout the world behave and change.

Golding, William. *Lord of the Flies*. London: Faber and Faber, 1954.

This is a novel based on a plot which places a number of children alone on a Pacific island. The story of the gradual shedding of culture that occurs as the children become more and more barbaric in their behaviour is a fascinating one for the sociologist.

Graubard, Allen, "The Free School Movement," *Harvard Educational Review*, 43, no. 3 (1972): 351-373.

This article begins with factual data on the number, growth, location, staffing, size and financing of free schools in the United States. The author then develops a four-fold typology of free schools; (a) the "classical" type (a Summerhill-influenced community); (b) the "parent-teacher co-op" (formed by young, white, middle-class parents who do not want their children subjected to normal school requirements); (c) the "free high school" (high school counterpart of the classical free school, oriented to white middle-class and "hip" youth culture); and (d) "community elementary schools" (where concern is with parent-control of the schools). The author discusses the varying concepts of social change associated with each.

Kneller, George. "Education and Cultural Change," in D. F. Swift, ed., *Basic Readings in the Sociology of Education*, pp. 248-259. London: Routledge and Kegan Paul, 1970.

A discussion of the relationship between education and social change, with comments on various views as to the nature of this relationship.

Lane, Robert A. "Canadian Indians," *The Canadian Psychologist* 13, no. 4 (October 1972): 350-359.

The author claims that in the consideration of Indians as a single cultural group in research, two points are frequently neglected. First, culture is always dynamic. Secondly, there is a great deal of cultural diversity within the classification of North American Indians. Further, it is suggested that rather than consider what it is about Indian culture that causes school failure, a close examination should be made of characteristics of the educator's culture that makes it difficult to teach children that are different.

Michener, James A. *Kent State.* Greenwich, Conn.: Fawcett Publishing, 1971.
This tragic story, so well documented and presented here, offers many insights into the sources and consequences of one particular type of intra-cultural conflict within most urban societies today—that between upper-middle class youth and their parents.

Moore, G. Alexander. "An Anthropological View of Urban Education." *Education and Urban Society* 1, no. 4 (1969): 423-439.
The author states that the interests of sociologists and anthropologists converge in the study of communities. He views the school as a major agency by means of which the child is separated from the confines of the family and equipped to function as a member of the community.

Morgan, Elaine. *The Descent of Woman.* Toronto: J. M. Dent and Sons, 1972.
This book may well be a landmark in the clarification of the relationship between the evolution of biological aspects of the human species and the evolution of culture. The author strips away many misleading anthropological assumptions which have been founded more on the mythology of the anthropologist's culture than on biological knowledge.

Morris, Audry Y. *The Gentle Pioneers.* Don Mills, Ontario: General Publishing Co. Ltd., 1966.
The author tells the story of some of the upper middle-class English settlers in early nineteenth century Ontario whose influence on the shaping of Canadian culture (like that of the United Empire Loyalists before them) was probably greatly out of proportion to their numbers. The indications of severe culture-conflict experienced by the "gentle" settlers in the pioneer communities are of interest.

Murdock, George Peter. *Culture and Society.* Pittsburgh: University of Pittsburgh Press, 1965.
This is a wide-ranging book, which includes a cross-section of interesting anthropological studies as well as theory on the topic of culture.

Rossides, Daniel W. "The Functional Adaptation of Canadian Education," in *Society as a Functional Process,* pp. 232-237 Toronto: McGraw-Hill. 1968.
The author asserts that a real crisis may occur when it is found that a schooling system which has not yet been able to adapt successfully to the needs of an industrial society may suddenly be confronted with the new and unknown needs of the post-industrial society.

Smollett, Tobias. *Humphrey Clinker.* New York: Dolphin Books (first published in 1771).
This novel transports the reader to another culture; not in another *place* than the western, industrialized world but to another *time* in the evolution of that world. We often tend to be too ahistorical in our study of cultural variation and

change. This classic allows us to live vicariously in the society of eighteenth-century Britain, and to realize that the change in the culture of that one society in two hundred years is of greater magnitude in many ways than are the cultural differences among most of the world's societies today.

Spindler, George D., ed. *Education and Culture*. Toronto: Holt, Rinehart and Winston, 1963.

This is a collection of valuable articles on this topic, some of which are classics in the field.

Stamp, R. M. "Education and Nation-Building in Canada," in Gale E. Jensen, and W.K. Medlin, eds. *Readings on the Planning of Education for Community and National Development*, pp. 9-26. Ann Arbor, University of Michigan Press, 1969.

The author argues that education has played an important role in the nation-building process in Canada, and cites four examples: (1) the education of immigrants, (2) the strong British imperial sentiment present in pre-World War I Canada, (3) the revolution in French Canada in the 1960s, and (4) social change and education in pre-1914 Ontario.

Stanley, G. F. G. "The Métis and the Conflict of Cultures in Western Canada." *Canadian Historical Review* 28, no. 4 (1947): 428-433.

This is a review of the book by Marcell Girand, *Le Métis Canadien: Son Role dans l'Histoirie des Provinces de l'Ouest*, Paris: Université de Paris, Travaux de Memoires de l'Institute d'Ethnologie, tome XLIV, 1945. This book deals with the evolution of the French-Canadian half-breed from his origins to the present day, with the role he has played in the history of the prairie provinces, and with the factors (such as education) which contributed to his present position in Canadian society.

The Concept Reviewed

1 For the sociologist, the chief difference between the concepts of "society" and "culture" is:

a. "culture" is a more abstract concept than "society"

b. "society" (or "social system") refers to the pattern of relationships developed by a group of individuals interacting interdependently in a specific geographical setting (such as a neighbourhood or a country, or the planet Earth as a whole), while "culture" refers to a cumulative pool of shared beliefs produced by the ongoing interaction of each of these levels of community.

c. "society" is the name given by sociologists to the very same thing that anthropologists study under the name of "culture"

d. "society" is always evolving, while "culture" is static

e one can think of societies within societies as boxes within boxes, right up to the world community as the largest encompassing entity, but cultures are distinct and separate from one another, and associated only with differences among human ethnic groups.

2 An institution can be thought of as a group role because:
    a. it bridges both society and culture, just as a role contains both "objective" societal aspects and "subjective" cultural aspects
    b. it involves social organization as well as cultural ideals and customs, just as role is a function both of established patterns of societal interaction and of individual values and habits
    c. it performs a function for the society as a whole, just as the individual role performs a function for the smaller social system or formal organization
    d. it changes only gradually in response to alterations in environmental demands, just as roles change only gradually as the social and physical context in which individuals interact, undergo change
    e. both transcend the life span of the individuals who contribute to their form and nature and who are in turn shaped by them
    f. all of the above
    g. none of the above
    h. all but (b), (f) and (g).

3 Most anthropologists and ethnologists claim that the crucial key to culture is:
    a. conceptualizing ability
    b. habit-forming capacity
    c. ability to represent things and actions by symbols
    d. propensity to form social relationships.

4 The terms "integration" and "assimilation" are often used ambiguously. According to the explanation given in this chapter:
    a. integration is less desirable than assimilation
    b. assimilation among the various components of a social group is necessary if it is to form a society, while integration is not necessary
    c. integration is a social process, while assimilation represents a cultural change which may or may not result from integration
    d. assimilation always follows acculturation, while integration is the inevitable result of any social interaction
    e. all of the above
    f. none of the above
    g. all but (b), (e) and (f).

5 By "knowledge" we mean:
    a. highly tested and reliable group beliefs about desirable ways of doing things
    b. unique beliefs about the nature of relations holding among physical and social phenomena, held by individuals
    c. highly tested and reliable group beliefs about how to make specific

technical tools for coping with the environment

d. "self-evident" group beliefs about good ends for humans to strive for

e. highly tested and reliable group beliefs about the nature of the real world.

6 Education can be conceptualized as that institution designed to:

a. accomplish the transmission of culture from one generation to the next

b. destroy the totality of culture within a brief period, by alienating the younger generation from all of the beliefs of their fathers, replacing these beliefs with a new cultural whole

c. accomplish the continuous reconstruction of culture, by inculcating the scientific temper in the members of society, so that they will evaluate and select out undesirable and out-moded beliefs, replacing them with more adequate ones

d. provide a rational revitalization of culture in directions deemed desirable by the group as a whole

e. all of the above

f. none of the above

g. all but (b), (e) and (f).

7. Customs differ from norms in that:

a. customs are group habits which are acknowledged and believed to be appropriate by most members of the group, whereas norms represent regularities in group behaviour which can be unrecognized and/or unadmired by those manifesting them

b. customs can be conceptualized as aspects of culture, while norms can be conceptualized as aspects of society

c. customs are usually the long-term products of the operation of norms in social interaction

d. norms can be studied by observing overt group behaviour from the outside; the study of a group's customs requires the collection and analysis of verbal behaviours as well

e. all of the above

f. none of the above

g. all but (b), (e) and (f).

8. A culture which becomes maladaptive and non-gratifying from the standpoint of its carriers:

a. is likely to be perpetuated intact for many generations even without a concerted effort at inculcation through education

b. is likely to withstand assimilation even though its carriers are exposed to acculturation

c. is likely to retain the dynamism essential for cultural evolution

d. is likely to be replaced by a more gratifying and useful set of beliefs.

9 According to this chapter, education has seldom been used as an instrument of rational cultural evolution because:

a. education can have no possible role in cultural change, for it can only transmit beliefs

b. cultural change can only be the result of changes in social organization, which can be better accomplished by political revolution than by education

c. the carriers of most cultures have so far refused to accept the premise that what we believe to be true has any influence on what we believe to be desirable

d. educators will never possess the power and status required to be successful agents of change.

10 To the sociologist, education for a democratic, rather than a totalitarian, culture implies a socialization-enculturization process which:

a. inculcates specific beliefs about the perfection and ultimacy of the forms of democratic government currently prevailing in the society in question

b. encourages the development of everyone as a scientist in the broad sense

c. inculcates respect for the authority of the society's institutions as they presently exist

d. trains most of the society's youth as either physical scientists or humanitarians, each group highly skilled only in their own specialization.

Answers: 1. (b); 2. (f); 3. (c); 4. (c); 5. (e); 6. (e); 7. (g); 8. (d); 9. (c); 10. (b).

8 Values

The Concept Explained

In order to understand a society or a culture we look for regularities in group behaviour and for regularities amidst the accumulated store of beliefs shared and espoused by the group. In order to understand an individual personality we look for regularities in the behaviour of one unique human organism. The concept of "personality" encompasses those of "habit structure," "self," and "value system." All four of these concepts are attempts by behavioural scientists to make sense out of what causes human beings to behave as they do, or attempts to discover what is going on between the stimuli and the responses in that unobservable no-man's-land inside the individual.

According to psychologists and sociologists, habits are those relatively stable predispositions to behave in certain ways that have become so ingrained through repetition of the same response to a particular stimulus or choice situation whenever it occurs, that they no longer operate at the conscious level. No thought is required for habitual behaviour. Most of our actions are of this type; if it were not so—if we were forced to make conscious choices for every move throughout the day—we would be mentally exhausted in no time. Indeed, this is precisely what occurs for the individual experiencing culture shock. Suddenly he finds himself in a situation where all the old familiar cues that stimulated automatic responses on his part in the past are no longer present. Every behaviour now requires a conscious choice. Furthermore, the behaviours which he observes around him seem to make no sense; he can discern no meaningful patterns in them which might serve as guides for his own behaviour.

Habits, once instilled, are difficult to change, because they are so deeply embedded in our nervous systems and operate below the level of consciousness. Piaget hypothesizes that patterns or "schema" develop first in the thought processes, as a result of the repetition and generalization of choice behaviour as the individual acts upon his environment over time. Piaget calls these cognitive structures. It may be that parts of these same structures (as well-worn pathways in the nervous system) gradually sink below the level of consciousness to become the habits that Dewey wrote about.

Piaget also refers to affective elements which he calls the "energetics" which cause the cognitive structures (or reflective thought processes) to operate. Some combination of these logical schema (which reflect the connections made by the individual among experienced objects) and the propensities (feelings or emotions) which drive them, predisposes the individual to make certain choices rather than others. These general predispositions governing choice, which combine both cognitive and affective elements, we can call *values*. They differ from habits in that they are predispositions to choose rather than merely to behave non-reflectively in response to precipitating factors in the environment. However, they contribute to the formation of habits.

For example, a person might begin to value flashy, high-powered cars because he believes that there is a connection between possession of such a car and high status along with physical safety (cognition). He continues to value these cars because of the feeling of power, prestige and security that he experiences while driving them (affectivity). Eventually this attitude toward cars is generalized to form a predisposition to value and therefore acquire high-status possessions (a desire for privilege). It may gradually result in a habit of collecting expensive possessions. This value (and ultimately, the habit) would begin to change if the person's belief about the relevant social and physical relationships was changed due to an assimilation of new knowledge or his belief about the "goodness" of expensive possessions was altered as a result of the fact that behaviours following from his value choices were no longer paying off in a balance of gratification over pain.

Values are often confused with *attitudes*, as the two concepts are similar. It helps in distinguishing between them to think of attitudes as simply more concrete and specific manifestations of underlying values. One may have a negative preconception or attitude toward the Indian family which is moving in next door: an attitude resulting from one's value regarding the relative goodness of certain races (racism) or one's value regarding the goodness of certain positions in the social structure (status snobbery).

Belief is another concept sometimes confused with that of values. The important difference is that a belief is verbalized, whereas values are embedded deeper in the individual's schema, and may not even be recognized by him. A belief is an explanation of experienced regularities among phenomena. It may describe the nature of the connections among them ("prestigious and powerful people drive high powered cars," "large, high-powered cars are safer than small cars"), or it may express the desirability of the identified regularities ("prestigious and powerful people should drive high-powered cars"), or of the phenomena themselves ("high-powered cars are good"). In other words, beliefs may be about the nature of the real (social as well as physical environment) or about the good. One's beliefs affect one's attitudes, values and habits, and are derived from what one makes of ongoing experiences (vicarious as well as direct). Even sincerely espoused beliefs may not accurately reflect one's actual values at any point in time, and may be even less compatible with one's habitual behaviour. The reflective thinker that Dewey hoped would be developed through education would, however, continually seek to square his beliefs with verified knowledge on the one hand, and on the other hand, would strive to ensure that his value choices and habits were consistent with his beliefs.

Very often we assume that cultural *ideals* and values are the same thing. In the last chapter we defined ideals as those beliefs about what is desirable and possible for man which are shared by the members of the society in question to the degree that they are considered self evident. Another way to describe them is to say that they are group values, just as institutions are group roles and norms are group habits. Similarly, we can think of knowledge as group beliefs about the real, which differ from individual beliefs about the real in that they are widely communicated, publicly tested, and highly verified by the relevant community.

Only in an extremely monolithic community or nation would we find the values of the individual closely mirroring the group values (or the ideals of the ethnic or national culture). Where the containing culture tends to be pluralistic, as is clearly the case in Canada, most individuals encounter a wide variety of ideals during the course of their growing up, and being socialized and enculturated. Small subcultures such as those perpetuated by isolated ethnic communities, occupational associations or peer groups inculcate ideals which may be at variance with the ideals of the larger containing culture. Or ideals of the national culture which are at variance with those of certain sub-cultures or of the emerging global culture are inculcated by the educational system. (Canadian nationalism might be an example of an ideal incompatible with both internationalism and ethnic tribalisms or ethnocentrisms.) In addition, individuals who are socialized to be reflective thinkers and "valuers," rather than passive recipients of group values, tend increasingly, as they develop intellectually and morally, to reassess those values which reflect the ideals of their various relevant cultures, and to construct their own unique value system on the basis of a reconciliation of personal experience and their reading of the accumulated wisdom of the race.

The result of all these factors is that in a culture like the Canadian one, we find that values tend to be dynamic rather than static and to vary extensively from person to person. Furthermore, we find value conflicts and inconsistencies within groups, among groups, and between sub-groups and the larger containing society. This is to be expected in a pluralistic culture and is, to a large extent, desirable. However, the question of the objectives of education for children in a society where little value consensus exists has proven to be a thorny one.

Another problem of a pluralistic, dynamic culture is illustrated by the concept of future shock (a type of culture shock)[1]. Too rapid a rate of change in cultures may perhaps be as debilitating for their bearers as is cultural stagnation. Individuals in such a situation may find themselves operating with a set of inconsistent and even incompatible values. Extreme tension, or anxiety, is likely to develop due to erratic valuing behaviour. Either knowledge and cognition are applied to one's situation, forcing growth-enhancing reappraisals of one's entire value system, or symptoms of disorganization appear. In their extreme forms these may be expressed either as a debilitating inability to choose any course of action, or as a tendency to react inconsistently to the same stimuli. The first of these two extremes is characteristic of the individual whose value system is largely comprised of patterns of habitual responses internalized in toto from his culture. He is thereby highly resistant to change, in that unfamiliar stimuli immobilize rather than arouse him. (His valuing or choosing behaviour is all habitual, rather than reflective.) The other is the extreme of openness to change: the situation in which a coherent set of values has failed to evolve and therefore there is little probability that any consistent behavioural pattern will be discernible over time. At one extreme the individual lacks any "self-concept" apart from a static cultural tradition; at the other he is able to identify a "self" only fleetingly, through membership in transient groups. He "is" and "does" what the group which he happens to be participating in at the moment "is" and "does."

All this has important implications for education in a rapidly urbanizing society, especially for the education of ethnic minorities whose members have only recently been suddenly exposed to the majority culture. If the overall aim of education could be identified as the structuring of the socialization-enculturation process so that the individual will develop an internally consistent yet continuously evolving value system which will enable him to cope successfully at all levels of cultural existence, we might at least begin to tackle the problem. This would require that we not expose children to cultural discontinuities (situations where they are suddenly forced to adopt a whole package of new and different values in order to survive). Whether the new package is better (more reliable, workable, gratifying and appropriate for the environmental circumstances) than the

[1] See Alvin Toffler's *Future Shock* (New York: Random House, 1970)

older one is not the issue. The individual forced to undergo such a break with his own past experience is likely to develop a compartmentalized value system which will result at best in inconsistent and erratic behaviours and a lack of internal harmony, and at worst, neuroses or outright psychotic reactions.

This means that education must be the means, not of substituting one set of values for another, but of leading the individual through a gradual process of value confirmation, recognition, testing and reconstruction. The child's first values should not be destroyed by his school experience, but should be built upon, expanded and identified by him; then gradually he will be encouraged to apply his developing intellectual tools (his knowledge and reflective thinking abilities) to the task of testing and reconstructing values: a task that hopefully he will continue to engage in throughout his life. This approach means that teachers must stop thinking of values simply as individual carbon copies of the culture's ideals, copies which they as teachers have the right to inculcate in their captive student audience in the most efficient manner possible. Also they must stop thinking of pupils as clay to be molded in their own value image. They must be willing to see them, instead, as active and increasingly reflective valuers in their own right.

How can value-growth rather than value-substitution or inculcation be encouraged by means of education? At first glance it may seem to be impossibly difficult, as its implementation demands a high level of moral and intellectual development on the part of teachers. However, it has the advantage of not requiring the widespread societal value consensus which is so readily available in a monolithic culture (such as Mao's China) but so unattainable in the pluralistic Canadian one. It requires only a consensus on the desirability of internally consistent yet continuously evolving value systems for individuals, not a consensus on the content of the values contained in these systems. The former consensus is quite within the realm of possibility in Canada today. Most Canadians would agree that emotionally healthy and morally mature individuals are those whose values comprise a relatively integrated system rather than an aggregate of compartmentalized, disparate and conflicting elements. Most Canadians would also agree that emotional health and moral maturity require values which are amenable to gradual change in accordance with the changes in beliefs which occur as learning takes place in the individual.

This brings us to a recognition of the crucial function of the beliefs to which a child is exposed in school. For, if he is to be socialized to continually assess both his value choices and his habitual behaviour in terms of his beliefs about "reality," and to make the corresponding adjustments in values and habits, then it is imperative that he acquire only the most highly verified beliefs available in the culture. In other words, the teacher must be concerned with teaching the accumulated knowledge, technology and arts of the global culture of humanity, and with doing this as much as possible (in the early grades at least) in the context of the familiar—that is, the national and ethnic customs and ideals.

It is essential that the content and sequencing of this knowledge (the curriculum) be determined by the most competent people available—that it not be left to chance or to the personal bias of the individual teacher whose scholarly preparation is often questionable. It is necessary to sound a warning here, for there are many beliefs about the real and the good being expounded at every level of culture, which represent no more than the opinions of various individuals, or political and professional interest groups, and which have not undergone any systematic, public tests of reliability. Needless to say, such beliefs should not be given the official sanction of the educational institution, whether the individual teacher happens to hold them or not. If children are to be encouraged to recognize and assess their values in the context of their beliefs about the nature of the inorganic, organic and psycho-social environment, and to seek harmony and consistency among these values and beliefs, then it is absolutely essential that inaccurate, perverse, unverifiable, and unreliable beliefs not be inculcated in the classroom. By the same reckoning, it is imperative that those beliefs (termed knowledge) that have been most highly verified (either by the formal scientific enterprise or by the informally accumulated everyday experience of the human race) are taught to every individual at the most appropriate stage of his intellectual and moral development, and by the most appropriate means. This implies a school curriculum of beliefs, the content and sequencing of which evolves gradually in response to changes in the content of the global culture's universal knowledge pool. The procedures for teaching the curriculum would vary to some extent with the customs, ideals and arts of the ethnic and national cultures. Our universal pool of knowledge about how human beings learn and how public knowledge itself is structured would determine the sequencing of the curriculum, while the core beliefs of the entire knowledge pool would comprise the content.

In order to avoid the cultural discontinuities which create conflicts among values (and between values and beliefs) a strong effort should be made to build upon the valuing structure (and the symbolic or language structure) which each kindergarten child has evolved in the bosom of his family. An early concentration upon the tools of communication (speaking, listening, writing, reading, counting and measuring) would seem to be necessary. These tools should be developed first in the language of the family and ethnic culture, and only later in one or both of the national languages (where these differ). A few tried and tested beliefs about how humans have fed, sheltered, clothed, protected and governed themselves through the ages could be introduced gradually—with cultural commonalities rather than differences being stressed. This continuous development of his tools of communication in the context of encounters with the basic human occupations (or roles such as those of his mother, father and uncle) would keep the child in close relationship to his home environment while at the same time gradually expanding his horizons beyond his own sub-culture. The condition known as alienation occurs for the child or youth whose entire belief-and-value system is torn from him by the indoctrinating educator anxious to implant his own "better" or "truer" set. Ironically, the more effective this type of teacher, the more destructive he may be of the pupil's process of self-growth.

Only after his early values have been confirmed by the school should the young child be introduced to situations which would cause him to recognize differences in values among individuals. Carefully documented, up-to-date descriptions of other cultures could bring about this initial recognition which could subsequently effect a gradual identification by the child of his own attitudes and underlying values, the beliefs about reality upon which they rest, the habitual behaviour to which they have given rise in the past, and the choices among alternatives for action which they determine in the present. The child usually referred to by educators as creative is, in all probability, the one who, because of early exposure to a variety of cultures (through reading, TV viewing or travel) appears to demonstrate originality in response to routine situations.

Once the value-recognizing process has been initiated by the teacher, the more advanced stages involving the reflective assessment of values against beliefs, and the subsequent continuous construction and reconstruction of the value system, can be gradually encouraged. For example, a child from a very conventional type of family may have been brought, through education, to the point where he realizes that there are numerous possible sex-role relationships other than that operating within his own home. He may have taken part in class discussions in which he and his pals compared notes on the work that mothers and fathers do. The teacher may have provided the class with stories showing mothers as career women as well as in the role that he had always known his own mother, and depicting fathers as homemakers sometimes. During recess he may have been encouraged to play with dolls at times, and to allow the girls to play with the dump trucks. As he grew older, his teacher may have encouraged him to read about the contribution of women to Canadian culture throughout history. Eventually, as he witnessed the demonstration of a wide variety of female talents all around him, he would begin to acquire the belief that girls were in general equal in ability to boys. Perhaps a little later, the belief would gradually grow in him that boys and girls should not be restricted to specific play and work roles on the basis of sex. As the educational process continued he might be discovered making his behavioural choices on the basis of these new beliefs that were proving to be reliable: choices revealing a radical departure from his former, family-inculcated habit of treating girls as inferior beings or as possible possessions.

He would have achieved an integrated personality to the degree that his value system did not include incompatible predispositions to choose, based on conflicting beliefs, or on conflicts between his habits and beliefs. (As when at school he behaves and talks of girls as people who should have as wide a range of choices available to them as boys, but at home he treats his mother and sisters as his servants. Such an individual would tend to lack the identifiable self-concept necessary to prevent his being drawn hither and thither by precipitating factors in his environment).

A mature level of intellectual and moral development would be demonstrated by the ability to apply relevant verified beliefs to value choices, so that one's value system evolved as one's fund of knowledge evolved. This would prevent that other extreme of rigidity of self-concept which renders the individual incapable of coping with altered circumstances. It would also provide a built-in motivation to acquire ever more of the reliable knowledge currently available in the culture of humanity, so that one's choices would become ever wiser in consequence. A good deal of the lack of motivation to learn that teachers deplore is due to the fences that the pupil has constructed subconsciously to prevent the incursion of testable beliefs that might reveal the shaky foundations of his own cherished values.

This is not to say that all morally mature people will have identical values. A number of such individuals might exhibit predispositions to choose (values) which vary considerably from person to person, even though they all went through an identical valuing process. Most of the differences would be due to variations in the degree of knowledge about probable consequences of actions, possessed by the individual. Some would be due to differential assessments of the future impact of these consequences on the individual's own feelings, and on the feelings of others. For example, we could think of two relatively morally developed individuals, with integrated value systems, one of whom made choices which indicated that he valued privilege in society, while the other demonstrated the value of social equality, or egalitarianism. The first (on the basis of his beliefs about the nature of human behaviour) is committed to the position that the only incentive which will motivate people to be fulfilled in their work is the prospect of a better life style than one's fellows can achieve, and that the happiness created by a possession is directly related to its exclusiveness. The beliefs of the other support the contention that the social jungle inevitably created by the competition of "all against all" for scarce privilege will destroy the opportunity for personal fulfillment for both winners and losers in the contest. (Given the present "pre-scientific" state of our belief-testing in the social studies, there is more unsubstantiated opinion than reliable knowledge available for our predictions here; therefore, even people at a high level of intellectual and moral development can arrive at widely differing conclusions or value premises. This compounds the problem of belief-selection for the schools in the area of the social studies.)

It is possible, however, to identify a core of beliefs in the psycho-social realm upon which there is overwhelming agreement by behavioural scientists today, and which are extremely relevant to the valuing process. The following are suggested:

1   The senses are man's receivers or means of experiencing his surroundings, and therefore his ultimate check on the validity of his beliefs about the real. (Although this check is inevitably biased by the conditioning resulting from the socialization-enculturation process, it is still the best testing tool available to the human race, and we ignore it at our intellectual and moral peril.)

2   The individual is able to predict that one alternative act will make him feel better than another (a check on his beliefs about the good) because he is biologically equipped to experience sensations and to recall those experienced from similar acts in the past. However, feelings or emotions are not in themselves sufficient as guides to choosing, largely because of the factor of conditioning mentioned above.

3   The sharing of experiences by means of communication, and the process of relating cause to consequence, or applying reason to one's interpretation of present and future conditions is a fundamental prerequisite for the making of choices that will be good for tomorrow as well as today, and for others as well as oneself. (Involved in this belief is awareness that the greater the distance in time and space between cause and consequence, the more necessary are refined communication processes and the more elaborate is the reasoning process required to interpret and make the necessary connections.)

4   All components of the universe are interdependent; each individual's every act evokes irrevocable consequences for

the social and ecological environment. (This implies a human responsibility that has nothing to do with guilt, punishment or conscience, but has to do with being alive in an interacting, inextricably intertwined web of humanity.)

5   In the long run nothing can be best for the individual concerned if it injures others. This belief is strongly substantiated by evidence that retaliation is likely to follow such acts, that they contribute to the creating of a social environment in which no one is safe from injury, and that the ultimate in personal satisfaction is reached only when that feeling is shared by others.

6   Ideals and knowledge are social products which are based on a consensus of individual beliefs about what is good and real and which owe their validity not only to privately experienced feelings but to their public verifiability in terms of reliability for enabling individuals to deal effectively with their environment. (This means that knowledge and group values are continually evolving just as is the web of humanity and the individual selves which contribute to it.)

This core of beliefs would seem to have been proven sufficiently reliable by the experience of humanity for several million years, and to have achieved a sufficiently widespread consensus among Canadians, to be incorporated into our school curriculum as the moral foundation of our educational process. If this were done, the problems involved in our current controversies over drug education and sex education would not arise. Pupils would be taught consistently to evaluate any proposed present action according to its probable long-term consequences for themselves and the social group as a whole. The most reliable beliefs available about possible physiological, psychological, social and cultural effects of the use and abuse of drugs, tobacco and alcohol (and of the relative probabilities of experimentation inducing addiction) would be provided from the early grades on.

Teachers would no longer inculcate the belief either that drug-use is evil, or that drug-use is a mark of sophistication and therefore desirable. Pupils would instead be taught a valuing process and a fund of knowledge that would render such proscriptions and prescriptions unnecessary and ineffective, by the time they reached adolescence. They would view drug-abuse, or experimentation with drugs that are highly addictive or dangerous to health, as colossally and ridiculously stupid, and they would make their behavioural choices accordingly.

The same would apply to the moral problems surrounding the use and abuse of sex. If the sexual act were explained as the essentially social relationship which it obviously is, with the requirement for sustained and loving social interaction and the consequences for integrated group living that this implies, few adolescents would come to believe that mere frequency of achievement of that simple physical response common to all animals is the most desirable goal of human existence.

The emotionally confused and morally immature person is likely to be found espousing beliefs such as those associated with a predisposition not to exploit other people as mere means of temporary gratification, but behaving habitually in terms of the opposite value. Or talking egalitarianism while making behavioural choices that will serve to perpetuate aristrocracy and privilege.

It seems obvious that, when it comes to selecting candidates for teaching, an integrated and evolving value system (indicated by responsible moral behaviour) should be a major prerequisite. The content of the value system, however, should not be a criterion. That is, candidates should not be selected in terms of whether they demonstrate the value of aristocracy or egalitarianism. Rather they should be selected according to the degree to which their values and beliefs are consistent, the degree to which their beliefs reflect available knowledge rather than unsubstantiated personal opinion, and the degree to which they make their choices on the basis of awareness and concern for long-term consequences for themselves and others.

What does all this imply for the role of the teacher as a major educational agent? It means that the teacher does not implant values (such as that of privilege or social equality) but concentrates upon the intellectual and moral development of the child. In order to develop a reflective valuer or a continuously evolving, morally integrated person, the teacher will have to help the child to acquire as much as possible of the accumulated knowledge of the human race. Along with this knowledge the child should be helped to acquire the habit of applying reflective thought to his value choices: the habit of hypothesizing alternative actions, anticipating their consequences, and imagining their ultimate impact on the feelings of himself and others.

What the teacher does is to teach knowledge and reflective habits; to teach valuing rather than to inculcate specific values. This is not to deny that some values are better than others, or even that certain values are probably a prerequisite for the survival of civilization. It is rather to reject indoctrination as the road to these values, and to confirm a commitment to knowledge and reason as the only means which will not destroy the very values striven for through education.

The Concept Demonstrated

CASE STUDY ONE

Sam Oolik was five years old when the federal government assumed responsibility for territorial schooling in 1952. At that time Ottawa built schools at centres such as Yellowknife, Fort Smith and Inuvik, and arranged for Eskimo children to be flown hundreds of miles to attend them. Sam became one of the group who lived in a hostel in Inuvik, about a hundred miles from his home, for ten months of every year. He learned to read by means of the same "Dick and Jane" readers that were being used at the time in southern Canada. The residential school which he attended was operated by the Anglicans, and Sam was accepted as a committed member of the Anglican church by the time he was twelve.

Sam's visits home during the summer holidays became rather unhappy occasions as he grew older. His parents spoke an Eskimo dialect which he had almost forgotten after five years of school. He did not enjoy fishing from his father's small boat, and his older brothers' laughter at his performance on hunting trips filled him with resentment. His family's way of life began to seem crude to him, their manners embarrassing and their food revolting. His overriding ambition came to be to get a job in Inuvik, so that he would not have to return to his home community when he finished school.

By the time he was seventeen Sam had a regular job driving a truck for an oil company. He married young and was able to support his wife and children adequately on his wages, as well as to donate regularly to the Anglican church. His wife sometimes supplemented their income with part-time typing jobs. His foreman and the southern workers on the crews liked and respected Sam and he enjoyed working with them.

When the Ooliks' eldest son started to school in 1973 Sam was surprised to learn that little Jamie was being required to learn the native dialect in grade one, even though it was not spoken at home. The curriculum had undergone a drastic change also. Gone were Dick and Jane and the framework of Christian beliefs within which Sam had learned his three R's. Gone, too, were the priests and nuns and the visiting missionary teachers from the south. Now the teachers from southern Canada seemed more interested in inculcating the Eskimo culture than the white man's religious beliefs and customs. To Sam they seemed more involved in shaping the skills needed for making and using the crude tools used by his son's hunting and fishing forefathers than in developing those needed for coping with modern technology. Many of the teachers were now native northerners. Elderly Eskimos were brought into the classroom to recite the legends of their people. Others taught how to catch, clean and sell fish, and how to hunt caribou.

Sam was shocked and confused by the suddenness of the turn about. He felt betrayed by the whites who now seemed to be implying that what he had learned was no longer right and good: that the successful Eskimos were, instead, those who had refused to adapt to change. He did not want his children to be educated for their grand-parents' world. With Jamie struggling in school to master the rudiments of the culture that he, himself, had rejected, Sam was aware of being more and more alone. He felt betrayed by the whites whom he had sought so successfully to imitate and rejected by the native people who now seemed devoted to the idea of using the schools to perpetuate the traditional way of life, regardless of the consequences for individuals like Jamie.

QUESTIONS FOR GROUP DISCUSSION

1   How can the concept of cultural discontinuity be applied here? What were its consequences for Sam? What do you predict might be the result for Jamie?

2   Was the educational process to which Sam was exposed as a child concerned chiefly with inculcating values or with developing independent valuers? What about the educational process to which Jamie was being exposed? Justify your answers by referring to the case.

3   To what degree did Sam's parents likely participate in the determination of educational objectives for Sam? To what degree were Jamie's parents given an opportunity to contribute to the selection of objectives for his school? Discuss the implications of your answer for the value systems of the Eskimo people.

4   Are curriculum developers in northern Canada addressing the right questions when they battle over which set of values should be indoctrinated by the schools? If not, what sorts of questions should they be asking?

CASE STUDY TWO

Terry Corning's family was among those moved by the Newfoundland government from an isolated outport huddled on an offshore island to a thriving fishing community near St. John's. Terry's new school was very different from anything that he had experienced previously. There were so many rooms and so many boys and girls dashing hither and thither, and so many teachers, that for a long time Terry had nightmares about wandering the halls for days without locating his own class.

What was taught seemed different too; the teachers' words were strange, and during lessons they and the other children referred constantly to events and objects that were foreign to Terry's ears. Somehow he could never quite learn what was expected of him. No matter how hard he tried to fade into his surroundings, he seemed always to find himself standing suddenly alone, against a rush of smothered laughter.

Terry failed grade four at the end of that first year. His teacher described him as shy and a slow learner. During the next year he still didn't talk very much, but he tried even more desperately to figure out what the teacher wanted without revealing that he just couldn't understand what was going on, nor why the other children laughed at him. When he pretended to know whatever it was that they knew they laughed even more.

By the time Terry was thirteen years old he wasn't playing that particular game any more. He had learned that his classmates no longer laughed at him if he acted tough. He had even learned that the more he "hassled" the teacher, the more some of the boys looked up to him and wanted to roam around with him after school. He had learned also that the rougher he treated some of the girls in his class, the more they ran after him. Now when they laughed at his answers in class, it was usually the harassed teacher who was the butt of the joke.

Terry soon found other things that he could do that would provoke admiration from his friends. From shoplifting through vandalism to stealing cars he progressed rapidly. By the time he was fifteen his hours in school were merely boring, unreal preludes to the outside world of minor criminality in which he had carved out a place of sorts.

Suddenly, however, the world changed for Terry Corning. A new principal at the school persuaded some of the staff, parents, business people and fishermen in the community to try an experiment aimed at pupils whom the school did not seem to be helping. It was called a work-study program. Terry was one of the boys selected to work part time on one of the fishing trawlers and on other days to take school classes designed to teach him the kinds of skills he required for the job. Within a year Terry was a changed person, beginning to demonstrate a diligence and ability that his teachers hadn't known he possessed. Within two years he astounded his parents by informing them that he planned to take the upgrading program at the College of Fisheries on the Southside Campus at St. John's and eventually to enrol in marine engineering.

QUESTIONS FOR GROUP DISCUSSION

1   In your opinion, what constituted the major failure of Terry's teachers: their inability to help him develop morally or intellectually? By referring to this case, discuss how these two aspects of the individual's valuing process are related.

2   Would classes in religious education, sex education, and drug education at the junior high level likely have helped Terry? Discuss the strengths and limitations of this approach. Compare and contrast it to the work-study solution to the problem, in terms of consequences for the learner as a valuer.

3   Discuss the changes in the content of Terry's values (1) when he moved from the outport, and (2) as he became involved in the work-study program.

4   Why was Terry motivated to learn in the work-study program but not in the regular classroom situation? Discuss.

CASE STUDY THREE

When she was growing up in the Mennonite community near Kitchener, Ontario, no one would have dreamed that little Sarah Driedger would encounter anything but a life of productivity and contentment. She was raised on a farm with eight brothers and sisters, and was fondly recognized by her parents as the brightest of the lot. At the country and village schools that she attended from grade one through grade thirteen Sarah became accustomed to the praise of her teachers and to the respect and sometimes envy of her classmates. Her marks were invariably the highest, her work the neatest and most thorough.

It had always been expected that Sarah would go to university, so when she chose to enrol at the University of Toronto her parents felt a few qualms, but no surprise. After all, she was an obedient, sensible girl who had never given them a moment's trouble, and if she could not look after herself in the big city, they thought, what young person could?

However, after the first few weeks of living in residence among strangers, and racing to classes through roaring traffic, Sarah was no longer so sure about her ability to cope. For one thing, she had not been able to make any friends. Her long, straight hair and unmade-up face should have been in style, but somehow she sensed that her appearance was different from that of the other girls. She wore no jeans, for one thing; her parents would have been horrified at the idea that they should be used for anything but farm chores. She wore her hair in a neat bun at the back of her neck, not hanging loosely around her shoulders. Certainly she no longer wore braids, nor the long, black stockings of her childhood. But her clothes were different: handmade by her mother and her aunt. And the length of her skirts was obviously wrong.

Worst of all were the classes. Someone had advised a philosophy and a sociology, along with the more familiar subjects, and unquestioningly, Sarah had registered in them. What began to happen in these classes was terrible for Sarah. One professor said that there had always been as many Gods as there were men with the need to worship; another said that university students should examine critically the ideals and customs of their community and society; a third seemed to be assuming the truth of Darwin's theory of evolution. Sarah felt herself recoiling from such ideas in fear. To her they were not only a threat to everything she had been brought up to believe, but blasphemous as well. She began to feel that the place where such thoughts were uttered freely must surely be steeped in sin. The books that she was required to read and the papers that she had to write were not only disturbing to her, but seemed distinctly evil in their content.

The sensation of being somehow engulfed in sin remained with Sarah, deepening as her loneliness grew. Finally, the desperation of that loneliness drove her to accept an invitation, casually extended by a girl in her hall, to go to a dance on campus. With the almost certain knowledge that her sin was now so great that redemption was impossible, Sarah tried her first cigarette and her first drink that night. For the first time since coming to Toronto she experienced a glow of comradeship: a glow which deepened with the second drink, and remained with her throughout a confused evening.

As the winter wore on, confusion, interspersed with bouts of alcohol-induced euphoria, became the norm for Sarah. For companionship she found herself vacillating between a group of Lutheran students who had sought her out, and the "fun" group who made her hilariously welcome as they smoked pot or drank beer. With the Lutherans, she suffered from an awareness of her own guilt and hypocrisy; at the parties, unless she was stoned, she felt like a pretender and a misfit. Her desire to belong to the "fun" group drove her to lengths that horrified her in calmer moments. One night someone suggested popping a few pills, and even in that Sarah was eventually persuaded to join.

With spring came the realization that she was failing her classes. This was the final blow that Sarah knew she simply could not take. The thought of the disappointment in her parents' eyes was too great to be born. She could never face them after disgracing them so; of this Sarah was convinced. Her parents' fond dreams of the university education that was to have made their daughter a respected teacher, or perhaps even a doctor, she now knew would never be realized. She knew for certain that she had failed to make it; but would she ever, she wondered, really understand why?

QUESTIONS FOR GROUP DISCUSSION

1   Analyse Sarah's problems by applying the concept of the individual's value system.

2   What type of cultural environment would Sarah likely have had to remain within in order not to have encountered severe emotional stress? Why?

3   Discuss the nature of the socialization and educational processes to which Sarah had been exposed during her formative years. Identify some of the beliefs about the good and the real that she seems to have internalized during this time. Might any of these have been preventing further learning in the university setting?

4   Compare and contrast the experiences of culture shock suffered by Sam, Terry and Sarah. In each case, how did the shock affect the valuing process of the individual?

The Concept Applied
To Relevant Canadian Research

Anisfeld, E. and W. E. Lambert. "Evaluational Reactions of Bilingual
    and Monolingual Children to Spoken Languages." *Journal of Ab-
    normal and Social Psychology* (1964): 89-97.
The authors employed a research technique that they believe is capable of revealing the stereotyped characteristics which one linguistic-cultural group attributes to another. Monolingual and bilingual French-Canadian children listened to tape recordings of children's voices (in English and French) and rated each speaker's personality on fifteen traits. Bilinguals were found to evaluate English Canadians much more favourably than did monolinguals.

Berry, J. W. "Independence and Conformity in Subsistence-Level
    Societies." *Journal of Personality and Social Psychology* 7, no. 4 (1967):
    415-418.
Differences in conformity were investigated by using samples of the Temne people of Sierra Leone and the Baffin Island Eskimo. The degree of food accumulation and socialization practices of the two societies were used as a basis for predicting differences in conformity between them. The resulting group differences were significant, but differences between samples within each society (urban traditional versus rural traditional) were insignificant. It was concluded that sub-sistence level economies do tend to produce the degree of conformity required by their economics. (The Temne tended to accept the re-quirements of a group norm, the Eskimos to ignore it.)

Clifton, Rodney A. "The Social Adjustments of Native Students in a
    Northern Canadian Hostel." *Canadian Review of Sociology and An-
    thropology* 9, no. 2 (1972): 163-166.

In an analysis of a sample of 207 Eskimos from the Mackenzie River delta and Arctic coast, Indians from the Mackenzie River valley, and Métis from all three areas, it was found that there were significant differences in the social adjustment of members of the three groups.

Deval, W. B. "Support for Civil Liberties Among English-speaking Canadian University Students." *Canadian Journal of Political Science* 3, no. 3 (1970): 433-449.
A partial replication of a 1957 civil liberties survey of the University of California (Berkeley) students was carried out on a sample of 1325 undergraduate students in 13 Canadian English-language universities in 1969. General agreement was found with the earlier American study. Jewish students exhibited more civil libertarian responses than did Catholic or Protestant, as did students claiming that religion was of little importance in their lives. Social class appeared to be a less important determinant than area of study and years of schooling.

Driedger, Leo and Jacob Peters. "Ethnic Identity: A Comparison of Mennonite and other German Students." *Mennonite Quarterly Review* 47, no. 3 (July 1973): 225-244.
The researchers analysed data taken from the University of Manitoba Ethnic Survey conducted by the Ethnic Identity Research Team during 1970-71, with a total sample of 1,560 undergraduate students. Compared to other Canadians of German ethnic origin, twice as many Mennonites agreed to items concerning the value of parochial education, endogamy, in-group choice of friends and the use of the German language

Eberlein, L. et al. "Self-Ideal Congruence in Five Occupational Groups." *Alberta Journal of Educational Research* 17, no. 2 (1971): 95-104.
The researchers studied 584 subjects in five functionally different occupational groups: counsellors, teachers-in-training, priests, high school pupils and army officer cadets. Significant differences were found in the degree to which "congruent self-ideals" were held.

Friesen, David. "Value Climates in Canadian High Schools." *The Canadian Administrator* 6, no. 1 (October 1966): 1-4.
The author reports on a 1965-66 study of ten high schools situated in Alberta, Manitoba and Ontario. The sample included private, rural, small city and metropolitan high schools. He concludes that the peer group is a powerful element in adolescent society.

Gardner, R. C., et al. "Ethnic Stereotypes: Attitudes or Beliefs?" *Canadian Journal of Psychology* 24, no. 5 (1970): 321-324.

This study employed factor-analysis approach[2] to investigate the role of parents' and children's attitudes on the reactions of Canadian children to English-speaking and French-speaking people. The findings support the conclusion that two factors influence the tendency of children to ascribe traits to ethnic groups: (1) their parents' attitude toward the group and (2) community-wide stereotypes (beliefs?) about the group. It was found that children's authoritarian attitudes reflected those of their parents, but attitudes toward the other ethnic group were more highly related to those of their peers and surrounding community.

Gue, Leslie R. "Value Orientations in an Indian Community." *Alberta Journal of Educational Research* 17, no. 1 (1971): 19-32.
This study, using the theory and method of Florence Kluckhohn for identifying and comparing value orientations, sampled 138 Indian pupils, 30 Indian parents, and 129 teachers and administrators in a northern Canadian school system. Highly significant differences in value orientations were found between Indian and non-Indian samples in the "relational" value orientation area. [3] Differences were also found between Treaty and Métis pupils. However, similarities among all three groups were found in a number of the value orientation areas.

Henry, Franklin J. "University Influence on Student Opinion." *Canadian Review of Sociology and Anthropology* 8, no. 1 (1971): 18-31.
University influence on student position on the liberalism-conservatism value continuum was studied by means of a questionnaire distributed to first- and third-year McMaster University students. A larger percentage of third-year students were found to be relatively liberal. This relationship was found to persist even when the set of background factors most closely related to liberalism was empirically selected and held constant.

Holden, D. "Modernization Among Town and Bush Cree in Quebec." *Canadian Review of Sociology and Anthropology* 6, no. 4 (November 1969): 237-248.
This article takes data gathered on the Cree Indians of the Mistassini and Waswanipi areas of Quebec and analyses them in terms of role structure. A scale of modernization was developed and was found to

---

[2]Factor analysis is a statistical method of finding the common element or elements that underlie a given set of measures. For a fuller explanation, see R.B. Cattell, *Factor Analysis: An Introduction and Manual for the psychologist and Social Scientist* (Harper and Row, 1952).

[3]See the discussion of Kluckhohn's model in the Concept Amplified section of this chapter.

be associated with education, location of residence, occupational roles, and changes in attitudes and value orientations.

Hobart, C. W. "Attitudes Toward Parenthood Among Canadian Young People." *Journal of Marriage and the Family* 35, no. 1 (1973): 71-82.
The author gathered data by questionnaires from 162 university and 242 trade school French-Canadian students in Montreal and from 497 university and 203 trade school English-Canadian students in Alberta. It was found that both ethnic groups preferred medium-sized families, but the French Canadians were more opposed to the use of birth-control and had more traditional views concerning parental roles and child-rearing practices. In both samples university students were more accepting of contraception, permissiveness in child-rearing, egalitarian parental roles and divorce than were their trade school counterparts. The author concluded that the data indicate differential patterns of erosion of traditionalism in that (1) various influences differed in their salience (rurality and class had less power than religion); (2) on certain issues traditionalism was eroded more than others (ideal family size); and (3) erosion had gone further among the English than among the French Canadians.

Hutcheon, Pat Duffy. "Political Affiliation and Academic Discipline as Predictive of Faculty Radicalism." *Saskatchewan Journal of Educational Research and Development* 1, no. 2 (Spring 1971): 25-31.
This is a study which attempts to isolate the various components of and the background factors associated with the value currently labelled as "radical." The sample studied comprised 119 teaching members of a university faculty in western Canada.

Hughes, Judge E. N., et al. *Citizens' School Inquiry.* Saskatoon School Boards and Saskatchewan Teachers' Federation, 1973.
This is the report of an analysis of data gathered from two hundred written briefs submitted by organizations and individuals, a random survey, and a series of public meetings on the ends and means of schooling for Saskatoon. The findings included a consensus on general objectives such as increased emphasis on communicative skills, the development of learning or conceptualizing skills, consideration of a broad range of pupil-abilities and interests, development of values consistent with those taught in the home and society, plus equality of opportunity of access for everyone. There was indication of general satisfaction with the elementary school system, but less with the secondary system.

Johnstone, John C. *Young People's Images of Canadian Society,* Studies of
the Royal Commission on Bilingualism and Biculturalism, Information Canada, 1969.
This is a study of how a 1965 cohort of Canadian young people, aged 13
to 20, perceived their homeland. The conclusion: "Between these years
Anglophone youth could be said to expand their territorial horizons,
while Francophones seem to be limiting theirs."

King, A. J. C. "Ethnicity and School Adjustment." *Canadian Review of
Sociology and Anthropology* 5, no. 2 (May 1968): 84-89.
The researcher hypothesized that there are significant differences
among various ethnic groups in terms of their adjustment to, and
performance in, the Ontario school system. French and Jewish students were assumed to be "non-assimilative," while Ukrainian, German, Polish, Dutch, Slovak, and Hungarians were classified as "as-
similates." Research data were drawn from the Carnegie Human Resources Data Bank (gathered in a 1959-60 study of 90,719 Ontario grade
nine pupils). The findings of substantial differences among the groups
supported the hypothesis. Those classified as "assimilative" performed in school in a manner more closely approximating the
English-Canadian pupils than did the French or Jewish. The performance of the Jewish group was much superior to that of all the other
groups, while the school performance of the French was inferior.

Kitchen, Hubert W. "Relationships Between the Value Orientations of
Grade 9 Pupils in Newfoundland and the Characteristics of their
Primary and Secondary Groups." Ph. D. dissertation, University
of Alberta, Edmonton (January 1966).
This study, employing the Florence Kluckhohn model of value orientations, compared samples of urban and rural pupils including 2,151
pupils of 250 communities attending 175 Anglican schools offering
grade nine. It was found that urban pupils tended to be more "present" and "individualistically" oriented, more oriented toward "inter-
generational lineality," and less toward "bureaucratic lineality" than
the rural pupils.

Knill, W. "The Teen-age Subculture, Part IV: Values Held by High
School Students." *The Saskatchewan Bulletin* 29 (May 1963): 60-65.
This is the last of a series of articles presenting the results of a 1962
survey of Saskatoon high schools. The high school youth were found
to reflect society's values and in particular, those of their parents' SES.
The author concludes that "they are full of contradictions, being both
idealistic and security-oriented in their aspirations, viewing education
as instrumental in career achievement."

Kurokawa, Minako. "Psycho-Social Roles of Mennonite Children in a Changing Society." *Canadian Review of Sociology and Anthropology* 6, no. 1 (1969): 15-35.
The author reports on a study of 460 children and mothers belonging to three different Mennonite groups in Waterloo County, Ontario. He classifies the groups as "traditional," "transitional," and "progressive." The findings indicate that culture conflict is seen most clearly in the transitional group. Parents in this group seem to be authoritarian and inconsistent in disciplining. Their children tend to demonstrate value inconsistency, a sense of inadequacy, and covert symptoms of maladjustment.

Leard, H. H. and A. Farine, "The Generation Gap: Problem or Paradox?" *McGill Journal of Education* 7, no. 1 (1972): 46-60.
The authors report on the results of a questionnaire survey of 372 Francophone high school pupils from the Montreal region, and 42% of their parents. Responses were classified according to parent economic and educational levels. Support was found for the hypothesis that there is no significant gap between parents and youth with respect to value continuity in family relations and attitudes toward work. Although parents and youth both claimed there was a generation gap, outside their immediate family the response patterns disclosed no such gaps except in attitudes toward the use of drugs.

Mann, W. E. "Youth Attitudes and Values in Canada." *National Council of the Y.M.C.A.*, Toronto, 1961.
This study used a stratified sample of two thousand drawn from a population of nineteen thousand young people from all across Canada. The findings indicated that 31% believe that another war is unavoidable, and 42% believe that most people are becoming less honest.

Marjoribanks, K. "Achievement Orientation of Canadian Ethnic Groups." *Alberta Journal of Educational Research* 18, no. 3 (1972): 162-173.
The author reports on an examination made of interrrelationships among the constructs of ethnicity, social class, achievement orientation and intelligence. The sample included families classified as middle class and lower class, from five ethnic groups residing in Ontario. In general it was found that Jewish and white Anglo-Saxon Protestant groups, which are over-represented in the upper levels of the Canadian occupational hierarchy, had above average achievement orientation and intelligence scores. Canadian Indians, who are largely concentrated in the lower levels of the occupational structure, were found to exhibit below average achievement orientation and intelligence test scores.

Pedersen, Eigil, and Kenneth Etheridge. "Conformist and Deviant Behavior in High School: The Merton Typology Adapted to an Educational Context." *Canadian Review of Sociology and Anthropology* 7, no. 1 (1970): 72-80.
Data collected from 3,465 Quebec grade ten pupils were used to assess the applicability of Merton's typology[4] of behaviour to the Canadian educational context. The value of education as a "culturally defined goal" was compared to expectations concerning the use of college attendance as the "institutionally appropriate means" of achieving the goal. Four classifications of pupils were developed: "conformists" (high on both measures), "innovators" (high-low), "ritualists" (low-high) and "retreatists" (low-low). More than 25% of the pupils fell in the fourth category

Perkins, S. A. "A Pilot Study of the Values of Public and Separate School Grade Twelve Students." *Alberta Journal of Educational Research* 18, no. 3 (1972): 196-201.
The Differential Values Test devised by Thomas was administered to seventy-eight public school and sixty-two separate school students in Lethbridge, Alberta. Significant differences were found on the aesthetic, intelligence and material values scales, but not on the humanitarian, power and religious scales. Findings differed somewhat when respondents were grouped homogeneously according to sex.

Pratt, David. "Value Judgements in Textbooks: The Coefficient of Evaluation as a Quantitative Measure." *Interchange* 2, no. 3 (1971): 1-14
The author reports on the design and use of an objective instrument in the study of the treatment of four minority groups in the history textbooks in use in Ontario schools.

Rogers, T. B. "Some Thoughts on 'Culture-Fairness' of Personality Inventories." *The Canadian Psychologist* 13, no. 2 (April 1972): 116-120.
The author discusses issues attending the use of personality inventories in cultures other than the one in which they were sired. To demonstrate some of these points data were presented that indicated differential understandability of certain trait names even between two cultures as similar as those of Canada and the U.S. The need for a research-based program prior to the adoption of non-Canadian tests in Canadian settings was stressed.

[4]For an explanation of this typology, see Robert K. Merton, *Social Theory and Social Structure* (New York: Free Press, 1968), p. 140.

Saskatchewan Department of Continuing Education, *Report on the Plans of Graduating Grade 12 Students for Fall, 1973* (first report). Research and Evaluation Branch, June 1973.

The entire population of Saskatchewan grade twelve students planning to complete grade twelve in the current term (12,151) was surveyed in May 1973. It was found that approximately 41% planned to work rather than pursue further education, 24% planned to attend the University of Saskatchewan, 18% planned to attend a technical institute in Saskatchewan, 16% planned to attend some other post-secondary educational organization, and 2% planned on home-making or travel.

Schab, Fred. "Honour and Dishonour in the Secondary Schools of Three Cultures," *Adolescence* 6, no. 22 (1971): 145-154.

The purpose of this study was to examine the similarities and differences in the secondary school behaviour of 865 honour students in Georgia, U.S.A., 155 in Quebec, and 132 in Scotland. The data were gathered by means of a questionnaire which examined the students' beliefs concerning cheating, and attitudes about dishonesty in general. The findings suggest that the Scottish students were least tolerant of dishonesty, and the Quebec students most permissive.

Sydiaha, D., and J. Rempel. "Motivational and Attitudinal Characteristics of Indian School Children as Measured by the Thematic Apperception Test." *The Canadian Psychologist* 5, 3, (July 1964): 139-148.

The researchers studied 248 children in northern Saskatchewan. They state that the results of the thematic apperception test[5] indicated clear differences between Métis-Indian and northern ono-Indian students only for categories indicating awareness of poverty.

Wintrob, R. N., and P. S. Sindell, "Culture Change and Psychopathology: The Case of Cree Adolescent Students in Quebec," in Berry, J. W. and G. J. S. Wilde, eds. *Social Psychology: The Canadian Context*, pp. 259-271. Toronto: McClelland and Stewart, 1972.

This study examined the psychological consequences of students living alternately in the traditional milieu of the family and hunting groups, and in the urban school setting. Data were collected on all 109 Cree adolescents in the Mistassini and Waswanipi Bands who attended public school in 1967-1968. Forty-two per cent showed clear evidence of "identity conflict," 14% showed symptoms of "identity confusion."

---

[5]This is a projective technique which confronts the subject with a series of pictures about which he is asked to tell stories.

Yackley, Andrew and W. E. Lambert. "Inter-ethnic Group Competition and Levels of Aspiration." *Canadian Journal of Behavioural Science* 3, no. 2 (1971): 135-147.
Cultural variations of aspirations in a competitive situation were
studied, using nine-to-eleven-year-old French-Canadian and
English-Canadian boys of similar social class backgrounds. French-
Canadian boys were found to have higher aspirations for scoring
points in a team competition, especially when competing against the
English-Canadian teams: aspirations that proved to be unrealistic.

INDEPENDENT STUDY

Read carefully the article by the author described in the following section, and
entitled, "Value Theory: Toward Conceptual Clarification." Identify the nine
different types of phenomena commonly examined in research purporting to
be measuring values. Locate and read as many of the Canadian studies described in the preceding section as possible, classifying each as to which of the
nine types of phenomena the researcher is dealing with.

The Concept Amplified
By Further Reading

Dewey, John. *Freedom and Culture.* New York: Capricorn Books, 1963.
The central message of this valuable and still timely book is that human beings
will build and maintain free cultures only if they recognize that democracy
requires a conscious moral commitment and the will to achieve it through the
development of reflective individuals equipped, by means of the educational
process, with a scientific temper.

Dunlap, Riley. "Radical and Conservative Student Activists: A Comparison of
Family Backgrounds." *Pacific Sociological Review* 13, no. 3 (Summer 1970):
171-181.
This is the report of an attempt to check the hypothesis that the family
backgrounds of radical and conservative student activists might be changing.
(Keniston, Flacles, etc. had found that radicals tended to have left-wing,
affluent, highly educated parents who generally supported their activities,
while the conservatives came from working class, right-wing homes, also
supportive of their children's political stance.) The author's findings suggest
that more of the militant radicals than militant conservatives now come from
lower class backgrounds, with the parents of neither group supportive of their
offspring's activities.

Fichter, Joseph H. "High School Influence on Social Class Attitudes." *Sociological Analysis* 33, no. 4 (1973): 246-253.
American Catholic boys' high schools run by Jesuits declare their intention to

"improve" the social attitudes of their students. Two surveys of the freshmen and seniors in these schools in 1965 and 1968 provided data to test this stated objective. Using Lipset's categories[6] the author found that students from lower SES families tended to demonstrate economic liberalism (on questions of poverty) while those from higher SES families manifested non-economic liberalism (on questions of race). On all students the effect of four years attendance at Jesuit high schools was an increase of upper class non-economic liberalism and a decrease of lower-class economic liberalism.

Fuchs, Estelle. *Teachers Talk.* New York: Anchor Books, Doubleday and Co., 1969.
This is an excellent source of case studies pointing out value conflicts in the classroom, each chapter ending with an anthropological analysis of the classroom situation being described by the teacher in question.

Gallup Poll, 1970. "Public Attitudes Toward the Public Schools." *Phi Delta Kappan* 52, no. 2: 100-109.
The most interesting findings reported here are the expressions of strong feeling that there is not enough discipline in schools, that teachers and administrators should be held more accountable, that schools have become too expensive, and that there is *not* a problem of unwillingness to change nor obsolescence of curriculum.

Goertzel, Ted. "Changes in the Values of College Students." *Pacific Sociological Review* 15, no. 2 (April 1972): 235-244.
A fifty-item questionnaire on moral values, which had been administered to a sample of beginning students in a U.S. university in 1958, was used to measure the values of a 1970-71 sample. The most marked change was found to be to much more permissive sexual attitudes. Also, the findings indicated a general weakening of moral norms concerning bootlegging, lying about a child's age in order to secure reduced fare, keeping excess change, cheating on exams, income tax, and on insurance benefits. A strengthening of norms concerning the wrongness of war, and an overall hostility to institutions were also apparent.

Henry, Jules. "Attitude Organization in Elementary School Classrooms." *American Journal of Orthopsychiatry* 27 (January 1957): 117-133.
A searching and enlightening analysis of the ways in which teachers (often unconsciously) organize the same underlying emotional characteristics of children to achieve different organizations of emotions. One teacher so organizes the children's emotions as to accomplish an intensification of the fear of intra-group aggression, while she turns the children's hostility toward one another (by the witch hunt and intensification of competition). A different teacher may organize the emotions of the children so that a euphoria in which students and teacher are bathed in a wave of emotional gratification is achieved (through the development of unquestioning docility in the children).

[6]For further information on these categories, see S.M. Lipset, "The Value Patterns of Democracy," *American Sociological Review,* 28 no. 4 (August 1963), 515-531.

Hutcheon, Pat Duffy. "Value Theory: Towards Conceptual Clarification." *The British Journal of Sociology* 23, no. 2 (June 1972): 172-187.
A survey of the current state of theory and research in values, followed by the presentation of a model of the process of the growth of value systems and valuing in the human being.

Kluckhohn, Florence, and Fred Strodtbeck. *Variations in Value Orientations.* New York: Row, Peterson and Co., 1961.
This book develops the concept of value orientations and presents reports on studies comparing these across five cultures. The authors identify five problems (assumed to be present for every human group) as (1) what is the character of human nature, (2) how does man relate to nature, (3) what is the temporal focus on human life, (4) is man chiefly active or passive in his relationship with nature, and (5) how do men relate to one another? The dominant socio-cultural responses to these problems are considered to be the specific value orientations of the culture concerned. The authors cite three possible variations for each of the orientations, as follows:

1   for the human nature problem: "evil," "neutral" (or a mixture) and "good";
2   for man-nature: "subjugation to," "harmony with" or "mastery over";
3   for time: "past," "present" or "future";
4   for activity: "being," "being-in-becoming", or "doing"; and
5   for the relational problem: "lineality," "collaterality" or "individualism."

Mead, Margaret. "Our Educational Emphases in Primitive Perspective." *The American Journal of Sociology* 48, no. 6 (May 1943): 633-639.
The author discusses ways in which educational behaviour in our Western culture differs conspicuously from that of primitive communities. She cites the emphasis on proselytizing so-called unchanging and unchallengeable Truths so common to our culture, one of the results being that education becomes the concern of the teacher rather than the learner; our emphasis on the use of education as a means of vertical social mobility and of perpetuating social structures; our acceptance of cultural discontinuity between child and parent; our emphasis on "change" rather than on "growth" as the goal of education; our belief that education can accomplish miracles; and the belief in education as an instrument for the creation of new human values. She concludes that the sooner Americans can rid their society of present discrepancies in social rewards, and rid their culture of the belief that the schools should indoctrinate Truths, the more hope there will be that education will indeed function as the source of new and better human values.

Russell, Bertrand. *Education and the Social Order.* London: Unwin Books, 1970.
This little book sums up Lord Russell's views on the relationship between education and the socio-cultural environment. In it he identifies may of the undesirable consequences of the schooling procedures of the time for the social structure as well as for the shaping of values such as nationalism rather than international cooperation.

Spindler, George D. "Education in a Transforming American Culture." *The Harvard Educational Review*, 25, no. 3 (Summer 1955) 145-156.
The author discusses major shifts in the core values of the American culture, and the effect of these shifts on education. He identifies a set of what he calls "emergent values," and opposes these to the "traditional values" of the culture, He sees the professional culture of teachers as primarily "emergent," and discusses the culture-conflict situation in which young teachers often find themselves as a result. He deals as well with the various common adaptive responses made by such teachers ("ambivalent," "compensatory" and "adapted.")

Tomkins, George S "National Consciousness of the Curriculum and Canadian Studies." *Journal of Educational Thought* 7, no. 1 (1973): 5-24.
This article deals with a national survey of concepts of Canadian national consciousness and nationalism, anti-Americanism in relation to Canadian national consciousness, and the search for common approaches to curriculum in relation to national goals. It then describes the Canadian Studies Program which was initiated in 1968 to develop curricula for Canadian schools.

Thompson, J. D. and W. J. McEwen. "Organizational Goals and Environment; Goal-Setting as an Interaction Process," in M. Milstein, and J. Belasco, eds., *Educational Administration and the Behavioral Sciences: A Systems Perspective*, pp. 213-228. Boston: Allyn and Bacon, 1973.
The authors discuss goal-setting in a formal organization as a dynamic, interactive process, purposive in terms of the values and goals of individual members, but influenced continuously by the inputs and pressures of the surrounding socio-cultural and physical environment.

Vickers, Sir Geoffrey. *Value Systems and Social Process.* London: Tavistock Pub. Co., 1968.
This book contains nine papers bearing on "the process by which men and societies develop and change the values by which they live." Part III deals with the nature, nurture, and function of appreciative (valuing) behaviour, the emergence of norms, and their place in the control of systems. In the last chapter, the papers discuss psycho-social science as the source of an epistemology of all science.

The Concept Reviewed

1   According to the explanation in this chapter, values are:
    a.   relatively stable predispositions to behave in certain ways that have become so ingrained through repetition of the same response to a particular choice situation, that they no longer operate at the conscious level
    b.   the affective elements that influence reflective thought processes
    c.   general predispositions governing choice, which combine both affective and cognitive elements (or both feeling and thinking)

d.   verbalized explanations of experienced regularities among phenomena which may reflect images both of what "is" and what "ought to be" (the state of the present as well as those future states which are desirable and possible—given what is currently known to be the nature of reality).

2   The distinction made in this chapter between ideals and values is that:
a.   the first concern moral ends, or what is good and desirable, while the second concern what is real
b.   the first are general predispositions to choose (priorities) characteristic of the social group as a whole; the second are the personal priorities that determine individual choices
c.   the first are often subconsciously held, while the second are always acknowledged and verbalized
d.   the first are less likely to be accurate reflections of group beliefs and images than are the second.

3   For the individual, cultural discontinuities are likely to be upsetting in that:
a.   such breaks with one's past experience are likely to produce compartmentalized value systems and/or loss of identity
b.   human nature is essentially such that human beings cannot adapt to change
c.   they may cause a condition of culture shock, where the individual suffers from a lack of familiar cues to which he can respond habitually
d.   they may result in alienation, erratic behaviour, neuroses, and even psychoses
e.   all of the above
f.   none of the above
g.   all but (b), (e) and (f).

4   The selection of the content and sequencing of the beliefs to which pupils are to be exposed in the school is crucial because:
a.   there are so many beliefs of varying validity and reliability available, both in relatively democratic societies with pluralistic cultures, and in relatively totalitarian societies which censor belief-construction, prohibiting the entrance of the "undesirable" and the testing of the "desirable"
b.   beliefs acquired during the earlier years of life often change only with difficulty with the test of subsequent experience, partly because they contribute to the selection and shaping of that very experience
c.   if we seek to develop individuals who form and test their values continuously against an ever-expanding foundation of acquired knowledge, it is essential that this foundation indeed be constructed from the most reliable beliefs about reality available
d.   any field of study as "pre-scientific" as is education at present is likely to be prone to fads and bandwagons, as well as still riddled with beliefs which could best be described as myths and old wives' tales, all of which will be lobbied for by numerous teachers and interest groups

e.   all of the above

f.   none of the above

g.   all but (b), (e) and (f).

5   A moral foundation composed of an evolving set of highly verified and reliable beliefs about the nature of human beings and their social relationships, such as that suggested in this chapter, would seem to be necessary because:

a.   it provides a dynamic solution to the dilemma posed by the realization that if all and only those beliefs handed down by our ancestors are of value, our curriculum content is likely to be obsolete and unchallengeable, while if all extant beliefs are valued more or less equally we are left with no criteria at all for curriculum selection

b.   we all know that the particular beliefs mentioned in this chapter will always be true

c.   these beliefs will ensure that all Canadians will develop the same values, thereby generating socio-cultural harmony and unity

d.   any one set of beliefs is as good as another as the moral foundation of society (and, therefore, of the society's school curriculum); all that matters is that *some* set be established as the ultimate criterion for curriculum selection.

e.   these beliefs are a good basis for morality because they deal only with the good and not with the real

f.   all of the above

g.   none of the above

h.   all but (b), (f) and (g).

6   According to this chapter, motivation to learn is:

a.   something that teachers must arouse at the beginning of each lesson by the use of exciting teaching techniques

b.   something that the learner brings to the lesson if he has previously been involved in an ongoing valuing process which requires continuous assessment against reliable knowledge

c.   something that is seldom found in children

d.   something that is determined by the genetic structure of the individuals so that if a child does not have it there is little that can be done to develop it.

7   Creativity is explained within the framework of the concept of values as:

a.   the ability to arrive at solutions to problems which are innovative in terms of the culture of the social system concerned: an ability enhanced by early exposure of the individual to a variety of other cultural ways of doing things

b.   A God-given gift that some people have and some do not

c.   the ability to produce ideas or artifacts which are totally new to humanity

d.   something that teachers can recognize and work with where it is possessed by pupils, but which cannot be developed by means of the educational process

e.   all of the above

f. none of the above

g. all but (b), (e) and (f).

8 Culture conflict can best be described as:

a. two cultures meeting as the result of imperialistic ploys by the bearers of the more powerful culture

b. an inevitable correlate of acculturation

c. something that occurs for cultures but not for individuals

d. the encountering and acquisition, by an individual, of incompatible sets of beliefs representing conflicting group assumptions about reality and ways of life.

9 A major implication of the discussion of values in this chapter is that the issue of moral education for youngsters would be:

a. resolved by the inclusion of separate classes such as sex education and drug education

b. resolved by the educational process in its totality, as the objective of the entire process would be to develop knowledgeable and wise valuers in every area of life

c. resolved by including more classes on religion in the curriculum

d. resolved by a careful selection of teachers on the basis of the specific values that they possess.

10 According to this chapter, the most desirable role of the teacher in value development through education is:

a. the inculcation of the ideals of the parents

b. the inculcation of the national culture

c. the inculcation of the teacher's values

d. the development within the pupil of the intellectual tools, the knowledge base, and the humane concerns required for wise and responsible valuing.

Answers: 1. (c); 2. (b); 3. (g); 4. (e); 5. (a); 6. (b); 7. (b); 8. (d); 9. (d); 10. (d).

Part Five
Toward
Educational
Knowledge

We have discussed the nature and interrelationship of individual beliefs and values and the role of these in the determination of the content of the education of the social group, and thereby the future shape of its culture. What remains to be examined is the *source* of these beliefs and values. The common response of some of the earlier sociologists and anthropologists—that these individual propensities and justifications exactly mirror the ideals of the culture—simply will not do. For if this were true neither individual intellectual growth nor cultural change would be possible; the socialization-enculturation process would ensure an exact duplication across and within generations. But even the most superficial familiarity with history and psychology demonstrates clearly that this is not the case. Cultural diversity and cultural change are observable everywhere, as are individual differences in values. Obviously the relationship between culture and individual value systems is far more complex than any such static picture of simple lineal causality would indicate.

Interposed between the values of the individual and the culture of the group is a phenomenon which could provide the key to the entire network of relations involved. This phenomenon is the *belief*—that consciously held explanation of relations in reality which is acquired through experience. The experience may be vicarious (as in the teachings of significant others, whether through example, command or literature), or be obtained by means of direct action upon one's environment. The beliefs so acquired may be private or public.

Because a privately formulated belief can become public, it has the capacity of being amenable to the test of the experience of others. It is possible for a belief to become public because it is capable of verbalization; because it can be expressed in symbols whose meanings are shared by the group. In other words, because beliefs can be *communicated*, the regularities among experienced phenomena to which they attest can be subjected to group tests of reliability. A privately held or subjective explanation can be made increasingly objective and public as it withstands the test of more and more experiencers. Beliefs which do not survive this check are gradually relinquished, and as this happens the subconsciously operating values derived from them undergo alteration as well.

However, a further complication arises from the fact that the relation between beliefs and values is reciprocal. Deeply embedded values can blind the individual to contrary evidence; to a large extent they determine even what he selects to experience from his surroundings. Again, the only means available to humans for lessening the effect on perception of built-in bias is the inter-subjective or public testing process, and the reflection on past experience of regularities which it requires and promotes. And a general attitude of reception to the test of shared experience—as well as the habit of reflective thought and precise communication—would seem to be a prerequisite for the construction of ever-more-reliable (although admittedly, still imperfect, partial, and tentative) beliefs about the nature of man's physical and social environment.

This reflecting and testing technique which produces increasingly reliable explanations and predictions of regularities on the basis of which man can make his individual choices is what we have come to know as the scientific process. John Dewey recognized it as a significant source of individual value change and of what we often refer to as individual creativity, as well as a possible source of rational cultural change—in directions valued by the carriers of the culture concerned. Thomas Kuhn sees it as the explanation of both the evolutionary progress of normal science by means of which structures of highly verified public beliefs gradually accumulate, and the revolutionary paradigm changes by which new containing structures for knowledge are formed.

For the educator, the concept that human beliefs form a continuum, from the most privately held explanations concerning relations among imagined phenomena quite inaccessible to the test of human experience to the most reliable and highly verified postulates of physical science known to man today, is an extremely important one. At some point along this movement toward inter-group sharing and checking, the belief in question achieves an acceptable degree of what we term *objectivity* (or inter-subjective testability). At this point, and until such time that it becomes discredited by feedback from further experience, we refer to the belief as *knowledge*. Such knowledge can be the result of centuries of everyday group experience, and in that case is usually referred to as folk wisdom or common sense. Or it can be the meticulously measured and tested result of systematic laboratory experiment.

It is from this pool of knowledge that the educator selects those beliefs which are to comprise the school curriculum. As the knowledge pool evolves, so too must the curriculum. And because not all beliefs which have achieved the status of public knowledge are equally highly verified and reliable, nor equally appropriate to every stage of child development, nor equally conducive to the instigation of further intellectual and moral growth in the individual, curriculum-making inevitably and necessarily involves *selection*. It is to this vital question of which concepts (related sets of beliefs) educators should help each child to acquire at which stage of conceptual development and by which procedures that we desperately need answers. These are educational questions. The posing of them forces us to examine the problem of what precise kind of systematic study of human social relationships might provide us with reliable answers.

9 Sociology And A Science Of Education

In the quest for reliable educational knowledge, what is the most appropriate, logical and useful role of the study known as sociology? Sociologists of education generally have attempted to answer the question in one of two ways. Many have phrased it in terms of a distinction between educational sociology (viewed as a normative enterprise dealing with beliefs about the good) and sociology of education (supposedly an empirical study dealing with beliefs about the real).[1] Others have considered the relationship essentially as that between a practical, derivative science and its theoretical or pure science base.[2] The latter distinction assumes that education is concerned only with the practice of teaching, while sociology involves the construction and testing of relevant theories.

Both these popular views of the relationship between sociology and education beg the question of what it means to pursue either study in a scientific manner. Does it mean to be empirical, but not normative? Is it possible that any science could avoid elements of both? Or does it mean to be theoretical, but not practical? And is it possible for any fruitful scientific study to be built on concepts that have not been tested in the real world? It might be well, therefore, to begin one step further back, with the problem of what it means to be scientific in approach to the study of *any* segment or aspect of reality capable of being acted upon by man, and whether a commitment on the part of educators to move in this direction is desirable and necessary.

[1] This distinction has probably been explained best by Donald A. Hansen, in "The Responsibility of the Sociologist to Education" *Harvard Educational Review* 33 (Summer 1963), p. 313, as follows:

"In brutally simple terms, sociology from the one perspective might ask education, 'What can I do to serve you?' From the other perspective it might ask, 'What, in the name of society, *are* you, and what in the world are you doing?'"

[2] A textbook such as Dorothy Westby-Gibson's *Social Perspectives on Education* (New York: John Wiley and Sons, 1965) is founded on this assumption, with the contributions of the social sciences other than sociology being recognized by the author as well.

John Dewey devoted the greater part of his long life to this problem and this commitment. Initially he thought that what was required was merely for education to be accepted as an integral part of the organization of the university. He assumed that, once accommodated administratively and imbued with the aura of academic legitimacy, it would automatically develop in a systematic and scholarly way, as had other accepted disciplines. It is now apparent that the recommended organizational changes were accomplished with characteristic American enthusiasm for structural innovation, but that the systematic development of a scientific study of education failed to follow. Instead, there blossomed and grew within the favourable habitat of the North American university a veritable professional beanstalk; strangely rootless and hollow in its lack of grounding in integrated theory and in its lack of substance in the form of reliable knowledge, but over-nourished by the symbolic trappings of academia and the ingroup solidarity of the union movement.

Needless to say, this was not what John Dewey had envisaged when he called for a science of education. To him the scientific approach to knowing meant a process of systematic inquiry beginning and ending in experience: a process utilizing both conceptual and technical tools in the transition of problematic situations into ordered, determinate ones. He believed that this method could be refined continuously and be used by Everyman in the process of his creative adaptation to dynamic physical and cultural surroundings as well as by philosophers whose responsibility it was to render the cultural evolutionary process less random and costly in human terms.

However, Dewey nowhere presented a clear, concise recipe for applying this approach to the building of a science of education. He seemed to start with the assumption that the social "sciences" were indeed scientific (because they were labelled as such and housed in the university?). He proceeded to view education as some sort of derivative study which would synthesize hypotheses from a variety of these disciplines and provide, in the form of public classrooms, ready-made laboratories for the testing of these hypotheses and for the subsequent construction of knowledge in these respective foundational "sciences." This synthesizing of facts from other disciplines would be the major task of educational scholars at the university level, while that of the school level would be the testing and application of these facts in the teaching-learning situation.

Later, Dewey identified the central task of scholarly educational studies as being the articulation of the psychological with the sociological. By psychological he seems to have meant the developmental processes occurring within the individual due to the interaction of maturation and enculturation, and by sociological, both the structuring of the web of social interaction in which the individual is enmeshed and the logical structuring of the knowledge available in the culture.

Jean Piaget seems to be the only educational scholar of note to have accepted adequately this mandate of Dewey's. Piaget, in his own scholarship, unites and synthesizes current findings and ideas from biology, psychology, sociology and epistemology. Like Dewey, Piaget is concerned about the lack of a scientific basis for educational practice, and intimates that such an accomplishment is intrinsically related to progress in the biological and social studies, and in philosophy. But, also like Dewey, he fails to present a clear picture of precisely what a science of education would entail. He still seems to assume that the social and philosophical studies possess a scientific or at least a disciplinary status which education, by its very nature, could not hope to attain. It would follow that the scientific or theoretical base for education must, of necessity, be derived from these base disciplines.

It seems imperative to pose a few questions at this point. Just how scientific and systematic in their scholarship *are* the philosophical and social studies from which we are to derive our educational theory and practice? Could it be that the failure of education to become scientific and scholarly at the same rate that it became professionalized has been due partly to the corresponding failures of philosophy, anthropology, sociology, psychology and political economy?

Secondly, why is it that neither Dewey nor Piaget can be appropriately classified as scholars of any one of these base disciplines? What is the appropriate label for scholars with their particular model of the interdependence of growing, learning, knowing and valuing, if it is not theorist of education? How strange that both men devoted long and productive lifetimes to the experimental study of educational processes within an identifiable interactionist-evolutionary, bio-social-psychological-philosophical framework, but that neither has related that framework in a self-conscious, formal way to the study of the particular aspect of reality in question! It will be argued in this chapter that the key to the development of a science of education lies precisely here, in this major accomplishment and major blind spot of these two great educational scholars.

The idea of an encompassing conceptual framework, then, which relates, makes sense out of, or maps the phenomena under study, brings us right to the heart of what it means to be scientific. It leads us to the definition of a science as *a systematic study of some aspect or portion of reality which is pursued by means of a common theoretical model* which, although explicitly acknowledged and formalized in the developmental stage, is largely internalized by later practitioners, and treated by them as "reality" or the "the truth" rather than a model. This is the concept of science developed so powerfully and persuasively by Thomas Kuhn. A science of education, according to Kuhn's model, would require what most of the behavioural, humanistic and philosophical studies (including sociology) have not yet achieved. It would require the development, among educational scholars, of a consensus regarding an adequate and fruitful conceptual framework by means of which educational events can be explained and consequently rendered more predictable and controllable. This definition requires a great deal of clarification.

The term, conceptual framework (or paradigm in Kuhn's presentation) is an extremely ambiguous one. It defies explanation in purely philosophical, psychological, biological or sociological terms. There is simply no way to understand it without delving into the total, complex process of human experiencing (the subject matter of education?). For our paradigms are the sieves which filter and shape our very perceptions of the environment, and which are subsequently accommodated to changes in that environment. In the case of a science, the paradigm has been rendered explicit and exact for purposes of measuring, testing and communicating that which is experienced.

Most of us would agree that what we learn is dependent upon what we experience or perceive by means of all our senses. But not everyone is yet prepared to accept the idea that what we perceive is never simply a mirror image of that objective reality "out there"—a reality apart from us which is implanted whole upon us and is amenable to reception by any normal human being entering a given situation. There are also many who still believe that perception is merely the sum total of disparate sensations, transmitted by the situation, which would produce the identical response in all normally functioning participants.

Not only are the Gestaltist and Behaviourist positions misleading but so, too, is the subjectivist position adopted by many Existentialists today. This view assumes that what the individual perceives in a situation is totally dependent—not upon what is in the situation, but upon what is in the individual—upon what he brings to it. In other words, to the Existentialist the individual shapes the immediate situation, not vice versa as the Gestaltist and Behaviourist would have it.

Piaget's model of the individual human's role in the process of knowledge-construction, however, is neither "holistic," "atomistic" nor "subjectivist." Like Dewey and G. H. Mead before him, he starts from "interactionist" assumptions about the nature of the relationship between the knower and the known. But he has progressed beyond them in building upon that base a sophisticated and fruitful model of how the human being acts upon his world in the process of constructing beliefs about it.

Piaget's model sheds considerable light upon the idea of a conceptual framework. It can be described in his terms as a set of mental structures (boxes evolving out of and in turn encompassing antecedent boxes) resulting from generalized experience: a complex of structures which provides every human being with his "intuitive" sense of how the various "felt" aspects of reality fit together. This means that experience (the source of individual learning) could not possibly be equivalent merely to the external stimuli impinging on the learner at any particular moment in time, whether it be in the form of gestalts or atomistic sensations. It seems that experience is, instead, the sum total of what the learner does to and with that environmental raw material. And how the learner handles presently available raw material is greatly affected by all the previous experience which has shaped his mental structures (within the limitations of his maturation process).

This means that this complex of mental structures (or the total conceptual structure), which is rooted in genetic endowment and experience and applied by the individual to the current situation, determines to a large extent what he experiences of it. However, it does not mean that the external phenomena present in the situation are irrelevant. Reality (what is out there apart from the individual) does impose limits upon what the learner can experience; he cannot create his own reality. In fact, the major criterion for distinguishing sanity from insanity or a dreaming from a waking state is the ability to test one's private experience against that of others in the same situation. And in order for such inter-subjective reality testing to be possible, human beings must be able to communicate with one another concerning aspects of their experience.

This inevitably partial and imperfect sharing of experience requires shared conceptual frameworks. Very early in the child's development he acquires a whole nest of concepts shared by his group—by virtue of the fact that everyone in his social milieu acts in terms of them. Along with the social boundaries established by group interaction, the child encounters physical limits which force him into the patterns of action characteristic of his group. Some of these patterns produce the fundamental concepts of physical reality identified by Piaget: the permanent object, space, time and causality. Others are social concepts like mother, justice and authority which have become, through custom, almost equally self-evident to the group. Gradually the symbols which the group has agreed upon as representative of these concepts are learned by the child, and used to advantage in his subsequent testing and categorizing of experience.

All human beings, with the help of the more experienced group members, from birth onward construct their worlds. They do this by constructing generalizations from, or categories of relationships among, experiences. However, for the very survival of the individual and his social group, these categories must permit the effective prediction and control of physical and social relationships. This means they must be communicable in order to allow for continuous development, refinement, and public testing, and for their transmission and accumulation in the form of a cultural pool of verified and reliable tools for coping with a dynamic environment. And in order for very complex sets of logically related concepts to be communicable, they must be explicitly defined in terms of exact symbols and used in precisely the same way by all members of the relevant community. To the degree that this is so we can say that the area of study so conceptualized has become a science, and is thereby capable of generating the kind of knowledge that gives man the power to shape the course of his own cultural evolution.

This model sets up no dichotomy between scientific and unscientific belief-construction, but rather, pictures a continuum from the most private and uncommunicable concepts imaginable to those that are explicitly defined within a logically consistent theoretical structure, shared and symbolized in testable form by a relatively small community of researchers specializing in some highly esoteric study. It is the degree to which there is consensus on the model or conceptual framework used to order the phenomena studied, plus the degree of formalization of the structure of that model (so that valid and reliable public testing is possible) that makes a study scientific. Where there is no consensus on conceptual structure there can be no regularities among phenomena discernible by the group, and *where there are no regularities there is no knowledge.* There are only subjective or private beliefs about the nature and meaning of one's experience, each of which is as good as the next man's, and none of which allow the choice-maker to predict reliably the consequences of alternative courses of action. (Small wonder that, in the absence of such knowledge in the realm of social relations, man has tried to avoid facing up to his plight and his negligence by manufacturing myths which place the responsibility for human actions with the gods or with destiny!).

Both objective knowledge and subjective beliefs can be subsumed under the category of *explanations.* All human attempts to explain experienced regularities fall somewhere along the continuum from the extreme of subjectivity to the extreme of scientific objectivity described above. All such explanations result from efforts by human beings to satisfy curiosity, or relieve tension.

To a very significant degree unscientific educational practice, or schooling, has been the cause as well as the effect of the unscientific nature of the study of education. The problem is related in a very complex way to this human drive to satisfy curiosity.

We all know that people differ markedly as to the type of explanation which will satisfy their curiosity. This is so because human beings can quite easily be enculturated in such a way that the urge to know with which the baby is equipped at birth can either be continually enhanced or increasingly stifled. Children can be taught to demand that every explanation squares with their own experience; or they can be taught to live happily with ambiguity and with contradictions between their beliefs and the evidence of their biologically based testing tools (the senses and the sense-based ability to apply logical operations). Unfortunately, this second type of enculturation is the more common in human groups. It has been pursued in a systematic way (through schooling) in most societies throughout history. It has been pursued in order to transmit packages of explanations designed to inculcate norms which were no longer working to the advantage of the group; cultural ideals which were no longer reflecting the operating values and goals of the group members; and beliefs about relations among objects and events which were continually refuted by the individual's everyday experience. (Harold Benjamin exposed the dangerous irrationality of this type of schooling in his little classic, *The Sabre Tooth Curriculum*, when he described the preoccupation with teaching "tiger-scaring by fire" long after the great sabre tooths had become extinct.)

All too often, then, children are enculturated not only in the school, but even earlier in the bosom of the family and neighbourhood to have their curiosity satisfied by and to live happily with irrational or magical types of explanation. We could locate these at the extreme of the subjective end of the continuum. (I became ill because I disobeyed Mother and am now being punished by the Superior Being who watches over me . . . . Easter eggs are laid and distributed by bunnies . . . . Santa Claus rides through the sky bringing presents to good children and neglecting bad ones . . . . Human beings differ from other forms of organic life in that after they die they come to life again . . . . The violent destruction of one class by another is the only means to a just and humanly fulfilling social structure . . . .)

Associated with the magical explanation is the idea of the high status individual as the source of authority. Some all-knowing person must receive the revealed message from the spirit world (or the God within) and interpret it to the group. Because it was revealed only to him, and through a secret procedure, no means of testing the validity of the message or explanation is available to the group. And because moral sanctions are usually imposed by that same authority even upon the very desire to test its reliability, the magical explanation carries its own built-in immunity to the test of experience.

Developmental psychologists now hypothesize that respect for the authority of significant adult others is a prerequisite for the initial learning of social limits so necessary for the building of basic cognitive and affective structures. However, it is recognized as well that in order for the child's intellectual and emotional growth not to be frozen at a primitive level, a gradual encouragement of curiosity and of the desire to experiment and to question human and institutional authorities is required. The magical explanation, then, has its place in the human developmental process, but the growing learner should be encouraged to question it, to find it wanting, and to grow beyond it. The autistic child could be viewed as the extreme example of development halted at the magical level of explanation-seeking, with the adult "bureaucratic personality" a much more common case of such arrested growth.

Another type of explanation which has great attraction is the *empathetic* one. It makes sense out of an event by identifying the events which led up to it and by encouraging the inquirer to feel for the participants or objects whose behaviour is being studied. (I understand the motives and needs of the Indian student who skips classes and assignments. I too would behave as he does if I had been raised on a reservation, or in a city slum.) This represents the first step in becoming capable of sharing concepts—the ability to enter to some degree into the private feeling domain of the other, the attempt to perceive the world through his senses, as it were.

The empathetic explanation is sometimes called intuitive. It has been identified by sociological theorists such as Max Weber as the only appropriate one for inquiries into social phenomena. However, it suffers from obvious limitations. It emphasizes differences among unique events rather than similarities, and therefore makes the identification of regularities impossible; it emphasizes the qualitative aspects of the unique event rather than the connections among events which allow for prediction. (It helps us to develop the concept of the frustration of the Indian student but does not lead to the development of a larger, more encompassing mental construct of the *connections* among childhood socialization, present frustration and learning which would enable us to deal effectively with the Indian boy's problem.)

This type of explanation is applicable to physical phenomena as well. (Our curiosity about the nature of rain is satisfied when we experience the preceding build-up of clouds and feel the wetness and mud underfoot.) It contributes to the construction of what Piaget calls physical concepts, but not to operational or "logico-mathematical" ones. In Dewey's terms it defines objects of value but not objects of knowledge. Or we could say it enriches our store of images and feelings concerning the unique quality of a phenomenon, but not our recognition of regularities in the occurrence of the general class of phenomena. Nor does the empathetic explanation contribute to the encompassing conceptual structure or mental map within which we must eventually fit the particular concept in order to give it meaning in terms of our other concepts.

The empathetic explanation is undeniably necessary at a certain stage of intellectual and emotional development. But, as with the magical explanation, if the individual's curiosity continues overlong to be satisfied with it, it becomes an obstacle to further intellectual and emotional growth for the individual and to the process of knowledge-construction for the group.

A third type of explanation is what Nettler calls the *definitional* one. He says simply that this amounts to the conversion of foreign symbols into familiar ones. This, too, is an adequate and fruitful type of curiosity-satisfier during a certain stage in an individual's cognitive and affective development, just as it is a prerequisite for the formal stage of the development of a disciplined area of study. Enhancement of the child's symbol-manipulating power is usually accompanied by the refinement and multiplication of concepts, as each newly acquired symbol tends to introduce into his conceptual structure some additional aspect of the phenomenon being experienced and categorized.

However, if the learner is too strongly conditioned to having his curiosity satisfied by such explanations he may become trapped in an intellectual dead end. He will be in trouble if he adopts the habit of making connections among symbols without internalizing through experience the conceptual structures which the symbols represent. Piaget calls this figurative rather than active or operative learning. An example of this is the child who is a whiz at solving equations, but is unable to translate a problem encountered in real life into mathematical form. Or the university student who can expound in sophisticated sociological terms on the concept of authority, but who cannot begin to apply the concept to his own role as a student-teacher.

Rigorous identification and refinement of the symbolic structure of a discipline is a prerequisite for the accurate communication and repetition of procedures and findings which lead to knowledge.

Young disciplines are often criticized for undue emphasis on the definition of their concepts. However, this stage is neglected—as it has been in education—at the peril of discipline concerned. Ambiguity, distortion of the meaning of everyday language, and sloganizing are likely to be rampant in a field of study still characterized by magical and empathetic explanations. The road to the consensus on conceptual framework so necessary for the building of a science must be by way of continuous reappraisal, refinement and communication of the definitions conveying the meaning of its concepts. However, it is always possible that scholars in a youthful discipline will see this definitional process as an end in itself rather than as a means to the goal of paradigm-consensus and subsequent knowledge-construction. Again, this is a danger relevant to education today, where the temptation to spin sophisticated symbolic structures, unhampered by the frustrating limitations of the classroom, is particularly appealing.

A major thesis of this chapter is that the type of explanation which individuals find satisfying to their curiosity is intimately related to the process by which the group constructs its knowledge. Perhaps a discussion of a fourth type of explanation will help to clarify this relationship.

Nettler writes also of *scientific* explanations. In our model of the continuum of explanations from the subjective to the objective pole, this type represents the extreme of objective knowledge. Nettler claims that scientific explanations involve a self-conscious use of facts (propositions about regularities among phenomena verifiable by reference to publicly replicable and communicable experience). He says, "To explain an object-event scientifically is to cite a nontautological empirical regularity of which the explanandum is an instance."[3] (This, in a nutshell, distinguishes the scientific explanation from the tautological definitional one.)

The scientific explanation is expressed as a proposition, or statement of relations among perceived regularities. Nettler claims that it is characterized by

1   *simplicity*
2   *clarity* as to the nature of the measurement being used. (He notes that the choice is never between measuring and non-measuring—since magical and empathetic explanations are shot through with crude ranking labels—but in knowing when one is measuring and by which standards and with which degree of accuracy.)
3   *accuracy* of observation
4   *objectivity* (defined as inter-subjective communicability and testability, which, in our terms, requires paradigm-consensus)
5   an interest in *enlarging the scope* of reliable observation, and
6   an ability to abide with the *selective* and the *abstract*.

The person satisfied with the magical or empathetic explanation is apt to criticize the scientific one on the basis of this latter characteristic. But the scientifically oriented individual believes that the only

[3]Gwynn Nettler, *Explanations* (Toronto: McGraw-Hill Lt., 1970), p. 44.

way human beings *can* experience their environment is through selective perception. And the only way they can make enough sense out of it for collective survival is to construct reliable explanations which allow them to predict the consequences of alternative actions without having to suffer each through trial and error. Furthermore, he believes that for an explanation to become reliable it must be capable of being communicated to and tested by other human experiencers. This means that it must be expressed in relational and abstract terms.

It is these scientific types of explanation, whether constructed by unschooled but methodical peasants or highly schooled laboratory researchers, which provide the social group with its fund of reliable, useful and aesthetically satisfying knowledge. From any one particular time and place to another, the content of that pool of explanations previously verified by the group may vary considerably. An explanation (the earth is flat) can be a highly verified part of the structure of knowledge of a culture in one era, and the nonsensical belief of a crackpot several centuries later. Those regularities among phenomena amenable to human perception are not likely to have changed (the sun still appears in the east and disappears in the west), but the human group's curiosity-satisfying explanations for these regularities have altered drastically. In every case these new explanations that succeeded in replacing the old did so because they proved to be more powerful as tools; they succeeded because they multiplied the possibilities for effective action.

The more highly developed the curiosity of the group members and the more refined the conceptual and technical instruments of observation, the more universally communicable and testable (and therefore powerful) the explanation is likely to be. The same applies to the entire knowledge structure into which it is fitted. But in spite of the paradigm-consensus upon which this refinement of tools depends, a different explanation which works better may appear tomorrow. To work better is to satisfy the curiosity of the inquirer better; to better resolve some recurring anomaly. (Fortunate indeed is the learner who has been conditioned not to ignore nor get defensive about such contradictions but to feel stimulated and challenged by their presence; fortunate too is the culture which has nourished him!)

This new explanation may eventually force a readjustment of the entire model held by the group of the way reality fits together. In such a manner—through an evolutionary refining, testing and constructing process interspersed with revolutionary paradigm changes—does human knowledge grow, according to Kuhn.

But in order for this process even to *begin*, it is necessary to move beyond the magical and empathetic stages in which the educational and social studies still operate. Kuhn says that the pre-paradigm or pre-scientific stages of a discipline's development are characterized by competing and incompatible schools of thought (models), none of which accept the others' definitions of the basic concepts used to order the phenomena studied. This is still very much the situation even in the most sophisticated of the social "sciences" today.

According to our model of the nature of knowledge, the impetus for knowledge-building in human cultures (or in what is rapidly becoming the global culture) is the tension produced in the individual learner when he encounters contradictions among the explanations made available to him through the medium of his culture or between these and his personal experience. This tension propels him into his environment to act upon it and to experience the consequences of his acting so as to construct more adequate explanations that satisfy the curiosity produced by his tension. But tension will only act as a spur to joyful inquiry to the degree that the individual has not been previously enculturated to be satisfied with magical, empathetic or definitional explanations, and thereby arrested at one of these more primitive levels. Where such crippling has occurred, the tension (characteristic of all organisms as they strive for equilibrium in a dynamic environment) tends to result in anxiety and conflict rather than in intellectual and emotional growth.

What are the implications of this model of knowledge-construction and acquisition for the development of a science of education? There are at least two that warrant close scrutiny by educational scholars. First, the model appears to offer significant insights into the reasons for the present stalemate in education. Secondly, it points out in a challenging way the road to eventual progress in the future.

An application of this model to education today reveals at least three major obstacles in the way of fruitful development. The first of these is that far too many of the licenced practitioners and scholars of education are themselves still operating at the magical and empathetic levels of curiosity-satisfaction. And of those concentrating upon definition, too many see the formalization of precise, logically complete symbolic systems as an end in itself, quite apart from its instrumental role in the development of a systematic study of educational relationships in the realm of human experience. This means that much of the literature being produced in the field is still loaded with old wives' tales and slogans. (Children are by nature kind, creative, and freedom-loving. . . . Teach the whole child. . . . Don't smile until Christmas . . . .) Or else it is full of exercises in symbol-manipulation, either in the form of premature use of sophisticated statistical analysis or of esoteric excursions into the logically necessary components of educational terms.

The second major obstacle is the prevalence of the idea that it is not necessary to become more systematic in our approach because education is a part of the humanities and an art and therefore can never be studied scientifically anyway. But surely all science includes much that is art! What could be more aesthetic than the drive toward unity and harmony that motivates the puzzle-solver and model-builder of physics? And what could be more human than to seek to move beyond random trial-and-error expediency and other-worldly mythologizing in the attempt to understand and improve the quality of human life on this planet?

Thirdly, there is the idea promoted by scholars such as Dewey and Piaget, even though they are in favour of education becoming more scientific, that it can never be more than a derivative field of study based on the "truly scientific" disciplines of psychology, sociology and anthropology. As Kuhn says, it is highly questionable whether a paradigm-consensus yet exists in any of these fields. True, developmental and associationist psychology are much further advanced definitionally than is education. But sociology, anthropology and differential psychology are, if anything, even more given to magical and empathetic explanation and internecine conflict among irreconcilable schools of thought.

How strange that it has not been obvious to the very scholars most responsible for the development of a comprehensive model of human knowing that only a discipline growing out of and contributing to that integrated model could possibly produce the knowledge required by those uniquely concerned with knowledge-construction and transmission! Those most uniquely concerned in every society are the educators. The model is above all an *educational* model. And the systematic study which could be generated by it would be nothing less than the long-awaited comprehensive discipline of education!

In addition to obstacles, our model reveals exciting prospects for future progress. It suggests that in order for the study of education to become scientific we will need a world community of educators who are enculturated not to be satisfied with magical, empathetic or definitional explanation. It suggests that we require a consensus within this community on a conceptual framework or paradigm in terms of which all educational questions are posed and pursued. However, educators must never assume that this paradigm-consensus which is a prerequisite for the development of a science can be imposed arbitrarily by an authoritative professional elite or sold through political pressure tactics by a group of powerful ideologues within the academic community. It can only evolve slowly and painstakingly as one model becomes dominant due to its demonstrated fruitfulness as a generator of reliable hypotheses.

The model outlined in this chapter also appears to permit a long-overdue clarification of the subject matter of education. Any discipline based on the interactionist-evolutionary conceptual framework would by definition deal with social interaction associated with change processes in individuals, organizations and cultures, and with the interdependence of change at these levels of complexity. The schooling enterprise has always represented the attempt by the decision-makers of a society to shape these change processes in directions deemed desirable by the group. It has generally been a hit-and-miss affair because of the lack of knowledge of how to direct change and because of the lack of systematic means of assessing the consequences of current schooling practice in the light of agreed-upon cultural goals. In other words, what has been lacking is a science of education capable of providing a sound basis for schooling: one which would involve the systematic study of humanly *controllable* change processes in individuals, organizations, and cultures.

No longer would schooling be considered the only legitimate concern of educational scholars. A science of education would of necessity deal with the processes of socialization, enculturation, organizational change and cultural evolution. Schooling (whether public, private or free) would be viewed as the experimental and practical context in which educational hypotheses would be tested, and verified knowledge put to use. This would be quite unlike the situation which prevails today, where we witness sporadic attempts to apply in our classrooms unrelated postulates from a mish-mash of contradictory theories from compartmentalized social studies, each dealing with an isolated aspect of the human change process.

We will begin to produce reliable knowledge about how to achieve cultural goals, to achieve controlled change toward a better human condition, only when all of the hypotheses being tested in schooling procedures are generated by an internally consistent and continually refined paradigm: a paradigm founded on basic interdisciplinary social science concepts. Although this necessary first step still seems to be far into the future, we may be encouraged somewhat by the realization that at least there is now a surprising degree of consensus about what constitutes that better human condition, considering the confusion presently surrounding the means of attaining it. However, the latter is now almost universally recognized as the planned socialization process (education) to which human beings are exposed from birth onwards. At least a significant part of this education occurs in schools. The model of the educational and knowledge-building process presented in this book implies that the crucial task of curriculum-selection for those schools must take into account the following concerns:

1   the proposition that values are intricately related to the beliefs about the nature of the real and the good held by the individual, and that, therefore, the worth of one's values (as

guides to the achievement of humanly fulfilling goals) is dependent upon the reliability of one's beliefs;

2   the proposition that many of the beliefs available in the human culture, and presently being pushed by numerous vested interests, as well as individual teachers, are unreliable as guides to action and unwarranted by the test of experience;

3   the proposition that it *is* possible to determine, for any particular period in time, what constitutes the human group's fund of relatively reliable and verified beliefs, and to identify the conceptual structure of such knowledge systems for the purpose of concept-development in learners;

4   the proposition that the conceptual structure of these knowledge systems should serve as the source of the learning *objectives* of the school curriculum, while the *means* (or experiences) selected to achieve these may well vary from subculture to subculture;

5   the proposition that human beings learn in orderly stages of development, with the internal construction of certain concepts (related sets of beliefs) about the nature of their environment being the prerequisites for others. This means that the process of concept-acquisition is developmental, and that the curriculum must be carefully sequenced accordingly. It means also that the curriculum must be flexible enough to allow for adaptation to individual variation in rates of growth;

6   the proposition that a tension-producing curiosity about one's surroundings is the *impetus* for all concept-acquisition, or learning; that the feeling of pleasure at having made sense out of a puzzling experience is the *motivation* for the continuation of learning; and that systematic action upon one's environment (accompanied by an orderly assessment of the consequences of that action) is the most effective *mode* of learning;

7   the proposition that members of Canadian society must be prepared to cope satisfactorily not just at one, but at three levels of culture: that of the family or ethnic group, the nation, and the world. This means that the experiences provided by the curriculum (the means such as language, artistic, musical and physical activities, and readings) should be drawn first from the family and immediate community, later from the national, and finally from the international scene.

The magnitude of the responsibility of curriculum-makers now becomes clear to the sociologically aware. Knowing that we are as yet without a sound base of knowledge about educational processes, we must nevertheless face the fact that educational decisions are everywhere immediate and pressing. Human interaction cannot stop and wait. Individual growth cannot be postponed until a science of education is adequately developed. Man forges his future by means of his schools and other educational agencies, or else he abdicates responsibility for that future to the vagaries of hit-and-miss socialization. The excuse that we as yet know so little does not let us off the hook.

In modern urban societies it is the school that provides an environment specifically designed by the social group for the intensification, acceleration and direction of the process of socialization-enculturation for the developing individual. The sum of all these individual processes of belief- and value-construction has considerable bearing upon the quality of life, the wisdom and justice of the political decisions made, the structure of the society, and the direction in which the culture evolves. True, there are many other socializing agencies which may obstruct, divert, or circumvent the educational attempt of the school, but the power of the educational establishment as a builder of personality and culture remains great. Whether that power will be used for good or ill in Canada in the future depends to a large extent upon the knowledge, wisdom and morality of those who select what will be taught in our schools and universities, and through the medium of our mass communications.

Suggestions for Further Reading

Dewey, John. *The Child and the Curriculum.* Chicago: University of Chicago Press, 1902.
The author discusses two conflicting camps in education: that which sees the child as the centre of all things, and that which focuses on subject matter to the exclusion of all else. He deplores this simplistic dualism as he does all dualisms in the culture, and he elaborates his "interactive" position which views subject matter merely as intensified experience, logically arranged by scholars and teachers so as best to enable the developing powers of the child to grasp it and make it his own.

———. *Democracy and Education.* New York: The Macmillan Co., 1916.
This is probably the most comprehensive and definitive of Dewey's works. In it he sets forth in depth the philosophical, psychological and sociological basis for his educational model. Essentially it is a model of learning, knowing, and valuing which no longer puts experience in opposition to reason and explanation, as the earlier empiricist and rationalist theories tend to do.

————. *The Sources of a Science of Education*. New York: Liveright Pub. Co., 1929.
In this book Dewey discusses education as partly a derivative study, with classrooms functioning as laboratories for the social sciences. He concludes that the science of education includes the subject matter which has been developed scientifically in these other fields, but that education itself is a process extending beyond its borrowed scientific components.

————. "Psychology and Social Practice," (speech at New Haven in 1899) in Joseph Ratner, (ed.), *John Dewey: Philosophy, Psychology and Social Practice*, pp. 295-315. New York: Capricorn Books, 1936.
In this essay Dewey presents the proposition that the classroom is the ideal milieu for the testing of psychological theory because it stands halfway between the artificial simplification of the laboratory and the extreme complexity of life in the urban society.

————. *The Theory of Inquiry*. New York: H. Holt and Co., 1938.
Here Dewey carefully spells out his view of the nature of scientific inquiry and of the role of logic in this process. He views logic as the intellectual tool by means of which sound beliefs on any subject are attained and tested. He concludes that logic must be based inclusively and exclusively on the operations of inquiry into experience; otherwise this powerful human instrument becomes the handmaiden of obscurantism; it promotes acceptance of unsound beliefs; and it relegates scientific inquiry to mere specialized technique.

————. *Experience and Nature*, pp. 78-165. New York: Dover Publications, 1958.
In the first of these two chapters the author develops his theory of the nature of values as ends or consummations of experience. In the second chapter he explains knowledge as the means or instrumentalities by which human beings achieve control of these end-states of feeling.

Kuhn, Thomas. *The Structure of Scientific Revolutions*. 2nd ed. Chicago: University of Chicago Press, 1970.
This is one of the most controversial books of the past decade, and one of the first to apply the implications of Dewey's theory of knowledge to the historical development of science. The author presents a radically new perspective on the nature of the process of scientific belief-construction. He views it as a combination of periods of evolutionary, step-by-step accumulation of findings arrived at through rigorous testing of hypotheses within the confines of an agreed-upon and demonstrably fruitful conceptual framework (normal science) interspersed with periods of revolutionary readjustment of this encompassing framework or paradigm.

Nettler, Gwynn. *Explanations*. Toronto: McGraw-Hill, 1970.
The author discusses a variety of types of explanation which human beings resort to in their attempts to satisfy curiosity. He makes no judgments about the relative adequacy of these forms of explanation, nor does he discuss them in terms of their consequences for cultural evolution.

Piaget, Jean. *Science of Education and the Philosophy of the Child*. New York: Orion
 Press, 1969.
The author summarizes the history of the development of the sciences of
pedagogy and psychology, and attempts to explain why there has been so little
relationship between the two. On pages 71-75 he deals with the concept of
figurative learning (the production of a precise copy, in mental images, of the
forms of the objects studied) and compares this to operative learning in which
the learner acts upon objects in order to transform and assimilate them into his
own logical schema.

————. *Structuralism*. New York: Basic Books, 1970.
The author examines the logical structures built by human beings in a number
of areas of knowing (notably mathematics and linguistics) along with physical,
biological, psychological, and social structures in the environment. He concludes that holistic and reductionist approaches to the understanding of these
phenomena (such as those of the Gestaltists and Behaviourists) are equally
misleading: that there can be no understanding of human knowledge structures without a corresponding understanding of the human process of constructing logical schema by means of the organism's developing mental structures.

————. *Insights and Illusions of Philosophy*. New York: World Pub., 1971.
Piaget brings his broad background of scholarship in biology, mathematics,
psychology, sociology and philosophy to bear on the issue of the relationship
between philosophy and science. He rejects the phenomenologist position
currently so prevalent in Europe: that philosophy can lay claim to specific
modes of knowledge above and beyond that constructed by the process of
scientific inquiry. He sounds a warning against the danger of believing that
human beings can deal with factual problems by reflection alone.

————. *The Principles of Genetic Epistemology*. New York: Basic Books, 1972.
Here Piaget provides the theoretical and evidential justification for his genetic
(or developmental) model of knowledge and knowledge building. His thesis is
that, although objective structures certainly exist in the real world apart from
the subject, they, nonetheless, come to be known by the subject only by way of
his fitting them into his own logical structures. The initial source of these
logical structures (or schema) is not a mysterious Kantian *a priori*, but rather the
natural biological functioning of the human organism.

Appendix

A. *Sources of Useful Information for the Sociologist of Canadian Education*

    1. Abel, R. L., ed., *Encyclopedia of Educational Research*. Toronto: Collier-Macmillan of Canada, 1969.

    2. Canadian Education Association, *The Directory of Education Studies in Canada*. C.E.A., 252 Bloor Street W., Toronto, Ontario, 1973.

    3. Kalbach, Warren C., and W. McVey. *The Demographic Bases of Canadian Society*. Toronto: McGraw-Hill Ltd., 1971.

    4. Statistics Canada. *Education in Canada*, Education, Science and Culture Division, Ottawa, Ontario, K1A 0T6, 1973.

B. A Sampling of Relevant Statistical Data

1. CHARACTERISTICS of the CANADIAN POPULATION.
    a. *Size* (estimate as of June 1, 1973)[1]
       CANADA 22,095,000

Newfoundland	541,000
Prince Edward Island	115,000
Nova Scotia	805,000
New Brunswick	652,000
Quebec	6,081,000
Ontario	7,939,000
Manitoba	998,000
Saskatchewan	908,000
Alberta	1,683,000
British Columbia	2,315,000
Yukon	20,000
Northwest Territories	38,000

    b. *Income*
      (i) For Canada as a whole (average per family, for 1973).[2]

(national average = $10,113)

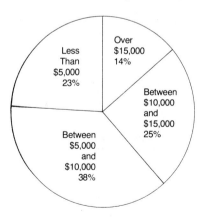

---

[1] Statistics Canada, Sept., 1973, Bulletin No. 8-3300-506.
[2] From items on Statistics Canada reports in the *LEADER POST* of January 26, 1974, p. 72, and January 30, 1974, p. 28.

1. b. (continued)
    (ii) By Province (and Territory)

	Per family	Per worker
Yukon	$ 11,194	—
Ontario	10,661	$8,839
British Columbia	10,019	9,630
Alberta	9,475	8,643
Quebec	9,260	8,273
Manitoba	8,646	7,732
Northwest Territories	8,449	—
Nova Scotia	7,859	7,400
New Brunswick	7,479	7,260
Saskatchewan	7,328	7,739
Prince Edward Island	6,989	5,947
Newfoundland	6,680	8,187

c. Religion	(Per cent of total)[3]	d. Ethnicity	(Per cent of total)[4]
Roman Catholic	46.2	British	44.6
United Church	17.5	French	28.7
Anglican	11.8	German	6.1
None	4.3	Italian	3.4
Presbyterian	4.0	Ukrainian	2.7
Lutheran	3.3	Dutch	2.0
Baptist	3.1	Scandinavian	1.8
Greek Orthodox	1.5	Polish	1.5
Jewish	1.3	Native	1.4
Ukrainian Catholic	1.1	Jewish	1.4
Menonite (and		Greek	0.6
Hutterite)	0.8	Hungarian	0.6
Jehovah's Witnesses	0.8	Other	5.4
Salvation Army	0.6		
Other	2.7		

2. Education Statistics
    a. Enrolment and Teachers, 1971-1972, for Canada and the Provinces (beginning-of-school-year estimates.)[5]

Province	Elementary enrolment	Secondary enrolment	Total enrolment	Elementary & secondary teachers	Pupils/ teachers
Newfoundland	128,410	33,130	161,540	6,562	24.6
Prince Edward Island	21,750	8,160	29,910	1,614	18.5
Nova Scotia	161,040	55,120	216,160	10,099	21.4
New Brunswick	126,620	50,450	177,070	7,910	22.4
Quebec	1,032,800	602,000	1,634,800	74,445	22.0
Ontario	1,463,140	620,220	2,083,360	98,445	21.2
Manitoba	187,690	72,480	260,170	11,939	21.8
Saskatchewan	174,210	73,460	247,670	11,050	22.4
Alberta	306,680	131,960	438,640	21,200	20.7
British Columbia	391,250	159,690	550,940	23,390	23.6
Yukon	4,140	1,150	5,290	260	20.3
Northwest Territories	10,500	1,210	11,710	630	18.6
Canada	4,011,830	1,810,030	5,821,860	267,854	21.7

[3] *Statistics Canada Daily*, July 3, 1973.
[4] *Ibid.*
[5] From Statistics Canada: *ADVANCE STATISTICS of EDUCATION*, 1971-1972, pp. 27-29.

b. Population Enrolled in Schools.[6]

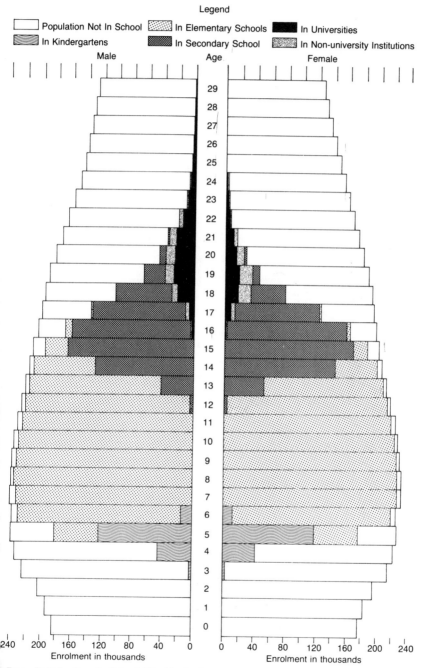

[6] From, Statistics Canada, *Estimated Participation Rate in Canadian Education*, 1968-69, p. 17

c. Full-time Post-secondary Enrolments (per 100,000 population)[7]

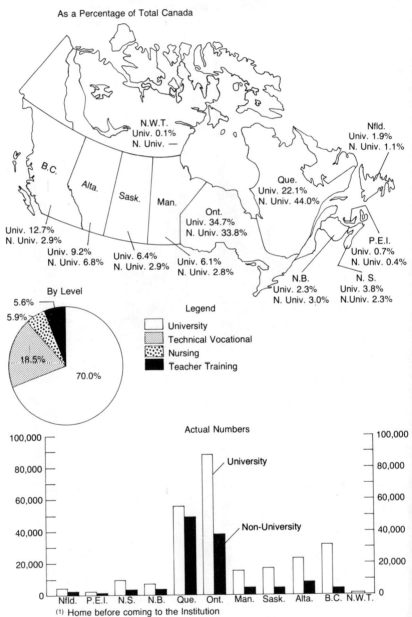

Full-time Post-secondary Students from Canada
Distributed by Province of Origin, Separately by Level, Canada, 1968-69

As a Percentage of Total Canada

N.W.T.
Univ. 0.1%
N. Univ. —

Nfld.
Univ. 1.9%
N. Univ. 1.1%

B.C.

Alta.

Sask.

Man.

Que.
Univ. 22.1%
N. Univ. 44.0%

Ont.
Univ. 34.7%
N. Univ. 33.8%

Univ. 12.7%
N. Univ. 2.9%

Univ. 9.2%
N. Univ. 6.8%

Univ. 6.4%
N. Univ. 2.9%

Univ. 6.1%
N. Univ. 2.8%

P.E.I.
Univ. 0.7%
N. Univ. 0.4%

N.B.
Univ. 2.3%
N. Univ. 3.0%

N. S.
Univ. 3.8%
N.Univ. 2.3%

By Level

5.6%
5.9%
18.5%
70.0%

Legend

University
Technical Vocational
Nursing
Teacher Training

Actual Numbers

100,000
80,000
60,000
40,000
20,000
0

University

Non-University

Nfld. P.E.I. N.S. N.B. Que. Ont. Man. Sask. Alta. B.C. N.W.T.

(1) Home before coming to the Institution

---

[7] From, Statistics Canada, *Estimated Participation Rates in Canadian Education*, 1968-1969, p. 32.

d. Indian and Eskimo Children in School[8]

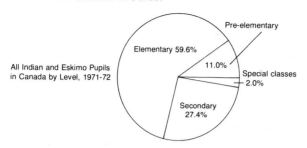

All Indian and Eskimo Pupils in Canada by Level, 1971-72

Pre-elementary

Elementary 59.6%

11.0%

Special classes 2.0%

Secondary 27.4%

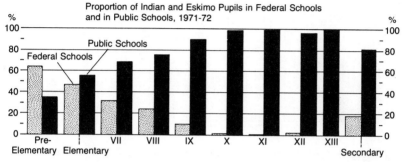

Proportion of Indian and Eskimo Pupils in Federal Schools and in Public Schools, 1971-72

Public Schools

Federal Schools

Pre-Elementary   Elementary   VII   VIII   IX   X   XI   XII   XIII   Secondary

e. Total Canadian Enrolment[9]

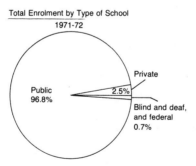

Total Enrolment by Type of School
1971-72

Public 96.8%

Private 2.5%

Blind and deaf, and federal 0.7%

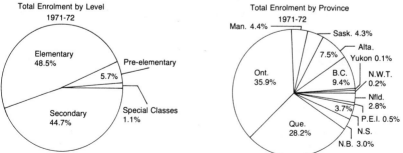

Total Enrolment by Level
1971-72

Elementary 48.5%

Pre-elementary 5.7%

Secondary 44.7%

Special Classes 1.1%

Total Enrolment by Province
1971-72

Man. 4.4%

Sask. 4.3%

Alta. 7.5%

Yukon 0.1%

Ont. 35.9%

B.C. 9.4%

N.W.T. 0.2%

Nfld. 2.8%

3.7%

P.E.I. 0.5%

Que. 28.2%

N.S.

N.B. 3.0%

[8] From, Statistics Canada, *Enrolment in Elementary and Secondary Schools in Canada*, 1971-72, p. 16.
[9] Ibid., p. 14.

f. Enrolment in Grade XII as Related to Population of 17-years-olds.[10]

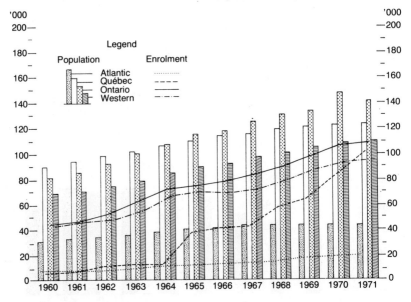

g. Sources of Funds and Expenditures for Education (based on beginning-of-school-year estimates)[11]

SOURCES OF FUNDS

	Millions of dollars
Local government taxation	2,154.6
Provincial and territorial governments	4,483.7
Federal government	830.3
Private	729.1
Total	8,197.7

EXPENDITURES

Elementary and secondary education	
Public	5,190.1
Private	99.5
Teacher training outside university	8.9
Post-secondary	
Non-university	393.8
Higher education	2,018.4
Other	45.0
Vocational training	442.0
(approximately $380 per capita) Total	8,197.7

[10] Ibid., p. 24.
[11] From Statistics Canada, *ADVANCE STATISTICS of EDUCATION*, 1971-1972, p.32.

Index

Law
  function of, 15, 93, 198
  institution of, 95, 96
Leadership, 54, 57-58, 101, 155, 161, 167
"Leading crowd", 21. *See also* Social
  organization, informal
Learning
  competition in the process of (*see*
    Competition in the learning process)
  cooperation in the process of (*see*
    Cooperation in the learning process)
  groups, 5, 18-20, 45, 47, 48, 50-51, 52, 54
  independent, 53, 82, 106
  process of, 7, 46, 178
Line positions, 98

Marx, Carl, 94, 96-97
Mead, G. H., 258
Media as socializing agents, 8, 12, 30, 198
Mennonites, 208, 209, 235-236, 242. *See also*
  Subcultures
Merit rating, 132
Meritocracy, 152, 153, 154, 159
Mickelson, N. I., 154
Mobility, social. *See* Social mobility
Moral development, 17, 29, 47, 158, 226, 228,
  231. *See also* Intellectual development *and*
  Emotional development
Motivation for learning, 16, 24, 26, 228, 242,
  244, 269
  of Native Canadians, 245
Murdock, George, 191-192, 194

Native Canadians, 18, 211, 213, 214, 232-233,
  237, 239, 244
  equality of opportunity for, 173
  intellectual development of, 28, 30, 179,
    211, 213
  motivation for learning of, 18-20, 175, 244
  school achievement of, 18-20, 207, 211
  schooling of, 166-167, 171-172, 173, 205-206,
    208, 209
Nettler, Gwynn, 263
Non-grading, 106. *See also* Evaluation
Norms, 42, 193, 223

Objectivity, 254, 259. *See also* Knowledge
Occupational associations, 124, 125, 134, 164
Organization, formal and informal. *See* Social
  organization
Organizational change, 76, 105-106, 111, 112
Organizational climate, 46, 48, 55, 56, 77
Organizational conflict. *See* Conflict,
  organizational
Organizational society, 149

Para-professional, 130, 132
Paradigm, 258, 259, 268. *See also* Conceptual
  framework
Parents
  as educational agents, 8, 9, 11-12
  as socializing agents, 8
  See also Family
Peers, as socializing agents, 9, 12, 29, 45, 238.
  See also "Friendship cliques"; "Leading
  crowd"; *and* Social organization, informal

Permissiveness, 102
Personality, 6, 221
Piaget, Jean, 257, 258, 262, 267
  on "assimilation and accommodation", 46
  on "energetics", 46, 222
  on "figurative" *and* "operative" learning, 16
  on the "formal" stage of development, 17
  on moral development, 17
  on "reciprocity", 17
  on "schema", 221
Poverty, 155, 159, 178
  culture of, 124
Power, 92, 93, 94, 98-99, 161. *See also*
  Centralization of control
Prejudice, 18-20, 24, 29, 167, 206
Principal, role of, 85, 86, 87, 100, 108, 142
Privilege, 155, 156, 159, 161, 165
Professional
  characteristics of, 126-127, 128, 130, 134
  role of, 122, 125, 127, 133, 135-136, 139, 187
  status of, 126, 129, 132, 150
  See also Para-professional
Professionalization, 123-147
Pupil, relationships of, 7

Reference group, 125
"Reflection", 223, 225, 229, 231. *See also*
  Dewey on
Religion, 198, 212
Role, 42, 69-91
  boundaries, 76
  change, 73, 74, 77
  conflict, 73, 74, 75, 76, 78, 81-82, 82-83, 106
  coordination, 76
  diversity, 73
  expectations, 71, 73, 74, 75-76, 198
  performance, 70, 72, 73, 74
  tension, 74-76, 78
  of the administrator (*see* Administrator)
  of the counsellor (*see* Counsellor)
  of the principal (*see* Principal)
  of the professional (*see* Professional)
  of the school board, 85
  of the schools, 153, 161
  of the student (*see* Student)
  of the teacher (*see* Teacher, role of)
Rural-urban differences, 73, 74, 125-126, 141,
  150, 153, 174
Russell, Bertrand, 95

School, 5, 44, 67, 72, 98-99, 121, 187
  achievement, 29, 153
  as a social system, 121
  Free (*see* Free schools)
  role of, 12, 97, 153, 161
  secondary, 110, 111, 158, 175, 213
School board, role of, 85, 110
Schooling
  of Native Canadians, 208, 232
  segregated, 201-203, 204, 205-206, 209, 210,
    211, 214
Science, definition of, 257, 260
Scientific inquiry, 16, 188, 201, 253, 254
  Dewey on, 13, 14, 17, 96, 196, 254, 256
Segregated schooling. *See* Schooling,
  segregated